Can Your Marriage Be Saved?

If you think your marriage is on the rocks, take this test and see where you stand. Put an X in the blank square that best applies.

Item	Not Much	Somewhat	Very Much
1. Every little thing my spouse does irritates me.			
2. I've lost any romantic feeling for my spouse.			
3. My spouse is less important to me than my other friends.			
4. I don't feel like sharing what I've done during the day with my spouse.			
5. The person I married seems gone forever.			
6. I am often attracted to someone of the opposite sex other than my spouse.			
7. I want to improve communications with my spouse but don't know how.			
8. Our sex life is dull.			
9. We are always criticizing each other.			
10. I am willing to go to a marriage counselor if that will help save my marriage.			

Five Steps to Take if You Decide to Divorce

1. Talk to your best friend, religious counselor, or therapist.
2. Consult an attorney.
3. Make copies of all your financial papers.
4. Take your money out of the joint bank account.
5. Talk to your accountant or bank manager to review your financial situation.

alpha books

tear here

Making It Easy on Your Children

➤ If possible, talk with your children about your impending separation with your spouse. Give them as much information as possible about how the divorce will concretely affect them.

➤ Never put your children in the middle of the conflict.

➤ Arrange a time-sharing plan that works with your children's developmental and temperamental needs and that will involve both parents in their lives.

➤ Make transitions between homes easier by having a positive attitude.

➤ Understand that custody is not ownership; it is just a legal term. Parents will be coparenting throughout their children's lives no matter what the official custody status is.

Five Tips to Reduce Legal Fees

1. Never use your lawyer as your therapist or friend.
2. Don't make motions unless less expensive means to your end have been tried.
3. Make a list of the points you want to discuss with your lawyer before you call.
4. Make sure that your telephone call is important.
5. Do as much paper copying and letter writing yourself as possible.

Recovery Zone

What have you done to get yourself back on track?

Item	Yes	No
1. See a therapist.		
2. Join a singles group or mailing list.		
3. Redecorate your apartment/house.		
4. Take a trip to an exotic destination.		
5. Take adult education courses.		

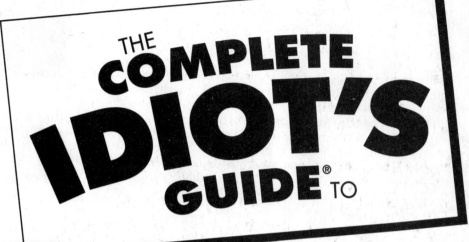

THE COMPLETE IDIOT'S GUIDE® TO

Surviving Divorce

Second Edition

by Pamela Weintraub and Terry Hillman
with Elayne J. Kesselman, Esquire

alpha books

A member of Penguin Group (USA) Inc.

We dedicate this book to all members of the Divorce Central.Com community (http://www.divorcecentral.com), who have taught us so much about the challenges and realities of divorce.

Copyright © 1999 by Alpha Books

International Standard Book Number: 0-02-863392-X
Library of Congress Catalog Card Number: 99-65990

06 05 04   8 7 6

Interpretation of the printing code: the rightmost number of the first series of numbers is the year of the book's printing; the rightmost number of the second series of numbers is the number of the book's printing. For example, a printing code of 99-1 shows that the first printing occurred in 1999.

Printed in the United States of America

Note: This publication contains the opinions and ideas of its authors. It is intended to provide helpful and informative material on the subject matter covered. It is sold with the understanding that the author and publisher are not engaged in rendering professional services in the book. If the reader requires personal assistance or advice, a competent professional should be consulted.

The authors and publisher specifically disclaim any responsibility for any liability, loss or risk, personal or otherwise, which is incurred as a consequence, directly or indirectly, of the use and application of any of the contents of this book.

Alpha Development Team

Publisher
Marie Butler-Knight

Editorial Director
Gary M. Krebs

Associate Managing Editor
Cari Shaw Fischer

Acquisitions Editors
Randy Ladenheim-Gil, Amy Gordon

Development Editor
Phil Kitchel, Amy Zavatto

Assistant Editor
Georgette Blau

Production Team

Development Editors
Phil Kitchel, Lynn Northrup

Production Editors
Tammy Ahrens, Mike Thomas

Copy Editor
Kris Simmons

Cover Designer
Mike Freeland

Photo Editor
Richard H. Fox

Illustrator
Jody P. Schaeffer

Book Designers
Scott Cook and Amy Adams of DesignLab

Indexer
Chris Wilcox

Layout/Proofreading
Angela Calvert, Juli Cook, Mary Hunt, Julie Swenson

Contents at a Glance

Appendixes

Contents

B The Divorce Network: A Guide to Divorce Organizations 287

C Suggested Readings and Online Resources 297

D A Guide to Divorce Laws on the World Wide Web 309

Foreword

As the American family approaches the new millennium, the statistic that half of all marriages in the United States end in divorce, unfortunately, has become a cliché. The staggering truth is that over two and a half million men and women, with more than one million children, struggle through divorce each year in this country. If you are going through a divorce, it may be the most grueling, emotionally exhausting, and expensive experience you will ever have. This book that you hold in your hands recognizes that though your divorce is a time of turmoil, you want to be informed and you need to make the best possible decisions to protect your interests.

With a title like *The Complete Idiot's Guide to Surviving Divorce,* I did not know what to expect. What I am pleased to find is a superb, practical, realistic, yet compassionate manual to guide men and women through the minefield of the divorce process. Whether yours will be an uncontested divorce or a high-conflict divorce, this book will help you understand the process and minimize your apprehension and anxiety. This book is filled with professional advice, interesting stories about real people, and a variety of strategies for negotiating the divorce experience. This book begins with a discussion of the pros and cons of deciding to divorce and ends with support for re-creating your life after your divorce. The chapters explain the divorce process step by step and answer your questions about numerous legal issues, including child custody, child support, alimony, and property division. Straightforward, sensible guidance is provided on a wide range of topics and concerns, such as how to select an attorney who is right for you, helping your children cope with the changes in their lives, and ensuring that you are protected after the divorce is final. The in-depth discussions about the alternatives for resolving your divorce through mediation and settlement, as well as litigating your case in court, will help you to have a better understanding of what is happening and to have more control of your case.

As President of the American Academy of Matrimonial Lawyers, I represent more than 1,500 lawyers, who are recognized by their peers as leading experts in the field of family and matrimonial law. On behalf of the Academy, I welcome this book, not to replace your lawyer, but to complement your working relationship with your lawyer. From my perspective, this book will help you to be a better client, and from your perspective, this book will help you to be a more informed consumer of your lawyer's services.

Your divorce may be the most stressful experience of your life, and the outcome may be the most important to your life. You deserve every benefit available to you. I recommend that you read this book from cover to cover at the very beginning of your divorce and re-read sections as the topics become relevant to your own situation. The understanding you will gain will make you stronger and more confident. In short, this book will help you to survive your divorce. In closing, I wish you well.

George S. Stern

George S. Stern is a senior partner in the Atlanta, Georgia law firm of Stern & Edlin, P.C, which limits its practice to complex family law cases. As a nationally recognized authority, he is a frequent lecturer and panelist at matrimonial law seminars, and a frequent contributor of articles on matrimonial law. Mr. Stern is the President of the American Academy of Matrimonial Lawyers, a prestigious organization consisting of the top family law attorneys in the country.

Introduction

One of the most striking facts about divorce is its sheer frequency. The statistics are staggering—more than 50 percent of all marriages end in failure. There are 1.2 million divorces, involving some 2.4 million adults and more than a million children each year. And the number of people dealing with fallout from past divorces registers in the tens of millions. Ongoing battles over spousal and child support, custody, and visitation are ongoing issues for untold numbers of American families. And the new American family—defined by single-parents, step-parents, step-siblings, and alternating homes—are more common than the nuclear family of the recent past.

Over the past four years we have had ample opportunity to serve the divorced and divorcing through our web site, Divorce Central. Our intimate work with this community has informed the overarching and utilitarian approach in *The Complete Idiot's Guide to Surviving Divorce*. First and foremost, we have come to understand, members of this huge and often-disenfranchised group are in need of basic information and expertise. The divorced and divorcing are often confused about their legal rights, intimidated at the prospect of finding an attorney, and baffled by the array of choices, from seemingly peaceful mediation to ferocious, litigation-based war. Frequently in the dark about how to even begin the process of divorce, they seek answers piecemeal through printed material, high-priced attorneys, and the nightmare stories of friends.

The Complete Idiot's Guide to Surviving Divorce aims to fill this void. One of the few books covering divorce from soup to nuts, this volume is a step-by-step primer on the strategic and emotional terrain. Written for the person who may be too shell-shocked or upset to develop elaborate strategies themselves, the Idiot's Guide presents a plan of action for those in crisis. It also lays out useful solutions for the spectrum of day-to-day issues likely to emerge in the months and years after the divorce has been decreed.

In an effort to cover the range of divorce issues, we have divided our volume into five discrete sections: Deciding to divorce, the legal issues, the financial issues, parenting issues, and recreating life after the divorce. Whatever your concerns, we have attempted to cover the basics. Because divorce is one of the most complex and emotionally loaded situations you will ever face, we have written our Idiot's Guide as a bastion of simplicity. In the end, of course, you will make decisions with the help of your attorney—but you'll find the Complete Idiot's Guide a useful touchstone, and the essential place to start.

How to Use This Book

As you read this book, you will find that many topics are universal; reestablishing self-esteem, making the best possible settlement, and managing your money affect the divorcing across the board. Other areas are more specialized. Not all divorced people, for instance, have children or wage custody wars; not all receive alimony; and not all must resolve their attachment to their ex's family.

We suggest, however, that you read this book thoroughly. We have tried to include enough anecdotes to make this book a page-turner. We suggest you turn every page.

Also, pay special attention to the sidebars scattered throughout. These will provide real-life anecdotes, help you avoid common pitfalls of the divorce process, and familiarize you with the legal lingo. They will get you going in a positive direction and will give you some comfort when you need it the most. You'll come to recognize these icons as you read:

You Can Do It!

Don't wallow in your misery. Take control of your life now! Up and at 'em! Pull yourself up by your bootstraps! Head 'em up, move 'em out! Et cetera, et cetera.

Divorce Dictionary

Here, you'll find definitions of commonly used legal terms in divorce.

Silver Linings

Every dark cloud has a silver lining. In these boxes, you'll find some ways to look on the positive side.

Red Alert

Know these pitfalls and you will be ahead of the game.

Acknowledgments

We want to thank psychologist Mitchell A. Baris, Ph.D., for sharing his ideas on the psychology of divorce, children of divorce, and parenting in the face of divorce; pioneering psychologist Janet Johnston for her insight and input; and financial analyst Ted Beecher, who helped make our chapters on money management and settlement as detailed and timely as possible. Special thanks to our editors, Jessica Faust, Phil Kitchel, and Lynn Northrup, and to our literary agent, Wendy Lipkind. Thanks also to Kathy Astor for help in researching the resource guide.

Trademarks

All terms mentioned in this book that are known to be or are suspected of being trademarks or service marks have been appropriately capitalized. Alpha Books and Penguin Group (USA) Inc. cannot attest to the accuracy of this information. Use of a term in this book should not be regarded as affecting the validity of any trademark or service mark.

Part 1
Making the Decision

According to statistics from the U.S. Census Bureau, about two and a half million people across all social and economic groups divorce each year. More than a million children are swept up in those divorces. The U.S. Census Bureau tells us that fully 50 percent of all those who marry will divorce an average of 11 years after the wedding.

Divorce should never be initiated lightly. For those who are separating, the fights can be draining, disruptive, and unbearable. For the one who's leaving, the guilt might be overpowering. For the one who is left, the rejection might be ego-shattering. In the wake of divorce, children might find themselves bereft of a parent. They might feel they have caused the divorce, that they are to blame. Divorce means divesting yourself of the comforts and accouterments of a life shared and starting out again—diminished in strength and number and alone. The death of a marriage inspires, among other emotions, anger, grief, and fear.

The decision to divorce, or to stay together and work it out, is the most important you may ever make. In Part 1, we will help you grapple with the decision to end it—or help you deal with the rejection if the decision has been thrust upon you by your spouse. Either way, we suggest some ways you can navigate your way to a new beginning.

Chapter 1

Saving Your Marriage: When There's Hope

In This Chapter

➤ When it's appropriate to try to save your marriage

➤ What therapy can do for you

➤ The pros and cons of divorce

➤ Telltale signs that your marriage should end

When you married a decade ago, it seemed to be for all the right reasons. Both ski enthusiasts, you spent all your weekends in Aspen. When in the city, you both loved the theater, opera, and museums. Because you were both in advertising, industry news was often the topic of conversation. Over the years, however, your styles have changed. You have become an increasingly ambitious account executive; the heady feeling of power in each new deal and acquisition keeps you primed. Your husband, meanwhile, has opted for the quieter life of a high school biology teacher. He loves nothing more than hiking in the mountains or helping his students protect the ecosystem of a local lake. There's no animosity—you still like each other—but you've grown apart. Your relationship has changed.

At first you thought it was exciting, that fiery temper that flared up whenever she sensed a universal injustice or personal slight. On campus, protesting the Vietnam War, she was first to join the march. Her boss fired a friend, and she quit, too. Yet now, that passion has turned to venom—and it has turned on you. Whenever you leave your coat in the living room or whenever you disagree with her politics or her taste in film, her eyes widen in anger, and before you know it, a book or shoe has flown across the room. You'd like to work it out, but she wants a divorce. What, if anything, can you do?

You thought you would be faithful forever, but suddenly, at the cusp of middle age, you have fallen in love. The new object of your affections is irreverent, exciting, forever into something exotic or new. An insatiable world traveler, he's spent years abroad, with extended periods in São Paulo, Jerusalem, Osaka, and Madrid. A jack-of-all-trades, he's worked as a photographer, gardener, stock broker, and now—in his latest incarnation—masseur. Oh, those massages! It's wonderful now, of course, but will you really abandon your reliable, loving husband—the father of your children—for this?

The Most Difficult Decision You Will Ever Make

The decision to divorce is never easy, and as anyone who has been through it will tell you, this wrenching, painful experience can leave scars on adults as well as children for years. Before you and your spouse decide to call it quits, consider whether your marriage can be saved.

Colorado psychologist Mitchell Baris, who works specifically with the divorced and the divorcing, has some guidelines for those wrestling with this difficult issue. When is it possible, through diligent, hard work in counseling, to save a marriage? And when is it generally impossible? When—despite the kids—are you doing the right thing by throwing in the towel?

There are, of course, many reasons for divorce, including sexual infidelity, a lack of interest, a difference in values, and even abuse. When are these chasms just too wide to bridge? When can bridges be mended and relationships restored? "The decision to divorce is personal," states Dr. Baris. "But I think the point of no return comes with the loss of respect and trust. Those two feelings are particularly difficult to rekindle. Trust can be built back, but it takes years. Often, if trust and respect are gone, rebuilding the marriage is hopeless."

Dr. Baris also feels it might be difficult to rebuild a marriage when the animosity between two people builds to the breaking point. "I find couples are most likely to split when the intensity of negativity between them escalates." One couple, for instance, fought relentlessly about their son's bedtime, his eating habits, the duties of the cleaning service they had hired, and even the cable TV bill. For such couples, discussion on any topic—from the children to the brand of dog food—might erupt into a negative and angry emotion. "These people will continually make destructive remarks about each other or just bring up the past," states Dr. Baris. "In therapy with them, you see this intense negativity and anger just pouring out."

What if children are involved? Dr. Baris explains the studies show that whether or not parents stay married is less important than whether they engage in fighting or conflict—and whether or not they drag the children in. The critical factor in the ultimate psychological health of a child is the degree of conflict in the environment.

In other words: Don't keep your marriage together for the children if that entails exposing them to constant conflict and wrath. It's better for your children if you divorce amicably than if you stay together and at war.

Divorce often means relinquishing the creature comforts that have defined your life in the past. Families who lived in the 'burbs as a unit now must sell the house, leave the neighborhood, and disperse out to harsher, less-expensive areas. Divorce means divesting the accoutrements of a shared life and starting out again—diminished in strength and number and alone. The death of a marriage inspires, among other emotions, anger, grief, and fear.

Silver Linings

As painful as it may be to admit that your marriage is at an end, sometimes ending a painful or difficult marriage is the only way you can empower yourself to move forward toward emotional health and growth. We know that leaving a familiar relationship for the isolation and stress of single life (and possibly single parenthood) is a rough road to travel. But once you have made the transition, you will find that you are open to new experiences and new relationships never before possible. If your marriage has been demeaning, painful, or even boring, take comfort in the knowledge that divorce might signify the beginning of something, not just the end.

Resolving Conflicts and Saving Your Marriage

Your marriage is at the brink of dissolution. You and your spouse have lost trust and faith in each other; your mutual anger is so palpable that you can no longer go out as a couple without breaking into a verbal sparring match or an out-and-out fight. Past hurts and wrongs haunt both of you, coloring your interpretation of the present; and perhaps most damaging, one or both of you have engaged in an extramarital affair.

Despite such problems, couples can and do put their marriages back together, although only through extremely hard work. That work must be done by both members of the couple, or it will be doomed from the start. Generally, the best approach is finding a marriage counselor to help you.

Therapists come in as many styles as this year's wall calendar. The question is, what should you look for in a marriage counselor? What kind of therapist is right for you?

Some of the best advice we've heard comes from Dr. Mitchell Baris, who works with the divorced and the divorcing every day. Couples should look for someone who can help them restructure their communication and react to their partner in terms of the real situation, not ghosts of the past, Baris advises. "Some counselors look into the couples' deep past; they help them go over their own childhood experiences, their early family dynamic. Couples might explore the impact their past had on their marital choice and on the negative (and positive) patterns they carried into their marriage and up to the present."

Divorce Dictionary

Conflict resolution: A peaceful and mutually satisfactory way to end or significantly—and hopefully permanently—de-escalate a conflict.

Although different marriage counselors emphasize different strategies, we have seen the highest levels of success among those who focus on *conflict resolution*. When one spouse gets excited or angry, the ideal strategy for the other is to try to defuse the anger by soothing his or her partner. Going to war—or worse yet, dredging up the past—will only fuel the fires of conflict and weaken the relationship already on its last legs.

Couples in trouble might also benefit from lessons in *fair fighting*. In this technique, each partner listens to the other without being vicious or defensive—or striking back with hurtful insults or references to the past. One well-known doctor, who pioneered the technique of "restructuring" couples so that they can fight fairly, has this amusing approach: He keeps a piece of linoleum in his office and hands it to one person at a time. "Here, you hold the floor," he says to the person holding the linoleum. The other person cannot speak until the linoleum is handed over. The lesson for couples here: Learn how to hear the other one through, and do *not* interrupt, especially to escalate the conflict.

How do you find the right therapist? The best way, our experts tell us, is to get referrals from satisfied friends. Make sure, of course, that you select someone who specializes in couples and relationships work and that he or she is well-regarded by other professionals. Make sure that whomever you choose feels "right." Is there a rapport among all three of you? Can you communicate easily with the therapist?

Once you find a therapist who meets these criteria, do give therapy a chance. Be open to the possibility that your marriage can be saved—and be ready to do the work that entails. Remember, therapy isn't always easy, especially if you're carrying painful emotional baggage from your childhood. But if you and your partner truly love each other and are willing to alter some basic patterns, therapy can succeed.

Point of No Return

Sometimes, the best-laid plans are laid to waste. Despite all your hopes and dreams in the beginning, and all your good intentions now, it seems impossible to continue your marriage. For many of us, the twentieth-century notion of "till death do us part" has become an anachronism: When life becomes too painful, with too many battles and battle scars, few of us question the notion, at least intellectually, of moving on.

Sometimes, Dr. Baris notes, so much hurt has been engendered over the years that it is simply impossible to get beyond it—at least in the context of your current relationship. When people harbor deep, abiding anger, and when, despite therapy, that anger cannot be resolved, it could be time to let go.

Even in the absence of anger, one or both partners might start to lose respect for the relationship and a spouse. That might signal the end as well. One couple we know, for instance, divorced after the husband made some poor investments and lost his business and the family home. The woman, who insisted she bore no anger, said she could no longer remain married to someone for whom she had "no respect." In another instance, a man divorced his wife, whom he'd met in the fiction-writing workshop at the University of Iowa, after she threw in her artistic career for a high-paying job in a public relations firm.

Sometimes, people divorce because they grow apart. A couple from the Chicago area spent 20 years in a traditional marriage; he went off to work, and she stayed home in the role of homemaker. They had it all, from the two kids to the house in the 'burbs to the cars. When the youngest child left for college and the couple had untold hours to spend together, focusing not on child or family issues but on each other, they found they had little in common. His involvement in the politics of advertising was simply boring to her, and he couldn't relate to her interests in gourmet cooking and international travel. Their taste in movies and even friends had become widely divergent. There were no affairs and no long-simmering anger or resentment. It's just that when both people reached this new crossroad, marked by the departure of their children, his arrow pointed east and hers west.

Younger people with relationships of much shorter duration often reach this juncture as well. When people get married too young, they might find they have gone through enormous changes during the relationship and have grown apart; they've simply gone through more personal development, they have a stronger sense of identity, and in light of that, they would not make the same marriage choice today. Frequently, in such cases, the decision to divorce is mutual. Often, these people can walk away from marriage without feeling particularly angry, especially if they don't have any children. They both just throw up their hands, shrug their shoulders, and say "This doesn't work."

When Is It Over?

How do you know when you've finally reached the point of no return, when putting your relationship together again is simply too much of a stretch? In the end, of course, the answer is personal. But if your answers to the following questions are irrefutably yes, it might be time to let go:

❑ Does every situation, no matter how seemingly trivial, evolve into a fight?

❑ Do you or your spouse continually refer to hurtful events in the past?

❑ Is all the respect gone from your relationship? Do you feel it is impossible to bring that respect back?

❑ Have your goals and directions changed whereas your partner's have stayed the same? (Or vice versa.)

❑ Is your partner no longer fostering your individual growth?

❑ Have you and your partner both changed so much that you no longer share moral, ethical, or lifestyle values?

❑ Have you and your spouse lost the art of compromise? When you disagree, are you unable to forge a path together that is acceptable to both?

❑ Do you and your spouse have a basic sexual incompatibility? Do you feel completely unattracted to each other? Despite help from professional therapists, have you stopped making love?

Don't Burn Your Bridges: Be Absolutely Certain

The decision to divorce should never be made in the aftermath of a fight. Divorce is final and should be considered carefully, not just for its impact on you, but also for its impact on your children. When you divorce, what ramifications will reverberate through your life and the life of your family? Will you have enough money to sustain your lifestyle—including important small details such as trips to the movies, piano lessons, or your weekly take-out Chinese food? Are you ready to leave the family house for a tiny apartment? Are you ready to divide the Impressionist paintings you've collected over the last 20 years, your mint collection of rock 'n' roll singles, or the living room set you bought from the furniture master in Milan?

The answers, for many, might be straightforward: The emotional relationship with their spouse is largely negative, for one or more of the reasons listed previously. Why else would divorce be in the air?

Nonetheless, sometimes couples in conflict can miss the positives. For instance, if you have a child, have you considered how difficult it might be to take total responsibility on one hand or restricted visitation on the other? Will you miss your in-laws, friends who might have to choose your spouse over you, or neighbors you might have to leave? Have you considered the stress of the dating scene? Perhaps most important, will you be relieved or paralyzed by the state of solitude you might be subject to, day in and day out, once you and your partner split?

During her years at college, Melanie was famous for her outgoing nature, flirtatious affect, and pure love of life. Yet when she met Brad, an accountant from the Midwest, she thought she had found a balance. Sober and sane, Brad seemed to have everything organized—where to buy a house and how much to pay for it; how many children to have, and when; where to vacation and when to buy a car. But it soon became clear that Brad had an agenda for Melanie, too. He always seemed to know where she might get her hair cut, and what style she might request; when she should ask for a raise; what committees she should volunteer for; and, in almost every situation, what she should say, think, and feel. It was Brad who insisted she work out of the house, spending less time with the kids, since it was so easy for him to conduct his business from home. Soon Melanie found playing Eliza to Brad's Doolittle a heavy load to bear. Repressed and confused, she suffered depression and self-doubt, all the while living the so-called dream. Despite her love for her children—at Brad's insistence, there were three—she felt strangely disenfranchised. No longer comfortable with her instinct and spontaneity, she felt like a stranger to herself.

It's no wonder she responded so strongly to Rick, an old flame from her glory days at school. He contacted her soon after his divorce—and seemed to love whatever she said or did. With a new love in her life, her motivation for divorcing Brad was high. Yet the price she paid to be rid of Brad was high, too. As the work-at-home parent (who had a higher income) he maintained sole custody of the children. In his usual, controlling fashion, he encouraged their animosity toward their mother. And he managed to secure a significant portion of Melanie's salary for child support.

There's no question that Melanie needed out of this marriage. But her haste caused her to suffer irretrievable losses, most notably her relationship with her children. Her relationship with Rick was never able to compensate her for the grief she experienced as her children increasingly shut her out. There's a lesson in this for most of us: When it comes to divorce, there is always a cost. You must calculate the cost/benefit ratio before you move forward with your divorce. If the price is too high, you may decide to hold off—or at least position yourself to rebalance the equation and come out ahead.

Take some time to consider your losses—and there are sure to be some—before you set your decision to divorce in stone.

When Divorce Is Urgent

We end this chapter with one final caveat: Occasionally, the decision to divorce is mandatory. In instances of spousal or child abuse (mental or physical)—in fact, whenever your safety is in jeopardy—you don't have the luxury of merely considering separation. If your life, limb, and sanity are threatened, it's important to make a quick and abrupt break. If you or your child are in danger, do not wait to organize your finances, collect your valuables, or even see a lawyer. Just get out.

Red Alert

Sometimes, people in destructive relationships have trouble removing the shackles and setting themselves free. If you're in that unfortunate club, you might want to heed the wisdom of Belle Burleson, program director for the National Domestic Violence Hotline (800-799-SAFE).

One woman we know had been abused for years when, in the aftermath of one final, brutalizing battle, she phoned her oldest friend and one-time college room-mate. The friend came with her husband and a couple of shopping bags and gathered what she could: a few clothes, a toothbrush, and some spare cash. Then, the friend and her husband hustled the badly beaten woman out the door. The woman never went back; however, to this day, she states that if she had not been ushered out by her friend, she might still be in that abusive relationship.

When it comes to domestic violence, women are victimized most. There are millions of such victims annually, Burleson says, adding that a woman is battered every nine seconds. Burleson adds that almost 5 percent of battering victims are men, and trauma can be similar no matter what the sex of the victim.

At the center of abusive relationships are issues of power and control. "The batterer uses violence to maintain power and control over the relationship and his partner," Burleson says. Victims are often in denial about their situation, but it is hard to deny some typical battering tactics:

➤ **Isolating the victim from family and friends** This helps keep the victim locked into the relationship because she is kept away from her support system.

➤ **Intimidation** The abuser intimidates the victim through looks, actions, and gestures. As an example, perhaps the couple is at a party and the wife is talking to a man across the room. The batterer looks across the room and clenches his fist. She sees this gesture and knows the subtext: She will be assaulted when they get home. He might also intimidate her by destroying her personal property or displaying weapons around the house.

➤ **Name calling** This is a prime feature of emotional abuse.

➤ **Threats** Batterers might threaten their partners as a means of coercion. Threats might be directed at the victim, at the victim's family and friends, or even at the batterer himself. Threatening to commit suicide if the victim leaves is not uncommon.

➤ **Economic abuse** Batterers often control family finances and might keep the victim on a weekly allowance to take care of the household. Victims of abuse might not have access to family bank accounts or might be prevented from taking and keeping a job.

➤ **Minimizing the violence** Almost universally, batterers minimize violence they perpetrate by saying such things as, "What's the big deal? I didn't really hit you;

I just slapped you." They will often deny the violence outright and tell their victims that it was all imagined.

➤ **Blaming the victim** Batterers will blame their partners for the violence, saying they were provoked.

➤ **Using the children** Batterers think nothing of using the children to relay intimidating messages or harassing the victim during child visitation.

What can family and friends do if they think someone's in an abusive relationship? First, provide unconditional support. And second, provide a safe haven so the victim has somewhere to go.

You Can Do It!

If you are the victim of verbal abuse from your spouse or ex, you should move to de-escalate the situation immediately. As soon as you notice the first sign of verbal abuse, put up your hand and say "stop." If the verbal abuse continues, you should deal with your spouse or ex only through a third party.

What can you do if you are the object of abuse? The first step is recognizing the telltale signs, and the second is seeking help and removing yourself from the situation as quickly as you can.

The Least You Need to Know

➤ Think long and hard before you move forward with your decision to divorce. Once you announce the decision to your spouse, it might be impossible to rescind.

➤ If you want to save your marriage, therapy based on conflict resolution might help.

➤ If your marriage is rife with conflict, don't stay together for the children. The conflict is worse for them than divorce could ever be.

➤ If your physical or mental safety is threatened, separation from your spouse is mandatory.

Planning for Divorce

There comes a time when you have to bite the bullet and admit that your marriage is at an end. You've tried living together and duking it out; you've tried couples therapy; and you've tried living apart. The truth is, unless you sever the ties and go your separate ways, you'll never have a shot at the happiness you both deserve.

Think Before You Act

Before you take the plunge, the savviest attorneys advise you would do well to make some preparations. It might seem heartless, but if you plan to ask your spouse for a divorce, or if you think your spouse might want one from you, there are some matters you should take care of first. Attend to these issues before your partner even realizes you're ready to call it quits, and you'll be ahead of the game during legal negotiations.

We know that the notion of a pending divorce—even one not yet broached with your spouse—can send you into a tailspin. The mere thought of divorce might evoke a range of emotions, including relief, fear, disappointment, excitement, and dread. After years of frustration, you're finally ready to divest yourself of some old and uncomfortable life choices for a world of new possibilities and, you hope, lower levels of conflict and pain. But no matter what you feel, you must push these emotions aside and take some practical and highly strategic steps before anyone gets the ball rolling.

1. Hire a Lawyer

Unless you have been married for only a short time, or you have no property or children, hire a lawyer. Even if you and your spouse have "worked everything out" or have chosen a mediator, your personal lawyer might tell you about rights you didn't even know you had. You don't need a Marvin Mitchelson or an F. Lee Bailey, but you should find someone who has handled divorces before, someone you can afford, and someone with whom you feel comfortable. Word of mouth is usually a good way to locate attorneys, but don't go by recommendations alone. Meet a few lawyers before making up your mind. You might have to pay for these consultations, but at least you'll learn a little about the differences in legal style and home in on the qualities you prefer.

2. Know Your Spouse's Annual Income

If he or she has a salaried position or is paid by the hour, the information should be on a recent pay stub. If you can't get your hands on one, last year's tax return should do. If your spouse is self-employed, a tax return might not tell you the full story. Do a little detective work. Does your spouse have a partner? Are you friendly with the partner's spouse? He or she might know about the business and be willing to share what he or she knows over a friendly lunch. Is someone else in the partnership divorced? Make an ally of that partner's former spouse, who will probably be full of information learned from his or her divorce and only too eager to share it.

Red Alert

When fishing for information about your spouse, do not explain, explicitly, why you need this information. Whoever you're asking might well figure out your motivation. Therefore, you must make it understood that discretion is essential. But do so subtly; the less said, the better. Remember, even a friend can be forced to testify against you under oath.

Finally, don't forget that the best source of financial information might be your spouse. If you haven't discussed your plans to divorce with your partner yet, put it off until after you obtain as much financial information as possible. One wife we know happened to be enrolled in a course on money management when she decided to move ahead with her divorce. Before she informed her husband, she asked him to help her fill out an income-disclosure form—ostensibly her "homework." When she began divorce proceedings, she had the information she needed—in her husband's handwriting, no less. Even if you're not enrolled in a class, requesting such information should be fairly straightforward. Why do you want the details? In this day and age, our financial status is something we must all be on top of. Just tell your partner you feel foolish without a handle on the economic underpinnings of your life.

3. Realistically Assess What You Can Earn

Have you been out of the job market for a while? Perhaps you need some time to get your skills up to speed before taking the plunge. Has business been off lately? Keep a record of that now so no one later accuses you of deliberately reducing your income to negotiate a more favorable settlement.

4. Learn About Your Family's Financial Holdings

Remember, as you wind your way through the divorce maze, you will only be able to share in assets you know about, so you must find out exactly what the two of you have. For most, that's probably easy. There's a house (owned by the bank), a car (still owned by the dealer), a pension (not yet vested), and a little bit of savings. But for some, property ownership is more complicated. In some states, a business created during the marriage is an asset to be valued, and a judge can distribute its value. The same may go for an academic degree or even part of the value of a summer house—one you inherited during the marriage.

5. Realistically Assess Your Family's Debt

Often, the allocation of debt is harder to prove or negotiate than the division of assets. What debts do you have? Credit card, personal loans, bank loans, car loans? How much does it cost to pay these debts each month?

A good source for this information is your family's tax return. Specifically, search under Schedule B for sources of interest income and jot down the information. If possible, locate the 1099 forms—the forms that banks use to report interest income each year. That form will have the name of the bank and the account number. If you don't have the tax return and are afraid of raising suspicions by asking for it, write the Internal Revenue Service. The IRS will provide you with a copy of the return (provided it was a joint return), but it takes several weeks to receive it. If you have a family accountant, you can also ask him or her to send you copies of returns and 1099 statements.

You can also check the mail each month to see who is billing you and for what. Open the bills and photocopy them. If your spouse asks why the envelope is open, say you wanted to see what the bill was for. Hey, you're entitled!

6. Make Photocopies of All Family Financial Records

Canceled checks, bank statements, tax returns, life insurance polices—if it's there, copy it. You might never need this information, but if you do, it's good to have it.

7. Take Stock of Your Family's Valuables

Inventory your safety deposit box or family safe, and take photographs of the contents. Do the same with jewelry or any furniture, paintings, or other items of value. You needn't list every worn-out piece of furniture, but anything with a value of more than

$300 should be included. Property-insurance policies can be helpful here because many companies ask you to list the valuables you want insured. Some people keep a list of belongings in a safe, also for insurance purposes. If you've done that, start with that list. There's no need to reinvent the wheel.

What stocks, checking accounts, savings accounts, and Christmas club accounts do either of you have? Do you have a stockbroker? What about life insurance and health insurance? Get detailed information on every policy you own, jointly or individually. Remember, get the name and phone number of your insurance broker now.

8. Learn How Much It Costs to Run Your Household Now

Whether you plan to stay in the house or leave, unless you know the monthly costs, you won't know how much money you need. If you pay the monthly bills, your job is easy. If you don't, look through the checkbook—how much is the monthly rent or mortgage; utilities, including electricity, heat, and phone; and sundry costs from snow plowing in winter to gardening in spring.

One woman we know, a well-educated social worker with a full-time career, didn't know the first thing about the family's monthly expenses because her husband's secretary made out the checks and paid the bills from the office. She was embarrassed to confess her "ignorance," but she is hardly alone. The point is, even if this woman hadn't been contemplating divorce, every adult should know these basic details.

9. Determine Where You Will Live Following Separation

If you're the spouse who plans to move out, decide where you're going to live and figure out how much it will cost, month-by-month, beforehand. Maybe you plan to move in with your romantic interest. Although that might be tempting—it might be the reason you want to divorce—it might also be a case of going from the frying pan into the fire. How is your spouse going to react when you want to bring the children there? Will this make your case a thousand times more difficult to settle? Will your spouse have an adultery claim that can hurt you later? If you answered any of these questions with a "yes" or an "I don't know," move somewhere else. Look through the real-estate advertisements to learn about rents. Consider what it will cost to move, and calculate start-up expenses, including telephone installation and turning on electricity and cable.

10. Start Saving Money

One unemployed wife of a physician wanted a divorce immediately. Her divorce lawyer, however, convinced her to change her mind. Instead, the attorney advised her, it would be best to wait a solid year before starting the divorce action. During that time, she was instructed to save money—enough, hopefully, to move out and go it alone. It wasn't easy, but the wife saved enough to move out a year later. After she was settled in her own apartment, her lawyer then went to court and got the judge to order the husband to pay her monthly rent until the divorce was final. If the wife had not moved out, the judge could not have directed the husband to pay her rent; she wouldn't have had any rent to pay. Instead, she would have been stuck in the house, with her husband, until the divorce was final; that could have taken far more than a year. (Although most jurisdictions will award a nonworking spouse temporary support, you cannot count on it.)

11. *Build Up Your Own Credit*

If you don't have credit cards in your own name, apply for them now. You might be able to get them based on your spouse's income, and you will probably need credit later. Use the cards instead of cash and pay the entire balance by the due date every month. Don't charge more than you can pay; you'll be creating even more problems for yourself!

12. *Stay Involved with Your Children*

First of all, this is important for your children—especially because they will need all the support and reassurance they can get during the turbulent times ahead. In addition, because courts consider the depth and quality of your relationship when making custody and visitation decisions, such involvement now could translate to continued involvement, at a higher level, after the divorce.

Do a self-check: Have you been so busy earning a living that you've let your spouse bear the brunt of child rearing? If so, now is the time to reallocate your priorities. If you have school-age children, help get them off to school in the morning, help them with homework at night, and help get them to bed. Learn who their teachers are, who their pediatrician is, who their friends are. If your children are not yet in school, spend as much time with them as you can before and after work. Even if you don't have much likelihood of getting custody, you'll become a better parent.

Red Alert

Take heed of the much-publicized custody battle involving film director Woody Allen and his former partner, Mia Farrow. Allen's case for joint custody was severely weakened when the judge learned he didn't know the names of his children's pets or teachers or their shoe sizes. Although many parents might not know their child's shoe size, Farrow's lawyer made a big deal out of it. Don't make the same mistake.

13. Withdraw Your Money from the Bank

If you fear your request for divorce will send your spouse straight to the bank, withdraw half of the money in all your savings accounts first. Place the money in a new account, and keep it there until you and your spouse can work out the distribution of property. Do not spend the money if at all possible. If the money is in a checking account and you know the account is nearly emptied every month to pay bills, do not withdraw any of that money; you'll create financial havoc if checks bounce.

14. Consider Canceling Charge Cards

If you pay the credit card bills, consider canceling your accounts—or at least reducing the spending limit. In one case, the husband's announcement that he wanted a divorce sent the wife on a $12,000 shopping spree—and he had to pay for the fur coat, the VCR, and the Jacuzzi (installed, incidentally, in a house he stood to lose). If you cancel or reduce lines of credit, of course, you must inform your spouse to save embarrassment and later, anger. You can say the family needs to cut back, which is probably going to be true.

15. Decide How to Tell Your Spouse

Here, you might need professional advice or advice from a battle-worn friend. Would your partner accept the news more easily in a public place, such as a restaurant, or in the privacy of your home? One husband we know delayed telling his wife he wanted a divorce because she threatened suicide each time he mentioned separating. The wife was an unsuccessful actress with a flair for the dramatic who dropped her suicide threats once the husband agreed she could take over their apartment. Still, some threats must be dealt with seriously. If you're afraid your announcement will send your spouse off the deep end, be sure that you have consulted a professional counselor beforehand. Although there is often no way to lessen the hurt and rejection, a professional therapist might be able to supply you with strategies for leaving your spouse with as much of your self-esteem as possible intact.

16. Decide How to Tell the Children

You might want to consult with a professional. (For more details, see Chapter 18.) Would the news be best coming from the two of you together or from one of you alone? One husband we know planned to tell the children that he was moving out on Christmas. He thought that would be a good time because the whole family would be together. His lawyer tactfully suggested he choose a different day.

17. Take Property That Belongs to You and Safeguard It

High school yearbooks, jewelry, computer disks, your collection of Beatles albums, your grandmother's family heirlooms, whatever—if it indisputably belongs to you and you fear your spouse might take it for spite or leverage, move it out of the house. If you have several such items, move them out slowly, over time, before you announce your plans. Depending on the size of the objects, you might store them in a safe-deposit box, a storage facility, or the home of a trusted friend.

18. Don't Make Any Unnecessary Major Purchases

Once there are suddenly two households to maintain, you might find your financial freedom drastically curtailed. The number of men who buy brand new cars while they're starting divorce proceedings is staggering. The payments financially devastate them, and their wives use the existence of the "car" as proof of ability to pay for all sorts of other expenses. Sorry, guys: Resist.

19. Make Sure That Your Spouse Is the First to Know Your Plans

Although you might consult with friends before you take the plunge, be sure that they know loose lips sink ships.

20. Stay in the Marital Residence If Possible

You will weaken your position on custody and possibly your personal or *marital property* if you move.

You Can Do It!

Before you start divorce proceedings you might want to consider the legal difference between divorce and separation. If you want finality in your marital status, it is certainly preferable to be divorced. Alternatively, if you do not wish to be divorced, but want no legal obligations to your spouse, a judgement of separation would be preferable. We suggest that, to the extent possible, you investigate these alternatives in advance.

Divorce Dictionary

Marital property: Also called **joint property**, it is generally what a husband and wife acquire during the marriage. In some jurisdictions, inheritances, disability awards, and gifts received from a third party—that is, not the spouse—are not considered marital or joint property, even if a spouse received them during the marriage. Other exceptions may exist as well.

Silver Linings

Planning for your divorce in advance will make the transition far easier. If you can keep your emotions in check long enough to build a safety net, you'll reap the benefits for years.

When It Comes As a Shock...

Every so often, the specter of divorce takes you by surprise. One man we know, a naturalist in California, lived high in the mountains of La Crescenta, teaching school children and giving tours. He was thrilled to receive a free cabin near the forest for himself and his new wife; life couldn't be grander. One day—out of the blue, it seemed—his wife announced she couldn't take another day and she wanted a divorce. It turned out she missed the city life—the shops, the restaurants, the bars. She packed her suitcase, and the next morning, she was gone.

You Can Do It!

As always, stay involved with your children. With a major disruption imminent, your kids will need the reassurance of your extra attention. Fear of abandonment by one or both parents is the number-one reaction of children faced with divorcing parents. On the legal front, the more involved you are with your kids now, the more chance you will have to stay involved—by court order, if necessary.

Another man, this one from Malibu, took his wife out to dinner with a couple of friends who were in town for the weekend. Halfway through the meal, she stood up, stretched and yawned, and announced. "I'm just so sleepy, I'll have to meet you guys back at home." When the man arrived back at his beach house, guests in tow, his wife was nowhere to be found. Indeed, despite the embarrassment she caused her husband in front of his friends, she didn't return home that night at all. In the morning, she called to say she was in love with someone else and wanted a divorce.

A third friend found herself in a similar situation. She thought she and her husband were, for the most part, getting along well, with only some small disagreements. They had a beautiful one-year-old son whom they both doted on. One night, her husband announced he wanted a divorce. At the same time, he refused to move out of the house for another year because he wanted to bond with his son. She had no recourse. She lived under those strained circumstances until they worked out a settlement. Only then did he move out.

No matter what your circumstances, if your spouse's desire for divorce takes you by surprise, you will probably feel as if the bottom has dropped out from under you. You're likely to need months to lick your emotional wounds, restore your self-esteem, and start to heal. Nonetheless, as raw and beaten as you might feel, you will need to follow a plan of action if you want to protect your legal rights, financial assets, and access to your children. We know you'll have plenty of time to think the details through, but for now, when the pain is so enormous you can hardly think at all, you must attend to the following items to shore up your strategic position for later.

The second you're told you will be involved in divorce, you must hire a lawyer. Be sure to tell your lawyer about any problems that might require relief from the court: the need for money for yourself or your children; the need to decide, at least on a temporary basis, who the children will live with and what the visitation arrangements will be; and, in some cases, the need for protection from the other spouse.

If you are a parent, the most important thing you will do is protect your relationship with your children. Consult your lawyer immediately to make sure that you are doing everything possible to protect your rights with regard to your children, and avoid trampling on the rights of your spouse—no matter how you feel about him or her.

Red Alert

Alberto was so furious at Sarah for divorcing him and then suing for 90 percent of the estate that he sent her a cockroach in the mail. Aware of her fear of insects, he chuckled to think of her reaction upon opening the clever "gift." But at trial, the so-called antic served merely to enrage the judge. He found the "trick" so reprehensible and Alberto's character and sense of justice so skewed that all discretionary decisions were made in favor of Sarah. Please keep your anger in check. Angry or aggressive acts can be used against you once the legal system is involved.

No matter how angry you are, don't lock out your spouse and don't abandon your marital residence with or without the children. If you do so, you stand to damage your position with regard to custody and assets. If you've locked out your spouse, he or she will get back in somehow, and living under one roof will be even more excruciating.

Never act out of revenge. Do not put the children in a loyalty bind. Resist any urge to do "revenge spending." It might be used against you later if your case goes to court.

It goes without saying, of course, that you will follow the strategic list provided at the top of this chapter: Protect your financial position by learning all you can about your family's finances. Be sure to photocopy all relevant documents and photograph your valuables, including those in the safe deposit box.

You must also protect yourself against any preemptive moves your spouse may have taken without your knowledge. Directly ask your spouse for any papers that are suddenly missing. Make sure that the safe deposit box or family safe has not been raided. With your lawyer's help, you can get restraining orders against the use of specific bank accounts.

Now is the time for some financial strikes of your own. If it's not too late, collect any journals, calendars, or other items and remove them from the house. If your spouse hasn't yet raided the bank accounts, withdraw half of the savings accounts and open a new account. Do not spend that money if at all possible. If the credit cards are in your name, or if you pay the credit card bills, cancel them. Tell your spouse you are doing that. Because he or she has announced plans to divorce, this should not come as a surprise. On the other hand, if you have not yet established credit in your own name, now is the time to do so; use your spouse's credit lines to build some credit of your own. Obtain and complete applications immediately.

If the two of you are going to live together until the divorce is final, decide where you'll sleep. Note that because your spouse told you that he or she wants the divorce, you have the upper hand and can probably successfully demand use of the bedroom. If you and your spouse can still have a civil conversation, decide how and what the two of you will tell the children.

Finally, consider therapy if you feel it might help. There are going to be many stresses in the future, emotional as well as financial, and the better you can cope with them, the smoother the divorce process will go for you.

Worksheet for Calculating Expenses

Item	Amount
Housing Expenses	
Rent	_____
Mortgage	_____
Property taxes	_____
Condominium charges	_____
Cooperative maintenance charges	_____
Outstanding loan payments	_____
Gardening	_____
Cleaning person	_____
Household repairs	_____
Painting	_____
Furniture, linens	_____
Cleaning supplies	_____
Utilities	
Water charges	_____
Electricity	_____
Telephone	_____
Cable	_____
Appliances and upkeep	_____
Transportation Expenses	
Car payments	_____
Car insurance	_____
Car repairs	_____
Fuel	_____
Public transportation	_____
Children	
Children tuition	_____
Summer camp	_____
Babysitter/childcare	_____
Allowance	_____
School transportation	_____

continues

Worksheet for Calculating Expenses   Continued

Item	Amount
Child support (from previous relationships)	_____
Lessons (music, dance, etc.)	_____
Sporting goods	_____

Personal Expenses

Food	_____
Clothing	_____
Laundry	_____
Dry cleaning	_____
Books	_____
Magazines	_____
Newspapers	_____
Cigarettes	_____
Gifts	_____
Beauty parlor	_____
Lunches at work	_____
Courses	_____
Hobbies	_____

Insurance

Life insurance	_____
Personal property insurance	_____
Fire, theft, liability insurance	_____

Medical Expenses

Medical insurance	_____
Medical	_____
Dental	_____
Optical	_____
Pharmaceutical	_____

Entertainment

Vacation	_____
Movies	_____
VCR rentals	_____

Item	Amount
Theater	_____
Dining out	_____
Parties/entertaining	_____
Miscellaneous Debts and Expenses	
Credit card debt	_____
Alimony (from previous relationships)	_____
Church or temple dues	_____
Charitable contributions	_____
Income taxes	_____
Other (Have we missed something essential to your life? You fill in the blanks.)	
_____	_____
_____	_____
_____	_____
Total:	_____

The Least You Need to Know

➤ As soon as you know you will be involved in a divorce, hire an attorney.

➤ Find out what assets the family has.

➤ Find out what expenses the family presently has and what expenses you can expect in the future.

➤ Photocopy all business records.

➤ Get any incriminating information—particularly personal diaries—out of the house.

Chapter 3

Love in Ruins

> ### In This Chapter
>
> ➤ Understanding the emotional journey to divorce for the "dumper" and the "dumpee"
>
> ➤ How to tell your partner it's over and the importance of honesty
>
> ➤ How to work through the pain and get on with your life
>
> ➤ Leaving the family home or staying until the divorce is final: pros and cons
>
> ➤ Protecting your custodial, property, and financial rights in the aftermath of separation

One of our friends was devastated when, during her last year of medical residency, her husband, a wealthy surgeon, left for someone else without explaining, even briefly, what went wrong. The couple became involved in a protracted court battle regarding finances and issues of child custody. As trial date after trial date was postponed, issues of spousal maintenance and child support, division of property, and a permanent custody decision were put on hold. In all that time, the ex-husband (by now remarried with a new family) refused to tell his former wife why he'd left her, for fear it would weaken his case. But here's a tip: This woman would have traded untold thousands of dollars for a simple explanation. "I'll tell you after the case is closed," her former spouse often promised during their infrequent moments of civility. If only that moment had arrived.

In truth, it's impossible for you to shield your partner from pain if you are rejecting him or her. It's going to hurt—especially if you are forthright and direct in your communication. And yet, as you help your partner face this final stage of your relationship, the most important gift you can give is honesty.

Breaking the News

Couples who plan to divorce will achieve their new balance during a period of separation—one of the first legal and emotional steps down the road to divorce. This break in the relationship is often experienced quite differently by the person who has done the rejecting (the "dumper" in divorce vernacular) and the rejected individual (the "dumpee"). If you are the partner initiating the divorce, the emotional journey from your marriage toward a new life began long ago. However, your spouse, although sensing difficulties, might not realize how far you have traveled from the nucleus of your relationship. Your spouse might feel not just hurt and angry, but also shocked, when you announce the news.

You owe that much to someone you have married but now want to cast aside. Again and again, divorce psychologists confide, the lament they hear most is this: "I want one adequate explanation. I never knew what went wrong."

After you have provided your spouse with an honest explanation of what went wrong, expect powerful emotions ranging from sadness to anger to fear. Remember, the divorce might sadden you, too, but you have had time to get used to the idea. Your partner has not. You will have to give some time and some leeway for your spouse to catch up.

Oh, the Agony!

If you are on the receiving end of the divorce announcement, on the other hand, you might find yourself reeling with disbelief, pain, and, after the shock wears off, anger. You must remember that these feelings are entirely normal. Indeed, the grief one feels at divorce is in some ways comparable to the grief experienced when a beloved spouse dies. According to psychologist Mitchell Baris, the grief is experienced in phases.

"Initially," he explains, "You go through a phase of sadness, anger, and heightened feelings of rejection. There may be very different rates of acceptance for one partner than for another," Baris states. Eventually, even the rejected individual will come to see separation and divorce in a more positive light. The divorce decision, often pushed by one of you, becomes mutual.

It only makes sense that the person who initially made the decision comes to accept the reality of divorce sooner. "That individual is a little bit more advanced; they have been working through their initial feelings of acceptance, of realization that the relationship is over," says Baris. "The sadness, the sense of failure, has begun to fade, and he or she has already begun to envision the single life—whether as a single parent or as a single individual. By the time that person has announced a desire to divorce to a spouse, the idea of separation has already been worked through. The rejected individual, on the other hand, is typically several months behind in terms of working through the grief."

Famed death researcher Elizabeth Kubler-Ross defined the stages in the grieving process over the death of a loved one. Those facing divorce, say psychologists, can expect much of the same:

➤ **Denial**   This is your basic state of shock. You cannot believe it's true.

➤ **Anger**   The rejected individual, "the dumpee," will direct anger at the rejecting spouse and the world. Get it out. It's okay.

➤ **Guilt**   Feelings of guilt cannot help but rear their head, more often in the one initiating the divorce, but in the recipient as well. It's important to turn guilt into something constructive: an examination of the role you played in the breakup of your marriage. Life is about growth, after all, and if you can't see yourself clearly, you won't be able to move on.

➤ **Acceptance**   Reality has sunk in. It's not one of those bad dreams from which you will awaken; it's real. You accept this as your reality and move on—however awkwardly, however tentatively—with your life.

In most situations, both people eventually accept the new reality, although for the rejected person, there may be scars. Ideally, in time, both will become centered in themselves and create a new lifestyle that includes an active social life, new friendships, and even romance.

Those who remain stuck in a morass of anger, self-pity, and self-imposed isolation might be helped by psychotherapy; through therapy, they should come to understand that they are just as valuable as their spouse and any other living soul. The right counselor can do wonders for someone who needs to change his or her view of the world, embrace creativity in life, and, most important, start feeling good!

Separation: Beginning of the End or a New Beginning?

Sometimes, of course, separation does not lead to divorce. Many times, couples will separate in the hope of saving a marriage. Sometimes, this can work. After all, just getting distance from a painful, antagonistic situation can provide you with enough perspective to come back together weeks or months later and sort things out.

One couple we know did just that. The man, a newspaper reporter, left his wife in Boston and went on assignment in Russia for a year. Their marriage had been on the rocks, but during the year apart, the two developed an email correspondence that brought them new intimacy and understanding. When they came back together after 12 months apart, they were ready to really commit to the relationship and even decided to start a family.

Most of the time, however, such plans backfire. Another couple we know, this time from Dallas, opted for a long-distance relationship as a means of gaining perspective. The decision was facilitated when the woman was offered a job in Des Moines. Unfortunately, her husband began feeling so resentful when she really left that ultimately, he could not accept her back into his life—and he felt this way despite the fact that he was the one who had encouraged her to leave in the first place.

In other marriages, separation—as opposed to divorce—becomes a permanent way of life. We know of a couple who stayed separate but married for some 20 years. (Indeed, they exist in that state to this day.) The woman, happily ensconced in a townhouse in Miami, played tennis during the day and spent evenings with her lover, another woman. The man, who enjoyed the city life in a Manhattan penthouse, ran a successful business and pursued a series of monogamous relationships that fell apart, one by one, when he refused to divorce. For this couple, divorce held nothing positive. It would have eroded their joint fortune and diminished the money available to their children (they had two), and, in the man's case, made him available for remarriage, an idea he hardly relished.

Deconstruction: Separation As the First Step

For most people, however, separation is a preamble to divorce. As the name implies, it is the first step along the journey to separate lives. Not quite permanent or irrevocable, separation enables the two individuals to get a taste of what it would be like to exist apart—to manage separate households, separate finances, separate selves.

Red Alert

If you think you are going to divorce eventually and you might want custody of your children, some judges might hold your move from your children's house against you. Be careful. Don't let a short-term goal interfere with what you really want.

We know one woman who married the first boyfriend she ever had right after college. As the marriage went on, he became increasingly critical and angry. (Psychological abuse is the phrase that comes to mind.) Yet because she'd never really been alone, she could not imagine life without him. Finally, through therapy, she was able to take what she thought would be a short hiatus from the marriage. She never imagined that during this break she would experience a return of self-esteem, enthusiasm, and even joy. This "brief" separation was just what she needed to realize she could go it alone over the long haul.

The Value of Separation

As we've already said, it only makes sense that the person who initiated the divorce comes to embrace single life sooner; that individual has been living with the decision for quite a while. Given this fact, the individual who has initiated the divorce should see the separation as a means of providing his or her partner with time. Even though you might be saying, "Okay, we're going to end the relationship. Let's get working on the terms of the separation. Let's see if we can mediate this," your partner is still reeling from the pain. At first, he or she will not be nearly as ready to negotiate the terms of the agreement—certainly not in any sense that could be favorable to you.

If you have been rejected by your spouse, on the other hand, use the separation period to help yourself heal. As you go through the stages of grief, you will come to see yourself as a solo act. You might need to utilize this time to brush up on job skills, gain self-confidence, or simply come to know yourself as an individual who stands alone. You'll know you have arrived when you, too, can say, "Okay, I can see our incompatibility. This needs to end. At this point, I would also choose to end this relationship and go on in a new direction."

Remember, the process is painful. If you're like most people, you won't pass quickly through the emotional gauntlet of separation. Typically, say psychologists, the first year following separation is most difficult. During this period, you're most prey to mood swings, sadness, feelings of loss, and anger. If you remain on this emotional roller-coaster for more than a year, however, you are not progressing fast enough. It is time to seek counseling or some other form of psychological help.

Published research bears this timetable out. According to a study from psychologist Joan Kelly of the Center for Marital Transition near San Francisco, couples in conflict report that conflict drastically reduces after 12 months. Other research indicates that conflict and anger tend to diffuse after a period of separation, and if couples have not continued to interact, at the end of two years, most of the conflict will be gone.

For couples with children, who must interact with each other to co-parent even in the face of divorce, a separation goes a long way toward easing conflict. Only after time apart can these parents come back and cooperate enough to co-parent again. A couple without children can make this break and need never come back together again. But for parents, this is impossible. If you're in this situation, you're stuck with your soon-to-be-ex-spouse for better or worse. You've got to figure out some way to manage the conflict and get over it so that you can see your ex from time to time and reestablish a businesslike relationship that works. Psychologists advise these parents to create every opportunity for complete separation so that full emotional disengagement can take place. After a period of time—generally about a year—they can relax the separation. Without the hiatus, such parents often keep the battle going, and the conflict never ends.

You Can Do It!

Make sure that even though you are moving out, your spouse understands that you are not giving up the right to property. Many spouses, out of guilt, give the other so much money that they have to move into a single room where they cannot bring the children to visit. Don't become one of them. Ask your attorney to protect you as vigorously as possible through a legally binding separation agreement.

31

In light of all the work you and your spouse will need to do during your separation, this is a poor time to invest in a new relationship. You must give yourself the time and space to find some new personal definition and direction. Separation is a perfect time to look inward, asking yourself how you contributed to the relationship's end. Some people have difficulty assuming responsibility for creating negative situations for themselves and so look to blame anybody or anything else. You must let go of this "victim" mentality if you are to avoid making the same mistakes again.

Surviving Forced Togetherness

Sometimes, despite the positive impact of formal separation, couples stay together for legal and financial reasons until the day of the divorce decree. There are a number of reasons why this is often legally advisable. If you seek full or joint custody of the children—or if you just want a generous visitation schedule—staying in the house will help your cause. Leaving, in fact, often puts you at a tremendous disadvantage in any legal proceeding. Although the opinions expressed here, as in the rest of the book, do not constitute legal advice, the decision to stay or leave is so important that we strongly advise you to consult your attorney before you do anything.

Your leaving might make it easier for your spouse to delay the signing of divorce papers, putting you at a strategic disadvantage. Indeed, many times, a spouse will just want you out of the house but because of economic circumstances will be reluctant to move forward with divorce. Once you leave, your spouse will have little incentive to move quickly. The longer your spouse delays the divorce, the more frustrated you will become and the more likely you will be to sign an agreement less favorable to yourself. On the other hand, if you stay in the home, your spouse will be the frustrated one; you will have the upper hand during negotiations.

Finally, for those who are particularly money conscious—and who isn't these days— the longer you and your spouse share the same home, the more money you will save.

If you've decided to stay in the house until the divorce is over, turn one section into your "camp." If you move out of the bedroom, do not—we repeat, do not—leave your clothes, jewelry, and other possessions in the dresser, especially if you plan to use them on a daily or weekly basis. Instead, choose a spot—the den, the guest room, or even the basement—and move all your clothes and possessions there so that you and your spouse have as little negative interaction as possible. (Weekday mornings are pretty negative even in the happiest marriages!)

If you have been advised by your attorney to stay in the house, try to do so as amicably as is humanly possible. One psychologist we have interviewed even suggests Yogic breathing exercises as a means of dealing with the stress this sort of situation brings. Remember, your code word is equanimity. Of course it will be difficult, but adding any more hatred or animosity to the marital pot is toxic.

If life in the house is intolerable and you know custody is not in the cards for you, a move might be wise. It could take one to three years for your divorce to be final, and neither you nor your spouse could cope with one to three more years of tension. More important, it's not good for the children. Again, check with your lawyer before making a decision.

Before you move, discuss the division of personal property with your spouse. You might not be able to take anything with you yet (one woman stayed with 10 friends during the 12 weeks it took her to locate an affordable apartment), but at least you'll both understand that by moving out, you're not giving up your rights to property. Your lawyer might want this in writing. If you don't have a lawyer, write down that you are not giving up any rights by moving out and ask your spouse to sign what you've written.

If life in the house is intolerable and you want custody of the children, talk to your lawyer about moving out with the children. Your lawyer might want to first obtain an order from a judge, giving you temporary custody of the children, thereby giving you the right to take the kids with you when you leave.

Silver Linings

During your first year of separation, you might find comfort and camaraderie in one of the myriad support groups for the divorced. See Appendix B to locate a group in your area. As you go about choosing a group, however, do be cautious. Some divorce groups are wonderfully supportive and nurture healing. Others foster conflict and fan the flames of anger. It will not help you to associate with a group that feeds the anger. What you really need—and what should be available in most areas—is a support team that facilitates positive, constructive solutions for your life so that you can get beyond this relationship and your divorce and move on.

The Least You Need to Know

➤ Be honest with your spouse about your reasons for moving on.

➤ Remember that most people get through the most intense part of their grief within a year and go on to experience personal renewal and growth.

➤ Stay in the house until the divorce is final if you have significant property or custodial rights to protect and if you can bear it.

➤ Protect your financial and property interests through any legal means available to you as soon and as strenuously as possible.

➤ If life in the house is intolerable and you want custody of the children, talk to your lawyer about moving out with the children.

Chapter 4

When There's No Turning Back

In This Chapter

➤ Financial archaeology: documenting your life from year one

➤ When to hire a private investigator

➤ How to review your prenuptial agreement

➤ How to practice discretion if you decide to date

➤ How to craft your own settlement agreement

Once the decision to divorce is made, you must—each of you, alone—take some practical steps to protect your interests. As unfortunate and as heartless as it sounds, you have moved on to another stage. You have stopped trying to patch things up in the realm of the heart and have begun instead to negotiate the real world of lawyers and courts, bank accounts and mortgage payments, and, most critically, the custodial fate of your children.

Where to Begin the End

If you and your spouse still get along and you are both fully aware of the family's financial situation, you can sit down and work out an allocation of assets and liabilities. You might also be able to agree on custody and visitation. The two of you together could conceivably decide who takes the children when and for how long; how to structure visitation; how to arrange for childcare; and how to cooperate so that you are there to back up each other in the parental role, although you no longer function as husband and wife. Each of you can then find a lawyer: One attorney will draw up documents, and the other will review them. Voilá, you're on your way.

The problem is, of course, things don't always go this smoothly. Even the best-intentioned couples find themselves arguing over anything from the custody of Rover to who gets the football season tickets. If you're like most people, sitting down over a cup of coffee and dividing up the hard-earned fruits of your marriage is just not going to happen.

What then? Follow the Scouting motto: Be prepared. In Chapter 5, we provide some additional tips to help you lay the groundwork for this preparation. We'll assume, of course, that you've already followed the steps recommended in Chapter 2. By now, you have hired a lawyer and have taken stock of your family's financial situation, including any income, property, or outstanding debt. But as the dust begins to clear, as reality sets in, you will be dealing with the details—the accumulations, the detritus, the remains of your relationship, and the vestiges of your shared life. As you set out to settle the score, divest some baggage, work through pain, or simply clear the field, you'll need to attend to the special issues discussed in this chapter.

Gathering Your Financial Documents

You've already collected financial statements readily available around the house. In some cases, it's important to have copies of tax returns, bank statements, insurance policies, and loan applications going back in the marriage as far as possible; if you or your spouse have destroyed documents after a decade, as some people do, it could work against you. Such documentation might be especially critical if there's a gap between your reported income and your standard of living.

The Bright family, for instance, reported income of $50,000, but the two children attend private school ($20,000 per year total); the Brights take two very nice vacations a year ($5,000 total); the monthly mortgage on their house is $1,000 ($12,000 total); the monthly mortgage on their summer house is $500 ($6,000 total); and each party drives a leased car at a combined cost of $500 a month ($6,000 total). Grand total: $49,000. That leaves $1,000 for taxes, food, utilities, clothing, pet supplies, and so on. Clearly, there's more income than has been reported. Bank statements, credit card receipts, canceled checks, and the like all help prove real, as opposed to reported, income. You might also need tax returns simply to prove how much income you or your spouse earns, even if you work for someone else.

If you can't find any of these documents (or you never saved them), you can write the Internal Revenue Service for copies of joint returns, or you can ask your accountant for copies. The bank might keep copies of loan applications and might be willing to release a copy of your application to you. For a fee, although it tends to get expensive, you can obtain copies of canceled checks and your bank statements. (Before incurring that expense, check with your attorney. He or she might be able to get the same information directly from your spouse's attorney. In most instances, the divorce law of your state entitles you to this information if your spouse has it or has access to it.)

As you document your deep financial history, make sure that you include these assets:

Cash	Options to buy stocks
Savings accounts	403 accounts
Checking accounts	401(k) accounts
CD accounts	Individual retirement accounts
Security deposits	Pension plans
Bonds	Cash value of life insurance
Notes	Businesses
Stocks	Loans to others
Jewelry	Expected inheritance
Antiques	Educational degrees
Judgments	Real property
Artwork	
Vehicles	
Business assets, including accounts receivable, work in process, inventory, hard assets, computer equipment, and software programs	

The point is, once the dust has cleared and you can focus, you might need to do a little digging in preparation for the legal proceedings to come. A divorce trial can sometimes be like a war, and you want to go to battle fully armed. Who wouldn't?

The Price of Dating Before the Divorce

As you continue to plan strategically for your divorce in these early stages, you need to consider the impact dating will have during your day in court. Just because you are divorcing, you do not have to be a hermit, unless your attorney tells you otherwise. Usually, discretion is the key. For example, if your divorce is not yet final, never have a friend of the opposite sex sleep at your home or spend time alone with you in your bedroom while the children are home. Similarly, if you are claiming that your spouse was unfaithful, and it is important to your case that you have been faithful, do not become involved with anyone until the divorce is final.

Even if your lawyer tells you it's okay to date, avoid going places where you might run into your spouse. In one case, a husband took his new girlfriend to his wife's favorite restaurant. (She found out when the credit card charges came through.) She was furious and refused to cooperate in settling the case.

Don't bring the children along on a date and don't introduce your friend to them. Unless your case is over or it has been dragging on for many years, it's too soon for the children, and it will only make your spouse mad. (You can be sure that your kids will give your spouse a full report.)

Hiring a Private Eye

You might feel that you want to do some digging in a host of personal realms. Perhaps you suspect that your spouse is having an affair, and you want the goods on him or her. Should you hire a private eye?

The days when you needed compromising pictures of your spouse in the arms of another are long gone. In all states, you can get a divorce on grounds other than adultery. Still, there are people, and you might be one of them, who firmly believe that if you could catch your spouse "in the act," he or she would "cave in" and give you an enormous settlement rather than risk disclosure of the infidelity.

Red Alert

You might worry that your spouse has hired a private detective or used other means to track you. Is your phone tapped? Are there hidden microphones in the walls? Sounds like paranoia, and for most people, it is. If you think your line is tapped, have the phone company check your line and phone. If you still feel paranoid, it might be worth your money to have your house checked, but never let your spouse know. (Do it when the children are away.)

In our opinion, this works on television and in the movies, but not in real life. Sometimes, the two-timing spouse is relieved to have his or her relationship out in the open; other times, he or she just doesn't care. Paying a private eye, at a hefty hourly rate, usually is not worth it.

There is one exception. If custody is going to be an issue in your case, the work of a private investigator might pay off. If you suspect that your spouse ignores the children or relegates their care to someone else (ranging from grandparents to babysitters), or if there is an unknown person living with your spouse and your young children, you might consider calling a detective. Evidence for any of these scenarios could be vitally important in a custody case, particularly if you and your spouse are otherwise equally capable parents.

Finally, here's a word to the wise: Never conduct surveillance yourself. Secret tape recordings of your spouse might prove harmful. In one difficult case, the husband, who sought custody of his two young sons, provoked his wife into an argument while the children were in the same room. Secretly, he taped 10 minutes of his wife yelling and the children crying. The husband played the tape in court. The wife's voice filled the courtroom, sounding shrill on the recording, while the children wailed in the background. The husband lost custody. The wife testified that the husband had started the argument. What kind of father, her lawyer argued, would deliberately subject his children to an argument between their parents to create evidence for court?

In some states, it is against the law to tap a phone line, and for that reason alone, you should never tap a phone line without first discussing the matter with your attorney. Furthermore, there is not much to be gained from a phone tap. A recorded phone conversation probably won't do you much good, unless it somehow directly bears on the issue of custody. The moral here is simple. Always consult with your attorney before engaging in any scheme involving a tape recorder. Even if taping is not against the law in your state, your plan might come back to haunt you.

Reviewing Your Prenuptial Agreement

If you and your spouse signed a *prenuptial agreement*, this is the time to pull it out. You might be surprised to read what the two of you signed in the throes of first love.

Prenups, as lawyers call them, used to be popular mostly with older people who were marrying for the second time and wanted to protect the inheritance rights of their children in the event they died. However, provisions for what would happen in the event the parties divorced began to pop up, and now, young people marrying for the first time often inquire about having a prenup. Some stand to inherit money from parents, and the parents want the prenup. Others are wealthy in their own right and have heard so many divorce horror stories that they want to protect their rights.

If you signed a properly executed prenup or postnuptial agreement (an agreement entered into after your marriage), there is little to discuss if the marriage fails. Judges will generally uphold the terms of the prenup with a couple of exceptions. In general, judges will not uphold provisions in a prenuptial agreement stating who is to have custody of children and how much child support is to be paid. The care and support of children is usually subject to court review. In addition, judges will not support your agreement if you can prove it was the product of fraud, coercion, distress, or some other unfairness the laws of your state allow you to assert.

Divorce Dictionary

Prenuptial agreement: A written contract entered into by a couple before marriage to establish their rights in the event of a death or divorce. The validity of such agreements depends on state law. It is advisable to sign a prenuptial agreement only if you are sure that you understand it, you know what assets your soon-to-be spouse has (and vice versa), and you have your own attorney review the document.

You Can Do It!

If you didn't have an attorney, you were unaware of your spouse's assets or liabilities, you did not understand the agreement, you were tricked into signing it, or you signed it very close to your wedding day, you might convince a judge to throw out the prenup.

Remember, all states subscribe to the Uniform Premarital Agreement Act. Some, such as California, do not include all its provisions, but such agreements between responsible adults represented by counsel and with full disclosure are favored by the courts these days.

What, exactly, will a judge consider unfair? Did you each have your own attorney when you signed the agreement? Did you each reveal how much money, assets, and debts you had before you signed the agreement? How close to your wedding date was the agreement signed? (Signing it on the day before might be construed as undue pressure.) Did you understand the agreement? Were you tricked into signing it? If you can prove any of these unfavorable conditions existed, a judge might invalidate the prenuptial agreement.

Starting the Divorce Action

To get the divorce process rolling, someone will need to file. The spouse who starts the legal proceedings is called the *plaintiff* or *petitioner*, and the one who responds is called the *defendant*, or *respondent*.

Your lawyer will decide when to start legal divorce proceedings, usually based on a number of different factors. Maybe you need some kind of immediate relief, such as support, and your spouse has refused to provide it. Your lawyer must go to court and ask a judge to order your spouse to pay. The only way the lawyer can go to court is to first start a divorce action, and therefore you would be the plaintiff, or petitioner.

Perhaps you've decided to start your divorce action a few months before you get that bonus, thus excluding the money from marital property. Depending on the laws of your state, such strategy may or may not be completely effective. Even if a bonus is paid after the date of separation, it might be deemed joint property because it was earned during the marriage.

Perhaps you and your spouse have worked out a mutually agreeable deal, and when it's time to file, the lawyer who has been doing the paperwork simply files for her client—whichever spouse that may be.

In short, who becomes plaintiff and who becomes defendant depends on a number of factors. Although it might not sit right with you to be the defendant or respondent, gone are the days when such labels mattered much.

Working Out a Settlement Agreement

In the best of all possible worlds, you and your spouse would sit down like two civilized adults and pound out a fair settlement between yourselves.

In one difficult case, a 60-year-old man was divorcing his second wife. (His first wife died after 30 years of marriage.) Discussions between the lawyers went nowhere, and the parties' grown children from their first marriages weren't helping with their endless "suggestions." Finally, the husband met his wife for breakfast at a diner one

Sunday morning. Monday, he came to see his lawyer with the details of a settlement scribbled on a napkin. The lawyers got busy writing up the settlement agreement.

The moral of the story? You and your spouse should do whatever you can to settle the case. You'll save legal fees and headaches. There is only one caveat. Do not sign anything until you speak to your lawyer.

Indeed, we conclude this chapter by stating the obvious: Always check with your attorney before signing any agreement or taking any major steps such as moving out, withdrawing money from joint accounts, stopping credit cards, hiring a private investigator, or trying to tape conversations.

The Least You Need to Know

➤ In the best of all possible worlds, you'll work out a settlement agreement with your spouse—but don't count on it.

➤ Photocopy all the financial documents you can find, particularly if actual income—as opposed to reported income—is going to be an issue.

➤ Be discreet if you date, and consider hiring a private investigator when appropriate in issues concerning child custody.

➤ Make sure to review your prenuptial agreement as early in the game as possible.

➤ Always check with your attorney before signing any agreement or taking any major steps such as moving out, withdrawing money from joint accounts, stopping credit cards, hiring a private investigator, or trying to tape conversations.

Part 2
Navigating the Law

After you digest the fact that your marriage is really ending, you must negotiate its conclusion as gracefully, efficiently, and inexpensively as you can—in a way advantageous to you. This simply won't be possible unless you learn all you can about matrimonial law. Only through such knowledge will you be able to protect your rights and your self-esteem.

Consider Part 2 your gentle introduction to divorce law. In the next nine chapters, we will help you take stock: Should you attempt to settle your case out of court, on your own? Or should you proceed to the battleground of a trial, armed with attorney, financial documents, and more stamina than you have ever needed before? We present a rundown of the most common legal problems and the pros and cons of such procedures as arbitration and mediation. Learn to understand and use the divorce lawyer, generally the architect of your fight for justice. Study the rules of divorce court. And acquire a taste for the distinctive and complex divorce-court culture that pervades the litigation experience in America today.

Chapter 5

Flip
Flip

How to Find and Retain an Attorney

In This Chapter

➤ Choosing a lawyer who's right for you

➤ What to expect from your lawyer

➤ An introduction to fees

➤ Evaluating references

➤ How to interview a prospective lawyer

If you had a sizable wedding, you probably followed these ancient rituals: You listened to various bands before choosing the music; you tasted food from different caterers before hiring a chef; and you studied sample photograph albums before selecting a photographer. In an ironic twist of fate, getting divorced is easier in at least one way. You need to find only one person: a competent lawyer you like, trust, and can afford. And your spouse doesn't have to agree!

Why a Lawyer Might Be Essential

If you've been married a relatively short time, or you don't have many assets or much debt, or you and your spouse have worked everything out, you might be able to proceed without a lawyer. Court clerks are usually not allowed to give legal advice, but that doesn't mean they can't tell you where to file what papers. Legal form publishers might have "divorce kits" that you can use to do all the paperwork yourself.

On the other hand, if you have children, you have acquired assets, even if only a house and a pension, or you and your spouse cannot agree on anything, you would be well advised to seek legal counsel. Even if you agree on everything, your money would still be well spent on a consultation. It's perfectly acceptable to present a lawyer with the agreement you and your spouse have drafted and ask for comments.

One young father assumed that if his wife had custody of their young son, she would be free to move anywhere in the country. He was surprised, and relieved, to learn that he could include in his agreement the stipulation that his wife not move more than 75 miles from her present location—provided he had not already moved himself. That was a provision he wanted, and got, in the agreement. For him, the attorney's fees spent were well worth it.

How to Choose the Best Lawyer for You

Even if your case seems pretty straightforward, go to someone who has handled matrimonial cases before. You don't need an attorney who works solely in that area, whose fees might be very high. But you do want someone who knows which papers have to be filed in which courthouse and who can take your case to trial if need be. Now is not the time to do your third cousin a favor by hiring her newly admitted son.

You Can Do It!

The American Academy of Matrimonial Lawyers in Chicago is a good source for names of qualified attorneys in your area. This organization has high standards that must be met by their members. You may reach them by phone at (312) 263-6477 or via their Web site at http://www.aaml.org.

Some very competent matrimonial lawyers will tell you from the outset that they do not go to court. They might be very good negotiators, but if your case doesn't settle, they will recommend another attorney, either in their firm or another, to take over the case. For some people, that's fine. Others prefer to have an attorney who will go the distance. Be sure to ask.

When you call the lawyer, ask whether there is a fee for the initial consultation. Don't be shy. Some lawyers will see you for free; others will charge their usual hourly rate (which might be as much as $300 an hour in major metropolitan areas). The reasoning: They've already done work on your behalf (albeit during the consultation) by collecting the background information they need to begin. Others will only bill you if they take your case.

As you search for a lawyer, also be sensitive to the amount of time you're kept in the waiting room. Your attorney's office shouldn't be Grand Central Station, after all. A small wait isn't always a bad sign, but if you are kept waiting more than 15 minutes, you might want to think twice about using that attorney. He or she should want to impress you most before you sign on. If you have to wait a long time before the initial consultation, what will it be like after you're a client?

You might want to work other factors into the equation as well. How does the office look? You don't need skyline views, but if the office is dirty, or the magazines are months old, be wary. Will your legal papers be cared for the same way? On the other hand, some attorneys do share space with others, and upkeep of the office is not within their control.

Once you begin your meeting inside the lawyer's private office, are you constantly interrupted as the attorney takes calls? An emergency call is one thing, but a constant stream of interruptions is another sign that this lawyer might just be too busy—or too disinterested in your case.

Your First Meeting

When you're with an attorney for the first time, he or she will ask you for some background information about your situation. You should be told, briefly, how the laws work in your state and what that will mean for your own case. The lawyer can also tell you which court will handle your case. Is the court in your jurisdiction backlogged? Knowing this could determine your strategy in resolving your case—is it helpful to drag out the divorce or to end it quickly?

Red Alert

Make sure you choose an attorney you can afford. Some lawyers want a large retainer, but their hourly rate is relatively low or they have a junior attorney who can do some of the work at a lower hourly rate. You might be better off with that than with an attorney with a small retainer and a high hourly rate. Be sure to ask how much the total is likely to be. Most attorneys will tell you that they honestly don't know; and in fact, the cost depends, to a large degree, on how quickly you and your spouse can come to an agreement. Nonetheless, the lawyer might be able to give you a figure based on similar cases.

A lawyer who knows the judges and their individual biases and personalities will be ahead of the game. Unfortunately, a carefully weighted decision by a judge can be less common in some jurisdictions. Some, for instance, may see all mothers as overprotective or all fathers as bill payers. Sometimes a decision can be made simply on the basis of whether the judge had a fight with his or her own spouse that day! A savvy attorney who has been around will be able to maneuver around a judge's personality or bias with more agility than someone who is new to the field or to the area.

Fees and Billing

During this first consultation, the lawyer should also explain his or her fees. Does she take a *retainer*—a lump-sum payment—up front? That practice is common. As the lawyer works on your case, she subtracts an amount equal to her hourly rate from the sum you have prepaid. For example,

Divorce Dictionary

Retainer: Money paid in advance to an attorney upon retaining the attorney. Future billed time is deducted from the retainer until the retainer is depleted.

if you paid Attorney Greenfield $1,000 and her hourly rate was $100, you would have bought 10 hours of work in advance. Most will quote a flat rate for the retainer.

Other lawyers do not take a retainer and simply bill you every month as the case moves along. Some lawyers require that a cushion remain in the retainer until the case is concluded—for example, a few thousand dollars to cover the closing of a matter or to refund to you at the conclusion of the case. Whatever the arrangement, determine the details now. Remember, never sign on with a lawyer unless you have these financial details in writing. You'll read more about fees in Chapter 7.

It's a Small World, After All

If your spouse has already hired an attorney, find out whether that individual has had any dealings with the lawyer you hope to hire. Remember, lawyers develop enemies and make friends. A lawyer will rarely come right out and say he hates your spouse's attorney and can't even call him or her, let alone negotiate, so you need to be crafty. Watch the attorney's reaction when you mention the lawyer's name. Ask whether they've had any cases against one another. Ask about the other lawyer's reputation.

You might even tell a white lie; say that you've heard the other attorney is impossible and ask whether there's any truth to it. A lawyer might be more willing to agree with an assessment that he or she thinks someone else has made.

Silver Linings

A lawyer who knows your spouse's lawyer and gets along with him or her will also put you and your spouse in a position to resolve the case efficiently.

Good Referral Sources

Many people find a divorce lawyer through recommendation of a professional. Clergy, therapists, and marriage counselors might all have divorce attorneys to suggest. Probably the most common way to get the name of a matrimonial attorney is through another attorney. You might already have a business lawyer, or maybe the lawyer who drew up your will is a friend and can recommend someone. Suppose you've gone to see one matrimonial lawyer, and you want the names of a few others. He or she will not be reluctant to give you some, especially if you explain that you can't afford the quoted fees.

Another source of referrals is friends who have been divorced. Sometimes, they will recommend their spouse's lawyer over their own, particularly if they thought they got the short end of the stick. This, too, is a good way to get started.

Your local bar association might also have the names of attorneys who do matrimonial work, but that's a step away from using the Yellow Pages. Remember, lawyers can generally make it into the bar association list simply by joining the association, not by showing any particular level of expertise. Still, many of those lawyers will provide a consultation at a low fee or for free, and you might find one who meets your criteria. Some state bar associations have formal specialty certifications. Look for a certified family law or matrimonial specialist who is certified by the state bar, if your state has such certifications.

As far as we're concerned, a better organization to tap is the American Academy of Matrimonial Attorneys, headquartered in Chicago. Each state has a chapter. Admission to the academy is highly selective. (See Appendix B for contact information.) Members must be in practice for a certain number of years; they must have worked largely if not solely in the field of matrimonial law; and they must pass a test. A member of this group will certainly be well qualified but might also be very expensive. One more caveat: In some chapters of the academy, politics play a role in who gets in and who stays out. The fact that an attorney is not a member does not necessarily mean that he or she is less qualified than a member. It could mean, however, that the lawyer and the president of the local chapter just don't get along.

Last but not least, the Yellow Pages can help. After all, you're only looking for an attorney with whom to have an initial consultation at this point. You're not actually hiring anyone blindly through any of these sources.

The Fox, the Shark, and the Lamb: A Look at Legal Styles

There are as many different legal styles as there are attorneys. Some attorneys are tough and aggressive and give you an immediate feeling of confidence or dislike, depending on your perspective. Others seem too nice or too soft-spoken, and you can't imagine them standing up to your spouse, let alone a judge.

Your attorney's legal style has to make you feel confident and at home. Of course, you want someone who will deftly help you negotiate and win power points in court. By the same token, if your lawyer is such a shark you're afraid to speak up and voice your concerns, all that aggression won't do you much good. In the end, it's a huge plus if you simply like your lawyer. Are you compatible? Can you be straightforward without feeling he or she is judgmental or condescending? Is your attorney genuinely concerned about you and the outcome of your case?

Some lawyers act one way when they are with clients, another when they're in front of a judge, and still another when they're with your spouse's lawyer. That's not always inconsistency; sometimes, it's just smarts. The best thing you can do is to watch prospective attorneys perform in court; this is difficult, of course, because legal schedules change at the drop of a hat.

You might also ask the lawyer for a client reference. Some attorneys might feel uncomfortable with the request because of confidentiality issues, but others might have clients who would be willing to talk.

How to Interview a Lawyer

What exactly do you need to know before you hire a lawyer? Here are some questions to ask before you write a retainer check or sign on the dotted line.

Red Alert

Resist the temptation to hire a lawyer based on your notion of how that lawyer might relate to your spouse. You might think it important for the lawyer to be able to stand up to your spouse. The truth is, the lawyer usually won't even speak to your spouse, only to his or her lawyer. Thus, the way your lawyer gets along with your spouse's lawyer is the real sticking point. Don't worry about your spouse's opinion of your lawyer.

Concerning general experience, ask these questions:

➤ How many matrimonial cases have you handled?

➤ How many of those cases went to trial? (An attorney who has done a lot of trials might not be a good negotiator. Keep that in mind, especially when the lawyer hasn't been in practice that long.)

➤ How many of these cases involved custody, support, large financial settlements, or whatever issue feels like your major concern?

➤ Where did you go to law school? (Don't ask if the diploma is staring you in the face.)

➤ Do you have the time to take on a new case now?

➤ Do you know my husband (or wife)?

➤ Do you know his or her attorney?

Ask about day-to-day operations:

➤ Will anyone (usually an associate) be assisting you on my case?

➤ What is his or her experience?

➤ Can I meet the associate now?

➤ What work would the associate do and what work would you do?

➤ Which one of you will negotiate the case? (If you want to be sure that the lawyer you are seeing is the negotiator, make that clear. You don't want an intern performing your quadruple bypass surgery, and you don't want an inexperienced associate you haven't met negotiating your divorce.)

➤ Who will try my case?

➤ Are you available to take phone calls?

➤ Is the associate available to take calls?

➤ What hours are you usually in the office?

➤ Do you have any time-consuming trials coming up?

➤ Will I get copies of all papers (letters, faxes, legal papers) in my case? (Be sure the answer is yes.)

Make sure the fees are clear:

➤ What is your hourly billing rate?

➤ What is the associate's billing rate?

➤ If both you and the associate are working on my case at the same time, am I billed at your combined rates? (Some firms do that only if two attorneys are needed, such as at trial. Others do it routinely, and others only bill you at the higher attorney's rate.)

➤ Is your fee for trial different from your hourly rate? (Some attorneys charge a set fee for every day they are in court.)

➤ Do you charge a retainer, and how much is it?

➤ Will the billing arrangements be set out in writing? (Insist that they be.)

➤ What happens when the retainer is used up?

➤ Will you keep me informed each month as to how much of the retainer has been used up?

➤ What happens if I get behind on the bills?

➤ Can you collect your fees from my spouse?

➤ How much am I billed for copies of all relevant documents? (If the fee is too high, you might want to make copies on your own.)

➤ What extra fees should I expect? (Typically, your retainer will not cover court filing fees, process server fees, excessive postage, messengers, stenographers, or similar out-of-pocket expenses.)

➤ Are those fees due in advance, and will I know in advance what they are?

➤ Am I billed for telephone calls?

➤ Do you have a minimum unit of time you bill me for? (Some lawyers will bill you for 5 or even 15 minutes when a call takes only 4 minutes. The theory is that you've taken them away from some other project, and they need time to "get back into it.")

➤ Do you take credit cards? Not many do now, but some do, and more will in the future. This can help you spread out your payments.

Ask these questions about handling the case:

➤ Will I have input in decisions concerning strategy in my case?

➤ Will I be kept informed of all developments?

➤ What problems do you foresee arising out of my case?

➤ What are your personal feelings about joint custody versus sole custody? Sometimes a lawyer has strong convictions one way or the other that could potentially affect the outcome of your case despite the fact that your wishes should prevail.

➤ Based on your experience, how much do you think my case will cost?

Before you make the final decision to sign on with a lawyer, be sure to fill out the following attorney checklist. It will guide you in your decision—and serve as a reminder about your agreement in the months to come.

Attorney Checklist

Name of attorney: _____

Address: _____

Size of firm: _____

Recommended by: _____

Date seen: _____

Consultation fee: _____

Office:

Is it an easy location for me to get to? _____

Was it relatively neat and clean? _____

Attorney:

Education: _____

Experience: _____

Was I kept waiting? _____

Were we interrupted? _____

Did I feel comfortable? _____

_____

Did the attorney listen to me? _____

_____

Fees:

Hourly billing rate: _____

Rates of others who might work on the case: _____

Retainer fee: _____

What happens when retainer is used up? _____

_____

How often am I billed? _____

What happens if I can't pay? _____

_____

Will attorney agree to collect from my spouse? _____

Who pays for disbursements and extra services? _____

Handling the case:

How long does the attorney think it will take to complete the case? _____

_____

Has the attorney handled cases like this before? _____

_____

You're Hired!

After you have decided whom you want, a reputable lawyer will send you his or her written agreement concerning fees and will give you time to ask questions about the agreement before you sign it. If a lawyer asks you to sign an agreement in his or her office without giving you the chance to think it over, look for another lawyer. Sometimes it's worth showing the agreement to your business or personal lawyer whom you trust. If and when you do return the written agreement, you usually have to include the retainer check required as your initial payment.

The Least You Need to Know

➤ Hire a competent attorney who makes you feel at ease, who you like, who's on your wavelength, and who your best instincts say you can trust.

➤ Make sure you can afford the attorney's fees or are able to work out an arrangement for payment. Ask about paying by credit card.

➤ Never pay a retainer fee without a guarantee that it will be refunded if it is not used up.

➤ Make sure the attorney-client agreement does not include the lawyer's ability to have a lien put on your house.

➤ It's more important that your attorney can work with your spouse's attorney than it is for your attorney to be able to impress your spouse.

➤ Know whether an associate will be working on your case and determine the associate's billing rate. Find out whether you'll be billed for both the associate's time and the primary attorney's time when both are working on the case.

Chapter 6

Your Lawyer's Obligations to You

In This Chapter

➤ How to make sure your lawyer is doing the right stuff

➤ Ethics questions

➤ When to find a new lawyer

After you hire your matrimonial attorney, get ready to have a long, intense relationship with the person who will be your closest ally in your battle for "justice" against your spouse. You will be putting all your trust and faith into this person—once a stranger, but now piloting your case against the person who was once your lover.

Great Expectations

This will no doubt be your first rebound relationship. Your divorce lawyer, and no one else, will be your most effective support during the separation and divorce process. Your relationship with your matrimonial attorney can be smooth or rocky, close or businesslike. You might come to think of your attorney as your confessor, therapist, Sir Galahad, or Amazon Woman.

But if you're going to make it through the divorce, you must banish these notions from your mind. Instead, it is to your advantage to learn (quickly) how to utilize your attorney in the most effective, cost-efficient way possible.

What Your Lawyer Should Be Doing and When

The practice of law is not a science, but it's not exactly an art either. There are certain things your attorney can and should be doing. For some guidelines, refer to the following list:

Red Alert

Don't confuse your lawyer with your shrink and waste your precious dollars using your attorney to vent your anger, assuage your guilt, or comfort your feelings of loss. Instead, seek the help of a qualified psycho-therapist.

1. Your lawyer should have an overall plan for your case. This might simply mean that she plans to meet with your spouse's lawyer within the next month and settle the case, have documents drawn up within two weeks after that meeting, have them signed within two weeks after that, and then submit them to court.

   Maybe it means she's going to make an immediate request for support on your behalf and start demanding financial documents, with the goal of having your case ready for trial within six months.

   Maybe your lawyer can't say when things will happen because too much depends on what the other side wants; still, she should have a general idea of how the case will proceed from your side given any number of scenarios.

One matrimonial lawyer tells us that clients often seek her out for a second opinion on their case. The most frequent complaint: Their case has no direction, they see no end in sight, and it seems like they're always responding to their spouse's action with no overriding plan of their own. One such client eventually terminated his relationship with a lawyer—after five years of delay, during which he waited in limbo for decisions on child custody, child support payments, visitation schedules, and more. Often as not, delays were caused by his own attorney's exhausting schedule as her city's superstar divorce diva. She was on every talk show and in every newspaper, but somehow, in terms of this client, she was unable to do her job.

2. Early in your case, your lawyer should demand any and all financial documents in your spouse's possession so that you can learn what there is between you to divide up.

3. If you or your spouse has a pension, your lawyer should get a copy of the pension plan and account statements for the past few years. We know of more than one case where the lawyers agreed a pension would be divided up, only to discover that under certain circumstances, the company had no obligation to pay the pension at all.

4. Your lawyer should assess whether any experts will be needed in your case. If your wife has a hat-making business she established during the marriage, depending on the laws of your state, you might need a business appraiser to estimate the value of that business. Your lawyer should locate a well-respected business appraiser now for possible later use.

   Maybe custody will be an issue, and you'll need an expert to testify on your behalf.

   In some jurisdictions, the judge will appoint an expert to report to the court, but you still might need someone to support your case. Your lawyer should start getting you the names of qualified people.

5. Your lawyer should, under almost all circumstances, tell your spouse's lawyer that you are willing to listen to any reasonable settlement proposal and to negotiate. Cases have been settled on the steps of the courthouse on the day of trial, so it's a good idea to leave the door open at all times.

6. Your lawyer should promptly respond to letters and phone calls and keep you informed of all such communication. Copies of letters should be sent to you within 24 hours of the lawyer's receipt. He or she should notify you about important phone calls—those concerning settlement proposals, for instance—as soon as possible. If the court hands down any decisions regarding your case, your lawyer should notify you at once.

   Your attorney should return your calls within 24 hours unless there's some reason why that's impossible—for instance, if she's in court or in the middle of a trial. On the other hand, you should only call when you have something to ask or something important to say. It's a good idea to write down questions and save them for a few days (unless they are urgent) so you can ask several at once. Many lawyers bill you a minimum of 15 minutes per call, so you might as well take up the time you'll be billed for anyway.

   One woman we know learned her divorce was final 20 days after her lawyer found out; she heard the news from a catty friend of her ex-husband's. The lawyer himself never called.

7. If your case is heading to trial, your attorney, with your input, should begin to interview and line up witnesses as needed. She should be sure to give your witnesses ample advance notice of the trial date.

8. If your case actually goes to trial, your lawyer should fully prepare you. If possible, you should visit the courthouse and even the courtroom in advance. Your lawyer should review the questions he himself plans to ask and alert you about what to expect during *cross-examination*.

One attorney we know even tells her clients how to dress on the day they will be in court. ("Go for the schoolteacher look," she likes to say, "and leave the jewelry and fur at home.")

Divorce Dictionary

Cross-examination: The act of being questioned by the attorney representing the person on whose behalf the witness is not testifying.

9. Throughout your case, your attorney should give you some sense of whether the law supports your position. No attorney worth her weight will guarantee you a victory, but a knowledgeable lawyer should be able to tell you whether there is a basis for your position and what is likely to happen if the case is tried.

10. If your case ends with a defeat at trial, or if there are any defeats along the way (say you lose a motion when the judge denies your request for something), your lawyer should be able to provide you with sound advice about whether to appeal.

Crossing the Line

Observe the following attorney-client protocol:

➤ Although your lawyer might know more about you than your accountant, your shrink, or even your spouse does, it's probably not a good idea to become drinking buddies. You want your lawyer to make objective decisions, not to kowtow to your demands because you've become best friends.

➤ In general, it's probably not a good idea for your lawyer to meet your kids. If the children are teenagers and their testimony is essential, then of course your attorney must meet them, but in other instances, they'll feel as though they're being made to take sides. Your attorney also runs the risk of being called as a witness in the case by virtue of his or her contact with the kids. (If your lawyer does become a witness, he or she will no longer be able to represent you.)

➤ Your attorney should not "come on" to you in any way whatsoever. (Agreeing to discuss your case on a Friday night at a fancy restaurant is not a good idea.) It doesn't matter if the attraction is mutual. If it's real, it can wait until your case is over.

➤ Your attorney should not be in contact with your spouse if he or she has an attorney, unless his or her attorney has agreed to such contact.

➤ Your attorney should not have a business relationship of any kind with your spouse or his or her family. For example, if the attorney you want to use drew your will and your spouse's will, he or she should probably not be representing you in the divorce. (If your spouse consents, it might be okay, but the wiser course would be to find someone else.)

If the attorney has had a prior business relation as counsel for a jointly owned business, the attorney might be disqualified from representing either party. It is better to stipulate that a lawyer who has been representing the spouses in business activities should not act as lawyer for one of the spouses.

What Your Attorney Needs to Know

For many clients, it's easy to know when to call with a question or problem. The problem is knowing when to call to tell the attorney something that might be important to your case, but you're not sure.

Your husband brought the kids back 10 minutes late. Should you tell your lawyer? It depends. If she is hard at work on a motion about visitation, it's important that your attorney know about the problem right away. If a conference between the lawyers is not going to take place for another two weeks, it's probably better to save the call for later, when you have more to add.

The bottom line is this: If you're not sure whether something merits a call, call your attorney. When you're through speaking about the problem, ask whether you should call about this sort of issue in the future. Maybe your lawyer will simply ask you to keep a diary, which you can hand over for later use in your case. Maybe he wants to be kept informed immediately, by phone.

Silver Linings

Many lawyers have experienced secretaries who can generously fill the gap between psychotherapist and attorney when you just need an ear. Usually, there is no charge to cry on a secretary's shoulder...but do find out. Some law firms' secretaries spend so much time listening to clients' heartbreak or anger at their spouse that the firm *does* charge for their time.

How and When to Talk to Your Lawyer

With luck, you have hired a lawyer with whom you feel comfortable, and you can talk to him as you would a friend. Nevertheless, it's important to maintain the boundaries that should exist between any professional and client. Keep your conversation focused on the reason for the call. Chatting about what a bad person your spouse is might feel good at the time, but it won't feel so good when you get the bill for the venting session.

Avoid raising issues your lawyer has already addressed. If your lawyer starts saying such things as "We're going in circles," or "I think we've covered that," it's a gentle hint to move on to the next topic or say goodbye.

When on the phone with your lawyer, do avoid the tendency to speculate. No single activity on the phone probably wastes more of your legal fee dollars than speculating on why your spouse has done something, what he or she might do, what a judge might do, or what the other lawyer might do. The list is endless. Discussing the merits of your position is one thing; trying to figure out why something was done or what someone else will do is usually a waste of time.

If too much time has elapsed since you and your lawyer agreed on a plan of action (your lawyer was supposed to call your husband's lawyer last week and hasn't done it yet), then make the call. The squeaky wheel gets oiled, but be reasonable. If your lawyer said he or she would call you as soon as there is a decision in your case, don't call every day to check whether the decision has come.

How to Annoy a Lawyer

Unfortunately, you and your lawyer are probably in it for the long haul; some people have a longer relationship with their matrimonial attorneys than they had with their spouses.

Many attorneys (like many psychotherapists) will never let you know when they are annoyed with you. After all, they get paid to listen to you, and the more they listen, the more money they'll make. Indeed, for some, your endless complaints about your ex might help fill an otherwise empty time sheet. But let's assume you hear testiness in your lawyer's voice, or you think he or she is tired of your case. What do you do?

The best thing to do is to raise your concern. "You sound upset. Does it have to do with my case?" is one good opener. "Have I done something to annoy you?" is another. If you have, your attorney will appreciate the opportunity to let you know. Maybe your payment check bounced; perhaps you've been yelling at the secretary or keeping the attorney on the phone too long. Perhaps you told your spouse something your lawyer said to keep under wraps.

Apologize and make sure that the problem has not become so big that your lawyer feels she can no longer enthusiastically represent your case.

When to Fire Your Lawyer

One woman we know is in the fourth year of her divorce case—and on her third lawyer. Is she an exception? Not necessarily. Firing a lawyer is more common than you might think. Why does this happen? When is it warranted? And how do you pull it off?

Sometimes, lawyers are let go due to a straightforward personality clash. Characteristics you were willing to overlook when you hired your lawyer (a brash, aggressive personality or perhaps a cloying patronage) now bother you so much that you can't talk to him anymore. Maybe you feel that your lawyer has mishandled your case. You've gotten a second opinion and learned about strategies that could have saved you time and money. When you ask your lawyer about them, she just shrugs. Sometimes, it's just a feeling that your case needs fresh ideas. Your attorney seems tired of the whole thing and no longer has the enthusiasm he had when you first hired him. You might also feel that your lawyer is giving in too easily to the other side or that trust has been breached. You tell your lawyer something you do not want repeated to your spouse's lawyer, and your attorney goes right ahead and does just that.

How do you fire your lawyer? The easiest way is to hire the replacement lawyer before you tell your present lawyer that you're making a change. Then, your new lawyer makes the call to your current lawyer and arranges to get your file, and you don't have to worry about the awkward moment of telling your lawyer it's over.

If you feel some personal statement or closure is in order, of course, you can send your attorney a short personal note. Depending on why you're "breaking up," you can simply send a thank-you note for past services or write a brief statement stating your beef. As with any close relationship, your lawyer might already be suspicious that you are unhappy with him, so your note or call might not be a total surprise.

Red Alert

The most common reason lawyers fire clients is their failure to pay bills. Even if you've spent thousands of dollars with this lawyer, if you are unable to meet a payment schedule, most lawyers will not continue to represent you.

Remember, most lawyers will expect to be paid in full before they release your file. Depending on where you live, your lawyer might be required to release your file even if you have yet to pay for all services—but the bill won't go away. If you have a problem paying the bill or a disagreement over the bill, discuss this with your present lawyer and work out an agreement. Otherwise, have your new lawyer work things out for you.

The Least You Need to Know

➤ Your lawyer should have a game plan, be on top of your case, and keep you informed of all developments.

➤ Write out questions and call your lawyer with several at once, if possible, to save time. When in doubt about whether to let your lawyer know something has happened, call.

➤ Don't stick with your attorney if lines of communication have broken down.

➤ Find a new attorney before you fire your old one.

Chapter 7

Paying the Bill

In This Chapter

➤ How divorce lawyers charge

➤ How you can save money on your legal fees

➤ How to negotiate a retainer agreement

➤ How to tell whether your attorney's charges are legitimate

Legal fees—the two most dreaded words in the English language. If you're going through a divorce and you get a staggering bill from your attorney, you might be hard-pressed to think of anything worse besides the breakup of your marriage itself. Why are lawyers so expensive, and how do they charge for services rendered? This chapter penetrates the most inscrutable secrets of this mysterious cabal—the cult of the divorce attorney.

Why Legal Representation Is So Costly

All lawyers do is talk, right? And don't they say talk is cheap? Not when there's a Juris Doctorate after the person's name.

Lawyers charge a lot because they usually have high overhead: an office, a receptionist, a secretary. Someone has to pay for it, and it won't be the lawyer. Lawyers have at least seven years of post-high school education (four years of college and three years of law school). For recent graduates, educational costs could have been as high as $120,000. The lawyer is recouping that investment.

Finally, lawyers charge what the traffic will bear. Put simply, moneyed clients are ready and willing to pay these high fees, and there are enough moneyed clients around to keep lawyers from having to worry about volume. As more attorneys enter the field, billing practices are beginning to change, and fees are coming down in some areas. But until that happens in more significant numbers, remember that you will need to pay your lawyer at the current market rate—if you want her to work for you at all.

Silver Linings

Some competent attorneys are willing to work out a payment plan in advance. It is to the attorney's advantage to make it as painless as possible for you to keep up with the bills. Many attorneys never collect the fully billed amount. If you should take responsibility by requesting a payment plan, the attorney is more likely to collect his fees, and might very well be agreeable.

How Matrimonial Lawyers Charge

Many lawyers charge an hourly rate and bill you for every hour worked. If Paula Smith's rate is $150 an hour and she does 10 hours of work for you, you'll get a bill for $1,500. It can be pretty straightforward.

Most lawyers want some payment up front. That fee is called a *retainer*. The amount will vary depending on where you live, your specific case, and the lawyer's hourly rate. In the New York City area, some matrimonial attorneys charge as much as a $7,500 to $10,000 retainer. In other states, some lawyers charge at least $25,000. (That's not the bad news; you'll probably spend much more than that for a protracted case!)

After you pay the retainer, your lawyer subtracts his hourly rate from what you've paid for each hour worked, until the case is over or he uses up your retainer, whichever happens first. If your lawyer has used up your retainer, you'll start getting bills. Some lawyers will want a new retainer; others might simply bill you on a weekly or monthly basis. Some lawyers will require replenishment of the retainer or a cushion to be maintained in the trust account until the case ends.

Wait a minute, you might think; doesn't the hourly billing rate encourage the lawyer to drag out my case to earn more money? Although this might seem easy, within the profession it is considered unethical for a lawyer to deliberately drag out ("churn," as lawyers say) a case. Another deterrent is that when a case drags on, lawyers can lose clients, or clients will not be able to afford to pay any longer. It's possible that the lawyer won't collect everything he's owed. Whatever he doesn't get is written off and in effect reduces his hourly rate. On the other hand, the lawyer who finishes her work within the amount of time the retainer covers gets her full hourly rate and comes out ahead.

Does that mean you don't have to pay your bill? It means if ethics don't stop a lawyer from dragging out a case, the practical realities of collection will.

In matrimonial law, it is very hard to predict how much time your lawyer will have to spend on your case. If you and your spouse have agreed on everything up front, the lawyer won't have to do much more than draft the legal documents, make sure you understand them, get them to the other lawyer, and then, eventually, submit them to the court. If you or your spouse are at war, a lot of time will be spent on your case, and you can end up spending an astronomical sum of money.

Before You Put Your Money Down

One of the most important things to understand as you enter a financial relationship with your matrimonial attorney is the retainer. If you do pay one, the first thing you will do is sign a *retainer agreement*. Remember, any agreement regarding your retainer must be in writing and should always provide for a refund if the fees are not used up.

The agreement should also stipulate what happens when the retainer is used up. Will you have to pay another lump sum, or will you be billed on a monthly or weekly basis? When it comes to your retainer, make sure that all the ground rules are spelled out first.

A reputable attorney will not only have no problem putting the retainer agreement in writing, but also will ask you to take the agreement home and study it before signing it. You should be invited to call and ask any questions you have. As eager as you might be to sign the retainer and write out a check, hold back until you read the agreement and thoroughly understand what it says.

Divorce Dictionary

Retainer agreement: A contract signed by an attorney and client setting forth the billing arrangement to be instituted between the lawyer and the client.

The Retainer Agreement: The Fine Print

At a minimum, this document should establish the amount of money you are paying up front and should stipulate hourly rates for the lawyer as well as others who might be assisting, including paralegals and junior attorneys. At a minimum, the retainer agreement should state that there might be ancillary staff involved and establish the range of their rates.

The agreement should also outline how you will pay for out-of-pocket expenses such as photocopying, process servers, stenographers, or court fees. Maybe those expenses will come out of your retainer, or maybe you'll have to pay them in addition to your retainer. Find out now.

A retainer agreement should explain how often you will be billed. Are you going to get a bill only when the retainer is used up, or will you be kept informed with a bill each month as the retainer dwindles?

What happens if you do not pay your bill? Does the lawyer have an automatic right to abandon your case? Does he or she have an obligation to work out a payment plan with you? Are you obligated to guarantee payment with collateral such as your house? Watch out for any lawyer who demands security in the form of something you cannot afford to lose.

Usually, you will be asked to countersign the retainer and send it back to the lawyer with the retainer check.

Elayne Kesselman, Esq.
Retainer Agreement

February 9, 1999

PERSONAL AND CONFIDENTIAL

John Doe
New York, New York
Re: Doe v. Doe

Dear Mr. Doe:

I appreciate your retaining me to represent you in connection with your matrimonial situation, and I write this letter in order to confirm our understanding regarding the financial arrangements between us with regard to that work.

As an initial retainer, you have agreed to pay, and I have agreed to accept, $1,500. Applied against this fee shall be my hourly billing rate. The rate presently applicable to my services is $150.00 per hour. Because of mounting costs, it may be necessary from time to time for the applicable time charges to be increased, and I will notify you of the same in advance of any such increase. You will be billed on or about the first day of each month for services rendered during the preceding month.

You will not be billed for any time spent discussing your bill.

I do not anticipate having anyone else work on your case, but should another attorney assist me in this matter, I will notify you of that in advance and of that attorney's billing rate.

You will also be charged separately for any out-of-pocket disbursements (such as court costs, messenger service, photocopier, long distance telephone calls, postage, service of papers, online computer assisted research, and so on) that are incurred on your behalf. In addition, you may be asked to pay certain disbursements directly to the vendor or provider of services involved (such as appraisers, process servers, transcripts of depositions or court proceedings, and the like), and you agree to do so upon my request. I will advise you of any such costs in advance of incurring the same.

If your retainer is used up and work remains to be done on your case, you will be billed on a monthly basis, and you agree to pay, the amount due for services rendered and disbursements incurred within thirty (30) days from receipt of the bill. In the event of your failure to make prompt and timely payment of a bill and should we fail to agree on suitable alternative arrangements for such payment, I reserve the right to cease work upon your matter and, if I am in the midst of litigation, to seek permission from the court to withdraw from your case. Should a dispute arise between us concerning the payment of attorney's fees in the sum of $3,000 or greater, you may seek to have the dispute resolved through arbitration, which shall be binding upon you and me. I shall provide you with information concerning fee arbitration in the event of such a dispute or upon your request.

You will be provided with copies of all correspondence and documents relating to the case, and you shall be kept apprised of the status of your case. You have the right to cancel this agreement at any time. Services rendered through the date of such cancellation and not yet billed will be billed to you upon such cancellation, and payment shall be due within thirty (30) days of receipt of the final bill.

I look forward to working with you and ask, if the contents of this letter accurately reflect our understanding, that you please sign the enclosed copy and return it to me.

Very truly yours,

_____
Elayne Kesselman

EK:ek

Enc.

CONSENTED AND AGREED TO:

_____
John Doe

Who Pays for What?

The assumption that the man has to pay all the legal bills is no longer true. Often, the spouse with the deeper pockets has to pay some or all the legal fees. In many cases, where the assets are going to be equally divided, the pockets are equally deep, and wives are shocked to learn that their share of the legal fees must come out of their share of the assets.

If a lawyer assures you that he will only collect what he can get from your spouse, have that put in writing. Most lawyers will not make that promise because they stand a chance of never getting paid. A reputable attorney will explain that payment will be due even if your spouse does not pay.

Sometimes, early in a case, a judge will order the wealthier spouse to pay temporary legal fees on behalf of the other spouse. By the time the case is over, however, both sides usually end up paying something.

Twelve Tips for Keeping Fees Under Control

We can't emphasize enough the importance of being vigilant about how and when you spend your hard-earned money on legal fees. Self-restraint is the order of the day. Here are some tips from the trenches of divorce. You may say, "I don't have the patience for all this detail," but take it from us, you will save thousands of dollars if you follow these guidelines.

You Can Do It!

For those of you who are of moderate income, consider that being reasonable in a divorce settlement could save you enormous sums in legal fees. How much in legal fees is it worth to get the sterling silver wedding present that cost $5,000? Is it worth $3,000 in legal fees? It could easily cost that. For your own sake, put away with anger and hurt and save yourself some money and aggravation. (We like to advise heading for the racquetball court immediately after a divorce settlement meeting ... and put a face on that ball!)

1. Hire a lawyer whose billing rate is manageable for you or who is willing to create a payment plan you can live with. For example, the lawyer will agree to be paid at the rate of $300 a month for however long it takes you to pay the bill.

2. Ask to receive a detailed bill every month; the bill should describe services rendered and disbursements paid. Tell your lawyer you want this even if your retainer is not yet used up.

3. Ask that, except in the case of emergencies, you be notified in advance of any major work to be done on your behalf. Typically, you and your lawyer have developed the plan of action, but it is possible your attorney might be ready to make a motion that you think unnecessary.

4. Ask for an estimate of the disbursements in advance. You don't have to be told about every postage stamp being billed to you, but your lawyer should tell you about process servers (whose fees can run from $50) or stenographers (deposition or trial transcripts can cost thousands of dollars). Maybe you have a friend who can serve the papers for free, for instance, or perhaps you know of a cheaper stenographer whose work is just as good.

5. Keep a record of the time you spend with your attorney on the phone and in person. When you get your bill, check it against your personal records.

   We know of one instance in which two attorneys representing opposing sides in a divorce case met to reach a settlement. After the meeting, they went out to dinner together. One of the lawyers had the audacity to charge his client for the time spent at dinner and for the dinner itself! Needless to say, the outraged client agreed to pay only for the time spent on his case. Then, he changed attorneys.

6. Before you sign the retainer agreement, ask whether you will be charged a minimum for phone calls and what that charge will be. Some lawyers charge a 15-minute minimum under the theory that your call has taken them away from other work and they need time to "get back into it." Others will charge a minimum of five minutes. Still others will only charge the actual time spent on the phone. If there is a 15-minute minimum, save your questions for one longer call rather than several short calls.

7. If you've gone to a firm with many attorneys, ask whether a good attorney with a lower billing rate will be able to do some of the work on your case. However, make it clear that for certain work—negotiations, for instance, or the actual trial—you want the attorney you hired.

8. If more than one attorney will be working on your case, find out before you sign the retainer how double services will be billed. If two attorneys are discussing your case, are you going to be billed at their total hourly rate or only at the higher attorney's rate?

9. Find out what you will be billed for photocopying and photocopy whatever you can yourself. Some firms charge as much as 25¢ a page. Time permitting, you could get copying done yourself for 4¢ per page overnight.

Red Alert

Can the divorcing couple use the same lawyer? It's possible, but it's not a good idea, no matter how friendly the divorce may be. Later, one of you might claim you didn't understand what you signed or that the lawyer or the deal was really one-sided. When claims of unfairness arise, judges usually don't like situations where there was only one lawyer. If your case is simple, one spouse may hire a lawyer and the other may represent himself or herself.

10. Ask your attorney to use faxes or express or overnight mail only when necessary.

11. Organize materials your attorney wants in the way she needs them to be organized. For example, if your attorney sends you a list of 20 documents demanded by your spouse's counsel, organize the records by year and category in separate folders. Your lawyer might want to change what you've done a little, but the cost will be far less than it would have been had you brought in a shopping bag full of receipts.

12. Don't engage your attorney in aimless phone calls. For example, don't start bad-mouthing your spouse, your spouse's attorney, the system, or the judge. Do not make small talk or discuss anything irrelevant to your case. You might feel better after the call; you won't when you get your bill.

How to Tell Whether Your Lawyer's Charges Are Legitimate

It's often hard to tell whether the amount of time your lawyer spent working for you was "legitimate." After all, you weren't there, and you're not a lawyer, so how are you supposed to know whether the charges are correct?

Although you can't keep track of every last microsecond, you can keep an eye on things. First, always ask your lawyer to discuss the amount of time and cost that will be incurred for a project your lawyer has in mind before he begins that project. Maybe your lawyer wants to make a motion asking the judge to order your spouse not to call the kids during dinner. The motion might cost a thousand dollars. You could ask the lawyer whether he can call your spouse's lawyer first or send a letter about the problem.

Check your bills carefully. Sometimes, law offices, like any business, can make a human error and charge for work not done on your behalf. If a lawyer tells you he has to be in court on your case and might have to sit there for three hours before the judge calls your case, ask whether he can do anyone else's work while he's there and not charge you for the waiting time. Some lawyers do just that and then "double bill"—bill you and the other person. An honest attorney won't do that, but it doesn't hurt to ask.

What if you're just not sure whether you're being ripped off? You probably need to reevaluate your relationship with your lawyer. If you think he or she is deliberately cheating you, why would you want that individual involved in your case?

Getting Your Money's Worth

Hourly rates depend on a lawyer's experience and education as well as the market itself. In a major urban setting such as Los Angeles, lawyers often charge $300 to $400 an hour. In smaller places, equally competent lawyers might only charge $150 an hour because no one will pay more.

If you hire an attorney from a major law firm, chances are that the rates will be higher than that of a solo practitioner or a small law firm. The larger firm has more overhead and has to add that to the bill. However, if the attorney at the larger firm is more competent than the attorney at the small firm, it might be worth the higher fees because he can cut the case shorter by virtue of his experience. This is not to say that small firms and solo practitioners are on the whole less experienced. It depends on the attorney.

The truth is, you should not judge an attorney by his or her hourly rate because that rate might be arbitrary. It's not as though the legal community got together and bestowed a high hourly rate on the best attorney, a little bit lower rate on the second best, and so on. It's more an ego and business decision, loosely translated as, "What can I get away with?"

For some, the hourly rate will always be considered an indication of talent and quality. A well-known lawyer might be just the one, you're thinking, to bully your spouse into settling. Maybe so, particularly if your spouse is a businessperson who is impressed by names, but it's a ploy that rarely pays off. In fact, if you hire a well-known lawyer, your case might get lost in the shuffle. The attorney's ability, integrity, and attention to your case—not his or her fee—is most important.

The Least You Need to Know

➤ Make sure that you can afford your attorney, and work out a suitable payment plan before you hire him.

➤ Put your fee arrangement in writing. Unearned retainer fees should be refundable to you.

➤ Ask your attorney to let you know in advance the cost of anticipated legal work or third-party expenses, such as process servers or stenographers.

➤ Keep a record of time spent with your attorney.

➤ Do not be impressed by hourly rates; high rates can indicate a lawyer too busy to call you back.

Chapter 8

The Art of the Deal: Settling Your Case Out of Court

> **In This Chapter**
>
> ➤ The no-fault divorce
>
> ➤ The quick divorce: when to pursue it and when to avoid it
>
> ➤ Constructive approaches to bargaining and compromise
>
> ➤ The cost of a quick divorce
>
> ➤ Your lawyer's role in a quick divorce

Most divorces end not with a bang, but with a whimper. After months or even years of negotiating, spouses reach agreements without anyone ever setting foot in a courthouse. This chapter tries to help you reach this goal quickly, saving tens of thousands of dollars and untold years.

"No-Fault" Divorce

In many states, provided you've resided in the state for a minimum amount of time (anywhere from six weeks, as in Nevada, to 18 months), you do not have to prove *grounds* to get divorced. All you have to plead is incompatibility or irreconcilable differences leading to the irremediable breakdown of the marriage, and a judge will grant you a divorce. This is quite a change from the days when private detectives hid in hotel room closets with cameras to prove adultery. Some states, however, still maintain a "fault" system. You have to prove one of several grounds to get divorced. Grounds usually include mental cruelty, abandonment, adultery, or imprisonment. When people living in "fault" states cannot prove grounds, they sometimes move to no-fault states to get their divorce.

You might qualify for a no-fault divorce, but that doesn't mean the real issues—custody, support, visitation—are going to be easily resolved. If any of those areas presents a problem, you might still need a judge, even though the divorce itself is a given.

Quick and Easy

Regardless of whether you live in a fault or a no-fault state, the real measure of how quickly you'll get your divorce through the courts is how quickly you and your spouse agree on the issues that exist between you. If you have no assets or debt, if you have no children, and if you've only been married a short time, your divorce should be relatively quick and easy. We know several couples who lived together peacefully for years, got married, and were divorced two or three years later. Maybe it was being married, or maybe the relationship had run its course. Whatever the reason, for those individuals the divorce was merely a matter of filling out the right papers and submitting them to the court. As long as you and your spouse agree that your marriage is over, you both know what assets and debt you have, and you agree on how you'll divide them, a quick divorce could work for you.

Not So Quick and Easy

A woman who had been married to a wealthy businessman for 12 years left him for her son's ninth-grade history teacher. She insisted that all she wanted was the Farberware. Her lawyer begged her to demand a fairer deal, wrote her letters stating she was making a mistake, and even threatened to stop working as her attorney if she took the deal. But she ran off with her friend and the pots and pans. Four months later, when her relationship with the teacher ended, she wanted to reopen her case—but it was four months too late. She got a quick divorce, but hardly a fair one.

What's the moral of the story? A quick divorce works fine if it's fair, but not when it occurs because one side feels guilty or pressured. Remember, never sign papers dividing assets or debt without first consulting an attorney. Never sign such papers while you are in an overly emotional state. It's okay to sign papers if you feel sad or even some-what depressed about the breakup, but if you're in a major depression, or you're enraged, spiteful, or blinded by love, wait until the sound and fury in your mind and heart have simmered down before you commit yourself to a deal you might regret.

Working Through the Issues

What if you and your spouse just can't agree? What if issues ranging from custody of the children and ownership of the dog to an inability to let go on the part of one spouse promise to complicate the situation for years to come? Can you get a quick divorce anyway? Sometimes, you can, with the help of a judge, but it depends on where you live.

In major metropolitan areas, where the court dockets are crowded, it could be months, even as long as a year, before your case can be tried. In smaller communities, it is possible you can get your day in court much sooner.

Silver Linings

If you have gotten the short end of the stick in a divorce decision, you will almost always get another chance. Even if your case has moved through the court system quickly the first time, if you have lost, you will usually have the right to appeal. If you have been treated unfairly, the situation might be rectified, although depending on how backlogged the appellate court is, it could take months or years.

Bargaining and Compromise

It's difficult to negotiate for yourself, particularly when emotions are involved, as they tend to be in a divorce. For many couples, trying to negotiate is like reliving the worst moments of the marriage. After all, if the two of you got along well enough to work out a divorce, you might not be divorcing in the first place. Does this mean you have to abandon all hope and leave everything to the attorneys? Not necessarily. Here are some tips that might help you reach a settlement without going to court:

1. *Never present your bottom line early in the negotiations.* It might sound childish, but it happens to be true. When negotiating, don't present your bottom line first; that could end up being the high figure, and it can drop from there.

2. *Argue issues, not positions.* It might sound obvious, but it isn't always. For example, you and your spouse are discussing who will pay for your children's college education. Your spouse says the two girls will go to state schools. You say they'll go to the best school they get into. The two of you are arguing positions, not issues. The issue is the cost of college and how you'll finance it.

3. *Make rules for your discussion.* If you and your spouse are meeting alone, write out a schedule of topics to be covered and stick to it. Agree that neither of you will interrupt the other. If you're meeting with your spouse and with the lawyers (commonly called a *four-way meeting*), you and your attorney should plan the meeting. You should have an agenda, preferably in writing, and you should know when to talk and when not to talk.

You Can Do It!

Focus on the problem, not on your feelings. For instance, you want to live in the family home until your youngest child graduates from college, but your husband wants to sell the house now. The problem should be whether you can afford the house and whether your spouse needs the sale proceeds, but your husband's real concern might be that you'll remarry and have someone else move into "his" house. If that issue surfaces, it can be addressed by agreeing that if you remarry, the house would then be sold.

Before one four-way meeting, one husband's lawyer asked him not to talk to his wife. Within three minutes of the meeting's start, the husband was shouting at his wife, and she was yelling right back. The husband's lawyer was doodling, and the wife's lawyer was trying to calm her client. Considering that the combined hourly billing rate of the two lawyers probably exceeded $500 an hour, the husband (and wife, for that matter) were spending their money at a rapid rate.

4. *Be flexible.* That doesn't mean cave in. It means be ready to compromise. Remember the example about the two girls and what college they'd attend? Suppose you don't want to pay anything for college, and your spouse wants you to pay half. What about paying one third? What about paying half only if your income is at a certain level by the time the girls go to college? What about agreeing to pay half but also stipulating that any loans or scholarships the girls receive offset your half?

As long as you stay locked into one position, it will be hard to settle your case. Be open to ideas. You might have to get some from your attorney, from your accountant, or from friends who have been divorced.

5. *Be ready to trade.* Say that you really want the gold necklace your husband bought you on your third wedding anniversary, and he really wants the engagement ring back. You want the engagement ring, too. Decide which one you want most, and, if the values are about equal, make the trade. It sounds obvious, but when emotions are running high, it might not be.

6. *Leave heated issues for last.* This is a lawyer's trick. Resolve everything you can and save the heavy issues for last. Maybe you both want custody of your child. If you start off discussing that sore point, you'll get nowhere with any other issues. If you first sort out the house, the car, and the debts, you might make better

progress on the last, toughest issue. After all, you've both spent so much time already, it would be a shame if you couldn't work it all out.

7. *Have a judge help resolve the issues you can't resolve.* Maybe you and your spouse have worked out everything except custody. A custody trial will still be cheaper than a trial on all the other issues, too. Don't throw in the towel on your settlement agreement just because you can't resolve everything.

8. *If things get too emotional, step back.* Maybe you and your spouse have met with the best intentions, but before you know it, you're back to the old routine that never got you anywhere in your marriage. Break for a few minutes or a few days before trying to hammer out an agreement again.

9. *Don't expect more than you would have had if you had stayed married.* Some spouses suddenly "forget" when getting divorced that they were married to the man who blew his paycheck every few weeks at the race track. When there's a missed support check, they're shocked. Maybe the two of you decided to put a lot of money into your house over the years. Suddenly, your spouse is shocked that there are no savings.

   Remember, getting divorced does not turn Cinderella into the prom queen or a frog into a prince. If you negotiate in good faith but lose track of who you are dealing with on the other side of the table, you could be in for disappointment.

10. *Give up if you're getting nowhere.* Maybe you've met alone, maybe with lawyers, maybe with a priest or an accountant, and you've agreed on nothing. It might be time to move on to the next step, which could be a trial in front of a judge. Some spouses need to be told by a judge the way it's going to be.

    In one case, the father would not voluntarily relinquish custody of the children (teenagers who wanted to live with their mother), no matter what. If a judge had told him he had to let them go, however, he would have complied.

    As it turned out, the case did not go to the court. The lawyers finally worked out an agreement without using the word "custody." The children stayed with their mother during the week and with their father most weekends. The father could live with that because technically both parties still had custody.

Impediments to Settlement

Once you both feel you know what is and is not in the marital pot, the biggest impediment to settlement usually is *emotion*.

Maybe you're not ready to see the marriage end, so just when it seems like you're about to make a deal, you find a problem with the agreement. If the real problem is that you do not want the marriage to end (whether it's because you still want to be married or you don't want to give her the satisfaction of being divorced), then you should tell your lawyer to stop negotiating for a while. You need time to think things through, and there is no sense incurring legal fees by having lawyers draft and redraft the agreement when you know you're never going to sign it.

Maybe you're ready to be divorced—maybe it was your idea—but you're convinced your spouse would not agree to a deal unless he was hiding something. Despite all the financial disclosure, you're just not sure that you really know what assets your spouse has.

If this is the problem, tell your lawyer you want a representation in the agreement that your spouse has fully disclosed assets and debt, and if it later turns out your spouse lied, you have the right to reopen the deal.

Silver Linings

As Freud once said, "Sometimes, a cigar is just a cigar." If your spouse isn't getting back to you about the agreement, saying he's too busy right now to look at it, maybe he is. One couple was on the verge of settling their case when tax season began. The husband was an accountant who relied heavily on returns for his income. He said he was just too busy to review the agreement; his wife was sure he was delaying. The truth was that the husband was too busy working to focus on the agreement, and negotiations had to wait until early May.

Some people reject settlements because they do not understand the law, and they think they'll do better in court. For many spouses living in states where no-fault divorce is available, it is difficult to understand how a spouse can just walk out of the marriage without paying some kind of penalty. The "penalty" sought is usually an extra share of the marital assets. The law might provide, however, that no matter the reason for the divorce, assets are to be divided on a nearly 50/50 basis. A client who refuses to accept this will never be able to settle on a 50/50 basis and might have to go through the expense of a trial just to hear a judge say the exact same thing.

Some people reject settlements because they feel the deal has been "shoved down their throats." Perhaps the lawyer was too pushy. Although the client didn't complain during the negotiations, when it comes time to signing, she balks. Whatever the problem, discuss it with your lawyer. If yours is a case that needs to be decided by a judge because you just can't work out or sign a settlement agreement, stop the settlement process now before any more money is spent.

No Deal!

At what point is it worth throwing in the towel during settlement negotiations? Here are some criteria to consider.

1. You think your spouse is hiding assets. You can have an expert locate them and testify to their existence in court. Remember, if you're sure that he's hiding assets but you can't prove it, a judge probably is not going to accept your position. Always consult with your lawyer.

2. The deal is too vague. For example, the proposal is that "visitation will be agreed upon later" or that "bank accounts will be divided according to the parties' wishes." Any "proposal" that's merely an agreement to agree is just putting off conflict, not resolving it. Reject it in favor of a specific proposal.

3. The deal is unfair. Although that might seem obvious, it's not always easy to know when a deal is unfair. Here are some examples:

   You and your spouse ran up the credit card bills together, buying things for the family, but only one of you is going to be responsible for all the debt.

   You filed "aggressive" joint tax returns, but now only one of you is expected to pay the debt.

   You own two apartments, and your spouse wants both of them.

   The test lawyers use for fairness is the law and the case law. You can use the "objective test": If you were not involved in this case, would you think the proposal was fair?

It's a Deal: Accepting the Package and Moving On

If the problem holding up the deal is your feeling that your spouse is hiding assets, but you can't prove it, you probably should take the deal.

If you're running out of money to pay a lawyer and the deal is reasonably fair, you probably should take it.

If neither one of you is completely happy—in fact, you're a little unhappy with the deal—you should probably take it. It's been said many times that the best deal is the one where both sides leave the table a little dissatisfied.

What Happens When the Settlement Is Reached?

When everyone agrees on the settlement, one of the lawyers usually writes it up in a document, called the *settlement agreement* or *stipulation of settlement*. Most of the agreement will have *boilerplate language*—language lawyers use all the time in agreements. For example, there's usually a provision that neither side will bother the other or that each side is responsible for his or her own debts. Lawyers can write the boilerplate provisions of the agreement very easily; the language is usually on a computer.

The heart of the agreement—usually custody, visitation, child support, or property distribution—can take a lawyer longer to draft. The agreement will be binding, just as though a judge had arrived at the decision after trial, so the lawyers need to make sure that there are no mistakes.

After one lawyer has drafted the agreement and reviewed it with you, he will send it to the other lawyer, who reviews it with your spouse. Finally, the terms and language of the agreement are acceptable to everyone, and you both sign on the dotted line. Usually, you need to sign five copies—one for the court, one for each lawyer, one for you, and one for your spouse. Some lawyers like clients to initial every page in addition to signing the agreement. That way, no one can claim he didn't know what was written.

Silver Linings

Sometimes, when a divorce settlement is ready for signature, one or both parties will look for excuses not to sign. Experienced attorneys have seen this often. It represents a sudden, deep realization that the marriage has truly ended. It is not uncommon for one or both attorneys to play the role of encouraging their clients to put pen to paper, have it done with, and go on with their lives.

This moment calls for reflection. It is a bittersweet moment: bitter because of the anger and hurt dragged out perhaps to keep the relationship, at whatever level, going; sweet because a great weight has miraculously evaporated from the shoulders of the embattled couple. Perhaps years of fighting and tortuous nights are about to come to an end. Oh, there will be flashbacks. But, over time those will fade into a daily routine that includes new projects and people.

So pick up the pen, and sign the agreement. It's okay to cry (or have a drink!).

The Cost of a Quick Divorce

Many couples we know have gotten their divorce for the cost of the court filing fees (usually under $300) and some photocopies. Others still needed a lawyer to work out the language of an agreement setting out their rights and responsibilities, tallying up costs of some $3,000 between the two of them.

In general, the less work the lawyers have to do, the cheaper your divorce will be.

Your Lawyer's Role

Even without a trial, if you have important issues to resolve, it's best to have a written agreement that you and your spouse can sign. The lawyer will draft that agreement, go over it with you, and send it to your spouse's lawyer, who will review it and then go over it with your spouse. After the document is agreeable to everyone, one of the lawyers will probably also have to draft papers that can be submitted to a judge, who will sign them and grant the divorce.

In some states, even when everything is agreed on, one of you might still have to go to court to testify. Your lawyer would conduct your examination, asking you legally required questions about the breakdown of your marriage while you sit witness in front of a judge.

Do you really need a lawyer if you and your spouse have agreed on everything? In that instance, is there really anything for an attorney to do? Of course, you can get a quick divorce without a lawyer, but if there's a chance you and your spouse will have outstanding issues, you're better off having legal counsel from the start.

The Default Divorce

Some spouses never answer the divorce papers they receive. They just don't care, or they figure they'll let you do all the work to get the divorce (maybe the way it was in the marriage). Do you have to wait until your spouse responds before you can move ahead?

Usually not. If you can prove that your spouse personally received the papers the law requires you to have served, you can probably get a divorce on default—your spouse's failure to respond. Although by law your spouse might have had 20 or 30 days to respond to the divorce papers before you are entitled to a default judgment, your judge might want you to wait three months before actually submitting the rest of the papers you need to be granted a divorce, just in case your spouse decides to respond after all.

There are some downsides to a default divorce, summarized below:

1. In some jurisdictions, your spouse can open the default within one year of its being granted if he or she can show "good cause" why it should be opened. That means your spouse can march into court and claim she never got the papers, or was sick at the time, or didn't understand them, and she wants a second chance. If the judge agrees that there is a reason to open the default, he will, and your divorce will in effect have to start all over again.

2. People tend to follow agreements more than they follow orders. If you and your spouse negotiated an agreement, the chances are better that your spouse will abide by it than if a judge set down in an order what your spouse has to pay because he didn't come to court.

3. You might actually do better if your spouse does show up in court. Maybe you can't prove how much money she earns, but if she were there, your lawyer could cross-examine her in such a way as to let the judge know that the tax return does not reflect all her income.

4. The judge might refer certain issues to another judge, such as a special referee, thereby prolonging the amount of time it will take to get the case over with. Maybe the judge wants to give your spouse another chance to show up, so he refers the support hearing to another judge and tells you to notify your spouse about the new date. It's not fair, but courts tend to try to ensure that everyone has his day in court, even when the person who's getting the second chance is the defaulting party.

The scenarios above provide some insight into what it takes to make a settlement happen. If you think you can settle and avoid litigation, it is in your best interest to make that settlement happen. Remember, the only winners in a protracted litigation are the lawyers! Judges in a trial will often try to give something to each party in the divorce, thereby imposing a form of settlement. Why not work out the issues yourselves? You and your spouse know better than anyone what's most important to each of you. If your marriage is at an end, orchestrate its conclusion in the least expensive, most expeditious way possible. Compromise where you feel comfortable—and weigh the cost of waging an all out war. Push your pride and hard stance aside, but don't give up what's most important to you.

The Least You Need to Know

➤ Even if you qualify for a no-fault divorce, you might still need to resolve other issues, such as custody, visitation, and support.

➤ Never sign important papers without first consulting an attorney.

➤ In negotiations, be flexible; come up with new ideas. Argue issues rather than positions.

➤ Even with a quick divorce, you might still need a lawyer to draft documents.

➤ If you want to reject a deal, make sure that the basis for the rejection is rational, not purely emotional.

Chapter 9

The Circle of Mediation

> **In This Chapter**
>
> ➤ The advantages of mediation
>
> ➤ How to know when mediation *is* wrong for you
>
> ➤ How to choose a mediator
>
> ➤ The mediation process from beginning to end
>
> ➤ When to go into arbitration

In the best of all possible worlds, couples facing divorce would work out agreements between themselves. That's often difficult, of course, because it's the very tendency to argue and diverge that leads to divorce in the first place. The most common solution is hiring attorneys—adversaries—who help the couple duke it out privately or in court. But for those who cherish the notion of an amicable parting, mediation is a popular and relatively inexpensive alternative.

Gentle Tactics

In *mediation*, you and your spouse settle the issues of your divorce with the help of a mediator, who could be a social worker or an attorney. Sometimes, a social worker and attorney pair up to help the divorcing couple. The mediator has multiple tasks, listed on the following page.

➤ Hearing the issues

➤ Understanding the personalities

➤ Explaining the divorce laws that, of necessity, form the background to the mediation sessions

➤ Facilitating discussions

➤ Suggesting solutions to disputed issues

➤ Bringing the parties to a settlement agreement

A deft mediator will be able to handle two individuals who have been a couple, sleuth out the dynamics of their marital relationship, and cleverly bring them beyond their impasse towards a final resolution of all issues that must be resolved in order to compose a settlement agreement. This process takes more than one session. How long the process takes depends on how willing the parties are to compromise in order to finalize a settlement. If one person will not budge in his or her position, the mediator will have to use all his or her resources to break down the barriers to compromise. This may, in the end be futile; but, if the couple is motivated to settle the case without litigation, eventually the mediator can help bring this about.

Say you want to keep the house and have primary custody of the children, but your spouse wants you to sell the house, split the sales proceeds, and have joint custody. There is a major challenge. The couple has a long way to go to reach an agreement. It's the mediator's job to find a practical solution that both parties can accept. At some point the mediator will explain the laws of the state regarding these issues and how a court might likely rule. Then it is up to the parties to decide if they can live with the state's idea of a resolution or if they are willing to modify their respective positions to reach a solution they both prefer.

Divorce Dictionary

Mediation: Divorce mediation is a process whereby a neutral person—the mediator, who is usually a lawyer and/or social worker—works with the divorcing couple towards reaching a settlement agreement.

Once an agreement is reached, each spouse brings the agreement to his or her own attorney for review. If the lawyers find no questions or problems with the document, one of the attorneys drafts the requisite paperwork for approval by the parties. If everyone is in accord, the settlement agreement is then submitted to the court for the judge to sign. Once it is entered into the court's records, it is finalized.

Advantages of Mediation

For certain people, mediation is an appropriate way to reach an agreement. The best candidates are those who are willing to negotiate directly with their spouse to save money and heartache and get on with their lives. They are people who understand the value of avoiding expensive, heated litigation and are willing to give something up in order to settle quickly and as amicably as possible. Typically, they value the fact that, even in their darkest hour as a couple, they can sit down and talk face to face instead of interacting solely through their attorneys. Mediation usually takes place in a friendlier setting than legal meetings, although if there are hard feelings because of a betrayal, there can be considerable tension. But, in a more relaxed environment, with the aid of a caring mediator, more might be accomplished.

As a process, mediation is also more flexible than the legal protocols that guide lawyers and courts. For example, you can set the pace of mediation sessions to correspond with your own emotional and logistical needs. After you enter the legal system, deadlines and delays come with the territory, imposed not just by individual judges, but also by the system's mandate to "move things along," or more likely, slowed by the huge backlog in the courts.

Finally, mediation might sometimes work better, even for the most calculating among us. Because mediators usually meet with both spouses at once, it's easier during these sessions to grasp just where the other is coming from. After all, you cannot read body language or facial expressions when your only communiqués come from the whir of a lawyer's fax machine. This might be a plus for those who can "just tell" when their spouse is bluffing or when he or she won't budge.

When Mediation Works Best

Despite the advantages, mediation is not for everyone. The system works best when you and your spouse have mutually agreed you want a divorce, when each of you is fully informed of the other's assets and debts, and when, despite some disputes, you're both flexible and eager to work it out as amicably as you can.

Mediation also works best when you and your spouse are convinced of the mediator's impartiality. One lawyer tells us the most common reason clients give for having left mediation is the feeling that the mediator had begun to favor the other spouse.

Mediation also works best when there are no urgent needs that must be resolved with a judge's help. For example, if your spouse has cut off support and refuses to reinstate it, you can't afford the luxury of meeting once a week with a mediator to resolve the issue. You need a lawyer to race into court and ask a judge to order your spouse to resume supporting you—now.

Finally, mediation works best when both individuals have had a relatively equal relationship. If one member of the couple has, historically, dominated the other, it may be more difficult for both to participate in the give-and-take of mediation.

Silver Linings

Mediation is not binding. If you are not satisfied with the outcome of your mediation, you might have wasted some time and money, but you can start all over by going to court.

When to Avoid Mediation

Take our "mediation-elimination" quiz. If you answer any of the following questions with a "No," mediation is not for you:

➤ Do we both want this divorce?

➤ Do I know what our assets and debts are?

➤ Are we communicating?

➤ Can we both be flexible if need be?

Red Alert

If you do not know the value of assets in your marriage—pension plans, a business—or your spouse's income, mediation is probably not for you. The reason: The mediator lacks any authority to make one of you reveal assets to the other. An attorney lacks that authority, too, but he or she can go to a judge. The judge, in turn, can render a ruling requiring your spouse to reveal assets. The judge can penalize your spouse for refusing to cooperate, or worse, for lying. The mediator has no such power.

Although wonderful in concept, mediation could be a disaster in certain situations. Even if you passed the "elimination quiz," take time to review the following list. As you consider your response to the questions, you might conclude that mediation is not for you:

1. If you and your spouse are not talking, mediation sessions are not the time to start, and mediation is probably not for you. Remember, the mediator is not a marriage counselor, but rather a conflict resolution specialist whose job it is to help the two of you address and resolve issues. If you're not even talking, there's not much the mediator can do.

2. If you or your spouse harbor extreme feelings of anger, mediation probably won't work.

3. If one of you does not want the divorce, mediation doesn't stand a chance.

4. If you're trying mediation but you feel the mediator is siding with your spouse, you should stop the process. Maybe you're being paranoid, but it doesn't matter. When one of you has lost confidence, you should each retain a lawyer.

5. Mediators do not have "attorney-client" privilege. That means that anything you tell the mediator can later come out in court. If you have secrets that impact your case, you should probably avoid mediation (or keep the secrets to yourself).

Mary Pauling found herself in that situation not long ago. She and her husband George decided to use mediation on the recommendation of friends—it worked for them. Each was in love with someone else, and there were no hard feelings. They had a four-year-old son, Evan, and they'd decided Mary would have custody. The only issue was the amount of support George would pay.

At the second session, before George arrived, Mary confided to the mediator that Evan was actually her boyfriend's son, not George's. The mediator felt obligated to share this information with George because it would have enormous impact on whether he even wanted to see Evan again, let alone provide for his support. Mary left before George arrived and hired a lawyer the next day, but that was a day too late. Had Mary gone to an attorney in the first place and made the same confession, the attorney could not have revealed anything without her consent.

Red Alert

Many believe that mediation is not a fair process for women. The reason given is that some men are able to bully the women during the mediation process, and some mediators will not be strong enough to counter the bullying or apprise the woman of her rights under the law. If you are a woman (or a man who lived with a bully for a wife), and this scenario rings true, be sure the mediator is aware of your concerns. Alternatively, you might decide this process won't work for you.

6. If your case is very simple, it might not pay to use a mediator because attorneys will have to review the agreement anyway, and you might be better off just starting out with those attorneys. Remember, mediation is useful when there are unresolved issues between you and your spouse. If there are no issues, you might as well go straight to lawyers to draft the agreement.

Choosing a Mediator

Unfortunately, there are no standards for mediators, and in most states, anyone can hang a shingle and call himself or herself a mediator. Your state or city might have an organization that admits mediators based on training and accumulated experience, and if so, look there for a list of references. Your local bar association might be able to give you the names of reputable mediators. Word of mouth is a good way to locate an appropriate professional as well.

The mediator should at least have a degree in social work, counseling, or psychology. It is helpful, but not imperative, that the mediator have a law degree as well. Even without a law degree, however, the mediator should be completely familiar with the divorce laws of your state.

How can you find out whether the mediator knows the law? Ask how long he has been doing mediation, how many cases he has handled, and how he keeps up with new developments in the law. The prospective mediator should be able to answer your questions without sounding defensive.

Find out what and how the mediator charges before you hire one. You and your spouse should agree on how the mediator's fees will be paid. Will you each pay half the fee at the end of each session, or will one of you pay all of it and be reimbursed when the case is over and the assets are divided? Will one of you foot the bill with no reimbursement? If you cannot work that out with the mediator's help, mediation might not be for you.

Finally, ask for references—and call those references. The mediator might not be willing to give you the names of clients (and should not do so without the clients' prior consent), but the mediator should be able to give you the names of attorneys familiar with his or her work. After all, the mediator should be sending couples to attorneys to review any agreement before it is signed. If the mediator doesn't know any attorneys or can't give you any names, interview someone else. Sometimes, it is useful to engage in a dual mediation process where there are two mediators, one a lawyer and one a psychologist. This raises the cost, but in the right case, it might be worth it.

Before choosing your mediator, fill out the candidate's credentials on the following checklist to decide whether a given mediator is for you:

Mediator Checklist

Mediator's name: _____

Address: _____

Date seen: _____

Mediator's education: _____

Mediator's experience: _____

Mediator's fees: _____

How fees will be paid: _____

Did I feel comfortable with the mediator? _____

Did the mediator seem to favor one of us over the other? _____

Was the mediator able to work out the payment of fees between us? _____

Does the mediator have an overall plan for our case? _____

Will the mediator draft an agreement if we come to one? _____

Mediation as a Process

What goes on in mediation—behind closed doors?

A mediator will often start the process by asking you to write out your goals—what you would like to come away with. You will be asked to anticipate such problem areas as custody or support. And you might be asked to set forth your assets and liabilities in a sworn (notarized) statement, just as you would have done with an attorney. This gives everyone involved a clear idea of what you're dealing with and how far apart you really are.

The mediator will work with both of you to divide assets, allocate support, and resolve custody and visitation or any other disputes. The mediator should not advocate one side over the other but should help you both by noting where compromise might work or by coming up with new solutions.

Red Alert

What if one of you really likes the mediator you're thinking of and the other doesn't? Don't be pressured. If you do not feel entirely comfortable, turn the mediator down. Besides, it's dangerous to start out with someone one of you likes better. As in the case of choosing an attorney, the mediator should be someone competent whom you both like and with whom you feel relatively comfortable.

If, at any point during the process, you don't like the way things are going, feel free to consult with an attorney. If you need to consult with your lawyer more than once or twice, however, you might be better off stopping the mediation and just using the attorney. After all, why pay for two professionals?

In any event, after you resolve all the issues, the mediator will draft a written agreement and suggest that you have it reviewed by an attorney. He or she will want to make sure that all possible issues have been covered. For example, some people don't realize they're entitled to part of their spouse's pension. Maybe the mediator overlooked this, or maybe you discussed it but you decided to waive any right to the pension. Either way, your lawyer should point out your rights and suggest that you pursue them or waive them in writing. It is then ready for signing by the parties and then brought before the judge for signing.

Can you go through the mediation process without ever using a lawyer? Possibly. But if you had enough issues to see a mediator, you're probably better off spending a little more on an attorney and making sure that everything is okay.

If you dislike the result of your mediation, *don't sign the agreement.* Say that you and your spouse have just spent four months and $2,000 on mediation, and as the process nears an end, you just don't feel comfortable. Perhaps you even feel the agreement is being "shoved down your throat." Maybe you began to think the mediator was siding with your spouse from the beginning, but you were afraid to say anything, or you feel as though your spouse is "pulling a fast one."

If there is some legitimate basis to your feeling, do not sign the agreement. Seek advice from an attorney. On the other hand, if the real problem is that you're just not ready to end the marriage, or you still hold the faint glimmer of hope that the marriage can be saved, you need to discuss these feelings with a therapist. The truth might be that you'll never be ready to sign an agreement, no matter how fair. If you are consciously or subconsciously subverting the negotiation process, don't take comfort in the thought that your spouse won't be able to get a divorce. You will simply be laying the groundwork for a litigated divorce. If you are in this situation, a consultation with a mental health professional might help you avoid the economic and emotional stress and time of going to court.

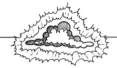

Silver Linings

The law is not the only consideration when trying to reach a settlement. If you can put any anger you might have aside, you might be able to appeal to your sense of fairness. The mediation process allows you to come to a settlement based on knowledge that only you and your spouse have about each other's temperaments and financial and emotional situations. If you can see past the breakup, both parties might come away from the process with less damage than simply relying on the laws of your state.

If You Think Your Spouse Is Lying

It might be your suspicion or your experience with your spouse that leads you to believe he or she is covering up the truth about finances or other matters. How is it possible to know, and, if it's true, how is it possible to continue using mediation as the vehicle to settle your case?

In a litigated divorce, the process of discovery is supposed to reveal the assets of both parties. This is a mandatory process that yields evidence admissible in court. During mediation, however, discovery is not required. The divorcing couple relies on mutual trust that the other will tell the truth and bring in all documents showing financial status.

How can you make sure that your spouse is telling the truth? If you are suspicious, hire an accountant to review the financial papers and books of your spouse, especially if you are not a financial expert. Not only will a professional be able to notice a deficiency, but the very fact that an accountant is scrutinizing your spouse's affairs will help to keep him or her honest during the negotiations.

Reliving Old Patterns During Your Mediation

It may not be surprising to you to hear that the patterns of interaction that typified your marriage will characterize your behavior as a couple during mediation. It is the job of a skillful mediator to help the couple break the pattern that put one of the spouses in the driver's seat and give strength to the other spouse. Accomplishing this doesn't mean the mediator is siding with one party or the other; instead, it is the only way that a fair settlement can be established.

Rebecca did not want to mediate her divorce with Michael, but he insisted she not hire an attorney and give mediation a chance. She hesitated for a long time, but finally gave in, as was usually the case in their marriage. Once at the mediator's office, Michael took center stage in presenting the "facts" to back up why he wanted a divorce and how the settlement should look. Rebecca disagreed with Michael's version of the "facts" but was reticent to speak up.

The mediator was skillful in noticing the pattern of interaction between the two and encouraged Rebecca to speak her mind. This skillful mediator simply would not allow Michael to gain the upper hand or let a subject drop without a full hearing from both Rebecca and Michael on all issues during the negotiation sessions. As a result, he was able to facilitate a fair settlement.

All About Arbitration

Arbitration is sometimes confused with mediation, but it's really quite different. In arbitration, an individual—the arbitrator—hears your case outside the court system and makes a decision that usually cannot be appealed. As in a court of law, you and your spouse would generally be represented by a lawyer, and depending on the arbitrator, he or she might even insist that the rules of evidence in your jurisdiction be followed by the book.

The arbitration itself usually takes place in an office around a conference table. In many ways, arbitration is like going to court, but unlike court, where you can appeal, the arbitrator's word is final.

Divorce Dictionary

Arbitration: A case is decided by an official arbitrator who hears all evidence and makes a decision. Individuals are represented by attorneys. Unlike litigating in court, there are no appeals.

Unlike lawyers, arbitrators do not make an effort to settle the case. They certainly do not do what mediators do—identify issues and then help you resolve them together. Instead, an arbitrator is more like a judge. You come to the table (with your lawyer), ready to present your side. The issues, whatever they might be, have already been determined by you and your lawyer. You must present the arbitrator with your position on those issues and argue your case as cogently as you can.

Given the restrictions, why would anyone ever choose to go into arbitration rather than to a judge? The reasons, for some, are compelling:

1. Depending on where you live, it could take as long as a year to go before a judge, whereas an arbitrator might be readily available.

2. You and your spouse might both feel that neither of you will appeal, no matter what the outcome. Maybe you have no more money or you simply can't withstand another round of litigation. Because you're not going to appeal, arbitration has no downside.

3. Arbitration might be cheaper than a trial. In some jurisdictions, trials do not take place day after day until they are finished. Rather, the judge might schedule one day for your case in January, one day in March, two days in April, and so on. You get the picture. Each time your lawyer has to refresh himself about your case, it costs you. Arbitrators, on the other hand, usually meet day after day until your case is fully heard. Your lawyer only has to prepare once.

4. Your case may have been in court (without being tried) for so long that you just want it over with, so you're more than willing to go to arbitration to save time.

After you and your spouse have agreed you want to have your case arbitrated, the lawyers usually pick the arbitrator. Often, arbitrators are retired judges or lawyers with an area of expertise, such as matrimonial law, and are thus quite competent. As with mediators, their fees must be paid by you and your spouse.

The Least You Need to Know

➤ Mediation works best when both of you can communicate, when you know what assets and liabilities you have, and when you are both willing to be flexible and you want the process to work.

➤ Mediators should have a degree in social work, counseling, psychology, and possibly law, but even without a law degree, they should be thoroughly familiar with the matrimonial laws of your state.

➤ Any agreement decided with a mediator should still be reviewed by an attorney.

➤ Do not sign an agreement with which you feel uncomfortable, but be sure that your discomfort is rooted in logic, not emotion.

➤ Consider arbitration if you and your spouse would not have appealed a trial judge's decision anyway, or if your case has dragged on due to a backlogged court.

Chapter 10

Taking Your Case to Court

In This Chapter

➤ The judge: If you two can't decide, he or she will do it for you

➤ Understanding courtspeak: conferences, motions, and discovery

➤ The difference between family and civil court

➤ Deciding to appeal: Is it worth it?

You and your spouse have tried for months, maybe even years, to settle your divorce on your own, but you've gotten nowhere. Your lawyer hasn't had any luck either. Finally, you've reached the end of the line: It's time to go to court.

Here Comes the Judge

Perhaps the most important person you'll deal with as you go to trial is the judge—just another human being, albeit one who has the power to make decisions for you and your spouse. In some states, your case might be tried by a jury, but if not, a judge will decide the outcome. As the decider (*trier of fact,* in courtspeak), the judge listens, takes notes, sometimes asks questions, and when the case is over, makes a decision. Because the judge is also the *referee,* he will set the schedule of the trial, make rulings when the lawyers disagree, and rap the gavel if the courtroom gets out of control. You might have one judge throughout the case or several different judges until trial, at which time you will have only one judge.

Behind Closed Doors: How Judges Resolve Issues

While those going through divorce await trial, they often find themselves unable to resolve even the most mundane issues on their own. When that happens, the judge on their case gets involved. For instance, John wanted to have his sons spend the last three weeks of the summer with him so that they could visit his sister (their aunt) and her family, who were in the United States for only a short time. Sara—the boys' mother—had already enrolled them in summer camp for those same weeks. Because John and Sara could not agree on a solution to this conflict, their lawyers were asked to intervene. Discussions between the lawyers also went nowhere.

Finally, John's lawyer asked for a conference with the judge. John brought a brochure from the summer camp, showing three sessions. He had contacted the camp and told the judge that the first and second sessions still had room for his sons. He explained that his sister, who lived in Spain, would only be in the United States for the last three weeks of the summer.

The judge immediately granted John his request. The cost to him? Less than $500 in legal fees. As an added bonus, he made a good impression on the judge (he had done his homework and had delivered his pitch calmly), whereas Sara seemed unreasonable and stressed. Not only would John get the boys when he wanted them, but he would also be walking into the upcoming trial with a reputation for reason, responsibility, and calmness.

Red Alert

If you attend a court conference, keep in mind that you will be in front of the judge who might eventually try your case. Do your best to make a good impression. Speak in a conversational tone and do not display emotion or make threats. Even if the current judge will not try your case, you stand a better chance of winning a request if the judge is happy with your demeanor.

How to Impress the Judge

Given the fact that your judge might be determining your fate and, if you have children, theirs too, making a good impression is vital. To make sure that you score points with this powerful figure, study the following helpful tips:

1. Avoid gesticulating wildly with your hands. The judge might not remember the issue raised in the conference, but if you make a spectacle of yourself, he might well remember that! Sometimes, it's hard to maintain control when you know your spouse is lying, but you have to do it.

2. If your lawyer is present, it's best that you follow accepted courtroom protocol and not speak at all unless your lawyer instructs you to or the judge asks you a question directly. If you think your lawyer is missing an issue (or the boat), nudge her gently and ask if you can speak to her for a minute. You can also write a note and push it over to your lawyer.

3. Remember, don't overreact.

Going Through the Motions

Sometimes, you will not be able to resolve pretrial conflicts in conferences, and your attorney will have to make a request in writing (a *motion*). If you want to obtain immediate, temporary support until the trial commences, temporary custody of the children, a visitation schedule, lawyer's fees, expert's fees, or any other temporary relief, written motions— although far more costly to the client than conferences—are the way to go.

Motion practice is like a tennis game, except paperwork—instead of a ball—flies back and forth. Say your spouse has stopped paying the mortgage on the marital residence. He has moved out, and he thinks you should pay for it because you're living there, but you don't want to use up your limited savings. It's been four months since he last paid the mortgage, and you're getting nasty letters from the bank. What to do?

Your lawyer will probably draft a motion asking the judge to immediately order your spouse to pay the back due mortgage and continue to make monthly payments. The motion will include your sworn statement, explaining that the mortgage has not been paid. Your lawyer will probably include the bank letters you've received as exhibits for the judge to see. Once your paperwork is completed, your lawyer sends a copy of the papers to your spouse's lawyer before giving the motion to the judge.

Divorce Dictionary

Motion: A request made of a judge at a time while an action is pending or at trial. Motions can be made in writing for the court to consider, or orally, such as at trial. In matrimonial cases, motions are typically made for temporary support, temporary custody, visitation rights, or to enjoin someone from taking money or property. A "motion" may also be called an "order to show cause."

Cross-motion: A counter request made of a judge in reaction to a motion made by the opposing party.

Your spouse's lawyer then has the chance to answer your paper. She will draft a sworn statement for your spouse to sign, opposing your motion. Maybe your husband will say he gave you the money to pay the mortgage each month, but you spent it on a vacation. He might include canceled checks as exhibits. If he wants additional relief, such as an order directing you to pay the utilities on the house, he can ask for that as well. That's called a *cross-motion*.

You then have the chance to respond to both his response to your motion—maybe those checks were used for food—and his cross-motion. He then responds to your response to the counter-motion. All the paperwork eventually goes to the judge, who makes a decision.

In some jurisdictions, even with all this paperwork, the lawyers still must appear in court and present oral arguments to the judge. You can well imagine that by the time all is said and done, you could have taken a trip to the US Open instead of paying legal fees in your own tennis match.

Divorce Dictionary

Discovery: The act of revealing information so that both parties are fully informed of facts before trial. Discovery can pertain to finances or to one's physical or mental condition when those issues are relevant, such as when a spouse claims an inability to work due to an injury. Depending on the jurisdiction, other areas may be discoverable as well. Discovery methods include depositions, answering interrogatories, producing documents, and/or undergoing a physical.

Divorce Dictionary

Deposition: Answering questions under oath. In matrimonial matters, a deposition usually centers on a party's finances and is conducted in a lawyer's office or in the courthouse, but a judge will not be present. In some jurisdictions, the grounds for divorce may also be the subject of the deposition. A stenographer takes down everything that is said and later types it up for review by the parties and their attorneys.

The Discovery Zone

Before your case can go to trial, you will go through the process of *discovery*. Here, you and your spouse, working through your attorneys, exchange information that might be important to your case. In some jurisdictions, discovery is limited to financial issues. In other places, the discovery can involve issues of physical and mental health, especially if these issues were part of the grounds for divorce.

How does discovery work? It's like a scavenger hunt. Your attorney will receive a list (usually long) from your spouse's attorney, setting out all the information that lawyer wants—bank statements, credit-card slips, canceled checks, loan applications, credit-card applications, deeds, wills, names of anyone with whom you own property; the list is limited only by the lawyer's imagination and the local law.

What if you don't have the materials requested? Unfortunately, your spouse probably won't believe you. You could end up before a judge, with your spouse's lawyer claiming you're hiding information and your lawyer explaining that you no longer have it. A judge will then rule for or against you.

Discovery is not limited to the production of written materials. You could also be *deposed*—be obligated to answer questions under oath in front of a stenographer, your spouse, and his lawyer. You could be served with extensive written questions, which you are obligated to answer truthfully.

Discovery could also involve a physical examination by a medical doctor (if, for example, the issue is your ability to work), a blood test (if the issue is paternity), and even a psychological examination (particularly if custody is at issue or you claim you need support because you have psychological problems).

A judge need not be involved in discovery if the lawyers agree on a schedule and stick to it and agree on what is to be disclosed. However, if one side doesn't agree on what is to be disclosed, then the decision will rest with the judge.

Trials and Tribulations: Your Day in Court

Judges generally try to help you resolve your case before the trial date, but that is often simply impossible. If, after months and even years of negotiations, conferences, and motions, you and your spouse or ex-spouse still have not reached an agreement, your last recourse is to have a trial. The trial gives the judge the opportunity to hear both parties' wish lists, substantiated by volumes of documents, possibly witnesses, and any other information the contenders think will persuade the judge in their favor.

After the judge ponders all this, she will make her decision. Because the judge has heard all the evidence and witnesses, a decision made after a trial is taken very seriously by the powers that be. This decision should put an end to conferences called for modifying temporary orders or changes in visitation schedules. Everyone has spent a lot of time, money, and effort at the trial, and asking for subsequent modification might not do you much good.

Your trial will be very much like those you've seen on television and in movies. If you are the *plaintiff*, or petitioner, the spouse who started the action, your lawyer presents your case first. He will probably call you to the witness stand, where you will be sworn in and asked to take a seat. After your lawyer has finished asking you questions (*direct examination*), your spouse's lawyer has the opportunity to ask you questions (*cross-examination*). Your lawyer has the right to object to improper questions, so give her time to do that before answering. It's also a good idea to take a moment before you answer to collect your thoughts.

After the cross-examination, your lawyer can ask you questions again; maybe your spouse's lawyer interrupted you while you were trying to explain something. Your lawyer can now give you the chance to present your explanation (your *re-direct examination*).

After your re-direct examination, there can be a re-cross-examination. The questioning can go back and forth for as long as the judge will allow it. When there are no more questions for you, your lawyer can call a witness to the stand on your behalf, and the whole process starts all over again.

Divorce Dictionary

Guardian ad litem: A person, often a lawyer, but in some states a psychologist or social worker, selected by the judge and assigned to represent "the best interests" of the children. Some states do not have guardians ad litem.

After you have presented all your witnesses (in divorce cases, it's often just you, your spouse, ;possibly your child's *guardian ad litem*, the court-appointed psychiatric evaluator, and expert witnesses such as an appraiser of real property or of a business), your side "rests." It is now your spouse's turn to present his witnesses. The same questioning occurs, only the roles are reversed. Your spouse's lawyer conducts the direct questioning, and your lawyer cross-examines the witness.

After your spouse (in this case, the defendant) presents her witnesses, your lawyer can call witnesses to refute what's been said (called *rebuttal witnesses*). After you've called your rebuttal witnesses, your spouse can do the same.

When both sides have rested, the judge might allow each attorney to make a short, closing speech. Alternatively, he might ask that the attorneys submit memoranda to him by a certain deadline. Sometime later, he makes his decision, usually in writing.

If your trial was by jury, the jury decides the outcome after all the witnesses have testified, closing speeches have been made, and the judge has instructed the jurors about their responsibilities.

Some judges might give you a "bench" (oral) decision at the end of your motion or trial, as though you had a jury. (Your lawyer should be able to find out, before the trial, if your judge makes bench decisions.)

Trials can be as short as half a day or as long as several months (although that would probably be unusual for a divorce trial). The length of a trial depends on the number of witnesses, how long each examination takes, and what motions are made during the course of the trial. The emotional and financial costs rapidly add up.

Judicial Bias

Do judges "play favorites" with lawyers? The answer is, probably not, but who knows? We like to think justice is blind, but there are some realities too. In some jurisdictions, the same judges tend to hear matrimonial cases, and the same lawyers tend to appear before them. Does that mean they're all buddies, and you had better find the lawyer the judge likes best? No. Cases are decided on their merits. It does mean, however, that if you've hired a well-respected attorney, the judge has probably already observed him at work and trusts his integrity.

Do some judges favor mothers over fathers in custody disputes? The answer to that question is probably "yes." Even though custody determinations are supposed to be gender neutral, the reality for many fathers is that they go off to work while the mother stays home. Even if the mother does work, she is the one who probably did most of the childcare. It follows that the mother has spent more time with the children, the main criterion for custody. Many judges also work under the assumption that young children (seven and under) belong with their mothers.

Will a judge ever admit to a bias? No. But most lawyers will tell you that if you're a father seeking custody, you'll probably need a good reason why the mother should not have custody. Should you throw in the towel? Consult with an attorney first.

What about other biases? Years on the bench, of course, can make one skeptical. Some judges have heard umpteen tales of the business that fails, miraculously, right before the divorce action, and a few years of seasoning means that they've seen the couple who's spent $100,000 a year while reporting income of $20,000 and even less. Does this mean you're doomed if your business really has taken a bad turn, or you had no idea what your spouse reported as income? No; but when you appear before a judge, you must be thoroughly prepared to prove your case.

Trial by Fire: When You're the Witness

As much as you might wish the witness seat would open up and swallow you, you will need to deal with the opposing attorney the best you can. What can you do when you're looking at a lawyer, but you feel as if you're peering into the mouth of a shark? Some pointers follow:

1. Take your time before answering questions. Think before you speak, and give your lawyer time to object to the question.

2. Do not let the lawyer get you riled. Control your emotions.

3. If you feel faint, tell the judge you need a break.

4. If there's water nearby, pour yourself a cup or ask the judge for some. Do not be shy about making these requests. Just be sure not to interrupt anyone else, unless it's an emergency.

5. Keep shaky hands inside the witness box so that the lawyer won't know what effect he's having on you.

6. Look at the judge, at the back of the room, or at your lawyer rather than at the lawyer who is questioning you.

7. Start crying. The judge is sure to call a recess, and you'll have a chance to pull yourself together. If you're a man, you probably think you'd never do that, but nothing will bring a divorce trial to a halt as quickly as a man crying, particularly if he does it while he's testifying about how much he loves his children.

Red Alert

Donna was more than a strict mother. She punished her children by hitting them—hard—for the least offense. That was one of the reasons Bill couldn't stand being in the marriage any longer. Bill was sensitive and could not tolerate the cold, abrasive, punishing mother that Donna was. He was asking for sole custody of the children.

While careful not to accuse Donna of physically abusing the children (his lawyers advised him that judges don't trust this overly used accusation in custody cases), Bill's lawyer asked Donna on the stand, "Isn't it true that you hit your children? Donna let slip out, "I haven't hit them for two years now."

While some judges adhere to the notion that hitting children is "parental style," this particular judge abhorred corporal punishment. Bill was awarded custody of his children.

Silver Linings

Although the issues being decided at your trial are extremely important and will affect you profoundly, this is not a criminal trial. No one is going to be sentenced to jail (unless this is a trial for contempt—a deliberate failure to make support payments, for example). Matrimonial judges might get annoyed at your bad behavior or obvious lies, but they are used to the deep feelings divorcing spouses have and are generally sympathetic and patient.

Traps You Can Avoid

A trial should be about the pursuit of truth and justice, not about who used what gimmick to "win." However, you can do things to help your case:

1. Visit the courthouse before the day of trial, when a trial is in progress, if possible. You'll feel better knowing you're not stepping into uncharted territory.

2. Tell your lawyer everything. If you have a secret bank account and you don't want to tell your lawyer (you're afraid she'll charge you more), keep in mind that your spouse might already know. It will be much worse for you if your lawyer hears about it for the first time while you're on the witness stand being cross-examined.

3. Dress appropriately. Our picks: white, Peter Pan collar blouse with wide skirt for women; suit and tie for men. If you're a man claiming poverty, a sports jacket (or even a sweater, if you're claiming extreme poverty) with slacks and a business shirt can work as well.

4. Leave expensive jewelry at home.

5. Be sure to bring all the documents needed. Pack them the night before. Bring paper, or ask your lawyer to bring an extra legal pad for you to take or write notes.

6. Pause before answering any questions. Give yourself time to think and give your lawyer time to object.

7. If you don't understand a question, tell the lawyer you do not understand and ask that it be repeated.

8. If your trial involves a jury, look at the jurors when you answer questions, but do not stare at any one juror. You don't want to make any juror feel uncomfortable.

9. Be aware that when your side is presenting its case, you're probably going to feel great during the direct examination by your lawyer and maybe even okay during the cross-examination, if your witness can hold his or her own. During the presentation of your spouse's case, you'll probably feel miserable.

10. During the week or so of the trial, get plenty of rest at night.

11. When the trial is over, try to put it out of your mind, at least until there is a decision (if you didn't get one at the end of the trial). You might keep thinking about what you should have said differently. Try to forget it.

Ten Common Mistakes You Must Not Make

The following points might seem obvious in the calm of your living room reading this book, but under the stress of a courtroom situation that is dealing with your marriage, divorce, and facing your "lying" spouse, for your sake, they must be subjected to memory.

1. Do not make faces, ever. If your wife lies like a rug, do not roll your eyes or shake your head (unless your attorney says it's okay). No matter how much you want to, a judge or jury might think you're being childish or that you're faking your reaction; you know she's told the truth, but you want to make it seem as if she hasn't.

2. Do not speak out in court. We know an attorney who represented the father during a custody hearing. While the lawyer was at the podium questioning the mother, her client began yelling at his wife to stop lying! When the case was over, the judge ordered the husband to attend an anger workshop. Needless to say, he did not win custody.

3. Follow your attorney's instincts. This is a tough one if you've been very involved in planning the strategy of your case and now your lawyer wants to do something you think is wrong. When you're at trial, it's not a good time for the camp to be divided. If you feel very strongly, and there's a sound basis to your thinking, present your idea to your attorney. However, unless you are also an attorney, or you are very certain you are right (which might be based on your knowledge of your spouse), do not give your attorney ultimatums.

4. Do not flirt with, excessively smile at, or in any way try to engage the judge or a juror.

5. If your trial is by jury, never speak to a juror while the trial is in progress.

6. Do not argue with your spouse's lawyer. If you're too angry to speak, wait or take a sip of water before continuing to testify.

7. Avoid sarcasm.

8. Avoid crossing your arms while you're on the witness stand.

9. Don't doodle. The judge or jurors might notice, and it will look as though you just don't care.

10. Don't talk to your spouse in court without good reason (scheduling the children, for example). Usually, there's just too much emotion for communication.

Family Court Versus Civil Court

Whether you go to family court is largely dependent on what state you live in and how far you have gotten in your case. In some states, you have to go to civil court if you want a divorce. In other states, all family-related matters may be handled in family court.

In general, family court might be a little more relaxed because many more people handle their own cases without a lawyer. The good news is that the courtrooms, whether by design or through lack of funding, might be much smaller than a "regular courtroom" and might feel less intimidating. The bad news is that while you wait for your case to be called, infants might be screaming all around you, and, depending on where you live, many cases might be ahead of yours. Civil court, on the other hand, tends to be quieter, less congested, and more professional.

Despite these outward differences, how the trial proceeds depends more on the judge than the courthouse. Some judges are very strict about the rules of evidence; others are more liberal. Some judges are very formal, wearing black robes and requiring you to rise when they enter the courtroom. Others are more relaxed and might not even wear a robe.

You're in the Army Now

If you're in the military, different divorce laws might apply, depending upon your state of residence. That's because when it comes to divorce—and everything else—military law is superimposed on top of state law, nationwide.

If you or your spouse are in the military, you should be aware of the following issues:

➤ **Retirement pay**   A federal statute limits the power of state courts to treat military retirement pay as marital property. Under certain circumstances—for instance, when the divorce is filed in the military employee's state of residence—the law allows military retirement pay to be divided with a spouse. But there are still significant restrictions: A spouse can get 50 percent of the retirement pay, at most, and can tap into these funds only if marriage and career overlap by at least a decade. The spouse must pay taxes on all military retirement pay received.

➤ **Legal representation**   If you are navigating divorce military style, you must find an expert familiar with military law.

➤ **Medical benefits** A former spouse is awarded lifetime medical benefits only if marriage and career overlapped at least 20 years. If marriage and career intersected by between 15 and 20 years, benefits will extend for one year. For an overlap that's less than 15 years, there are no benefits at all.

➤ **Death benefits** If a member of the military dies before retirement, no retirement benefits go to a former spouse. If the member dies after retirement, payments to the former spouse will stop. (Even if the military member is married at the time of death, all benefits to third parties cease; that is why private and government-sponsored insurance policies are generally used to protect a spouse.)

Should You Appeal?

As with so much in life, the answer is, "It depends."

If the issue is critically important to you, *and* your lawyer thinks you have a reasonable shot at getting a reversal, *and* you can afford it, *and* you have the emotional fortitude to continue, you probably should appeal.

On the other hand, if the issue is critically important to you, *but* your lawyer says you have virtually no chance of winning, *and* you'd need to mortgage your share of the house, you probably shouldn't appeal.

An appeal is expensive not only because your attorney has to do legal research and then write a brief, but also because you usually need the entire transcript of the trial. Depending on how many days the trial lasted, that alone could cost thousands of dollars. Then, you usually need to supply the appeals court with several copies of the transcript and the brief, adding hundreds of dollars more to your costs in photocopy fees. (Some jurisdictions have procedures whereby you can save money on the transcript or photocopying if you meet certain low-income requirements.)

To make matters worse, in some jurisdictions, the appellate courts are so backlogged that your appeal might not be decided for more than a year.

Can you do an appeal yourself? If you're a lawyer, maybe. However, it would be very hard for a layperson to do the legal research, and you would still be faced with transcript and photocopying costs.

When you consider whether to appeal, listen to your attorney and your head. As much as you might want to, this is not the time to vote with your heart.

The Least You Need to Know

➤ The judge is the final decision-maker if you and your spouse have not been able to come to an agreement.

➤ Motions tend to be expensive because lawyers have to put a lot of time into them. Settle whatever you can with your spouse to avoid motion practice.

➤ Always control your emotions in court. Never make faces in court.

➤ Pause before answering questions. Give your lawyer time to object and give yourself time to answer correctly.

➤ Consider the chances of success and the expense involved before you decide to appeal.

Chapter 11

When Divorce Turns Vicious

In This Chapter

➤ Levels of conflict

➤ How to obtain an order of protection

➤ The limitations of court-ordered protection

➤ How to use the resources of the legal system to reduce conflict

➤ Stalking: why it happens and protective laws

There's high-conflict divorce, and there's higher-conflict divorce. We'll touch on high-conflict divorce in the chapter on litigation—where such scenarios generally play out. When one spouse has been unfaithful and deceptive during the marriage, it is difficult for the "wronged" spouse to agree to an amicable divorce. This can lead to anger and resentment. Anger and resentment can turn to belligerence, which in turn angers the other spouse. Before you know it, neither party will cooperate with the other, and the divorcing couple is headed for protracted litigation.

Why protracted? Both people tend to dig in their heels on issues of importance to each. Add to that the huge backlog in the court system. Before you know it, you're in for the long haul. Sometimes it's the system itself that finally wears you down until you both yell "Uncle!"

Especially during the early years of a separation, fresh wounds from a betrayal or non-stop fighting during the marriage can generate such intense heat that neither person can be in the same room with the other. When children are an issue, things can get really nasty. (In another chapter, we discuss how harmful high-conflict situations are for the children and steps to mitigate the damaging effects on them.)

A custody battle can cause both parents to engage in extreme and hostile behavior never before seen by the other spouse. In some cases, a third party must be involved to help the children go from one parent to the next. Rude or aggressive behavior by one parent towards the other in front of the children is all too common in high-conflict divorce, and it is incumbent on both parents to walk away from situations where their "buttons" are being pushed.

Yet more conflict may arise when a spouse is completely unwilling to let go. Buckle your seat belt: When one spouse wants the divorce and the other opposes it, conflict can be extreme.

If you are the spouse who won't let go, our advice is simply to move on. By dragging out the proceedings, you are merely postponing the inevitable at enormous cost, not just emotionally, but also financially as you and your spouse dribble away your savings on legal fees.

If you are the partner who wants the divorce, step back and give your partner some time and space to get used to the idea. Pull back on significant legal action for a month or two.

Silver Linings

It takes two to have a fight. If your spouse or ex-spouse says something that makes you want to scream, don't! There can be no argument unless you respond in kind.

These high-conflict situations are bad enough, but it gets worse—much worse. One partner may have a genuine personality disorder or suffer mental illness. Now there's a dangerous situation—not just for the children, if there are any, but also for the other spouse.

Sometimes the battle is just a continuation of a long-standing abusive relationship. A spouse who has been battered for years finally has the courage to make a break. Other times a rejected spouse goes beyond what would be normal anger and even retribution into pathological behaviors that can lead to violence and even death. The remaining chapter will briefly touch on the issues involved with this extreme situation.

The Nightmare Begins

You've heard divorce horror stories, and you hoped you could avoid becoming one—but it looks as if your worst nightmare is coming true. Your spouse just won't leave you alone. He hangs out near your office and leers at you when you leave. She calls your new love interest on the phone in the middle of the night and mutters obscenities. He or she has threatened your physical safety and has even entered your apartment without your permission or against your will. Whatever harassment you might be experiencing, you will be able to deal with it most effectively after you have the legal system—and an attorney—on your side.

Red Alert

We don't mean to scare you, but if you have been accustomed to being abused, you must take the necessary steps immediately to get all the protection the law allows. If you think you are in imminent danger, contact the police, and go to a local abuse shelter. Hard though it may seem, you must break with any old habits you have of accepting your spouse back into your life. Now is the time to free yourself so you can live a happier life.

Harassment

Denise couldn't deal with Jack's leaving her. He was her entire life, or so she imagined. She couldn't live without him, and she told him so—over and over, in every form of communication possible. She called him night and day, both at home and at work. She sent him faxes, e-mails, and even called his friends to tell them what a so-and-so he was, yet how much she needed him. Jack could not escape her attempts to get at him. He was sleepless. He was afraid to go anywhere he thought she might be—restaurants they had frequented, the supermarket, cleaners, movie houses, and more. He dreaded stepping out of his office building for fear she would be waiting for him. Ditto his apartment building. In effect, he was under a terrorist attack.

Clearly he was dealing with a woman who had gone beyond the normal reaction of being rejected. What were his options?

Order of Protection

The first step toward protecting your rights and forcing your spouse to keep a distance is the *order of protection*, a document signed by a judge that prohibits your spouse from conducting himself or herself in a certain way in your presence. Judges don't always grant requests for orders of protection: You usually need to provide evidence to the judge showing that you have been or could be victimized by your spouse. If you have been beaten in the past, photographs of injuries, police reports, and hospital or doctor's reports concerning your injuries will help you present your case. Orders of protection can be gotten for less serious offenses, such as harassment and stalking.

Divorce Dictionary

Order of protection: An order directing one spouse to refrain from harassing the other. Violation of an order of protection can result in arrest and imprisonment.

Red Alert

The short-term order of protection that you or your attorney gets from the court contains a date for a court appearance. You're obligated to make sure your spouse is served with a copy of the restraining order. Under no circumstances should you give the order or a copy of the order to your spouse yourself. A process server can be hired by you or your attorney to deliver the order. When you return to court on the assigned date, you are required to present proof that your spouse has been personally served with the order. The proof is usually a sworn statement by the server. Your sworn statement will not be accepted as proof. One reason why you should not serve your spouse with the papers is that he or she might react violently; it's best if you're not around.

Typically, an order of protection may order your spouse to stay a certain distance from you, or it may order your spouse not to harass, menace, endanger, or in any way bother you. In some states, you can obtain an order of protection yourself by going to court (often the family court or criminal court) even if you and your spouse have not yet filed for divorce. If you have filed for divorce, the court where you filed usually has the authority to issue an order of protection, and in many states, criminal court judges have that power as well.

You can also obtain injunctive orders against the use of property, against the changing of beneficiaries on insurance policies, and against the removal of the children from the jurisdiction. Although violations of these orders will not usually result in arrest and imprisonment, it is important to have these in place as an incentive for spouses to refrain from such activities. These are typically called "temporary restraining orders."

Typically, you can get an *ex parte* temporary order of protection. Ex parte means that you (or you with your lawyer) have gone to court without first notifying your spouse. Based on what you present to the judge, he might give you an order enforceable only for a limited number of days or weeks. At the end of that time, you must return to court, and this time, your spouse will be present (or at least will have been notified in advance that he or she should be). The judge will listen to each of you and decide whether to issue another order of protection, usually good for a longer period of time.

Serving the Order

Who will serve the order of protection? At the courthouse, you can arrange for a police officer or sheriff to help. You can also have a friend do it, or, better still, bring the order of protection with a photograph of your spouse to a licensed *process server* who makes a living by serving court papers. Process servers often have offices near the courthouse, or you can locate one in the Yellow Pages. Even if the local police will not serve the order of protection for you, you should still bring or send a copy to your local precinct so that the police have it on record.

The person who serves the order of protection must sign a sworn statement telling when and where he served the order and how he knew the person who received the order was your spouse. You or your attorney will then bring that sworn statement to court on the day you are scheduled to be in court, thus documenting to the judge that your spouse received notification of the court date.

When an Order of Protection Is Not Enough

An order of protection is good 24 hours a day, 7 days a week, whether you are at home or at work. If you work in a state other than the one in which the order was issued, of course, that state might not be obligated to enforce the order. Depending on where you live, if your spouse violates the order of protection, the police might order an arrest, or they might do little at all. You should, of course, carry the order with you at all times; having it in your possession to show to authorities never hurts.

Still, the fact remains that having an order of protection might not solve your problems. You might need to supplement the order with other solutions. For instance, you can show the order to private security personnel at your office or apartment building and ask that they bar your spouse from the building. You might also want to request that your employer tell reception to screen your calls, or you can ask the receptionist directly. It might not be possible to keep your situation from the office rumor mill, but your safety comes first.

Divorce Dictionary

Process server: A company or individual who's profession it is to personally serve court papers.

You Can Do It!

You will need two things when filing a complaint with the authorities: A copy of your state's stalking statute, which you can get from any law library and some public libraries, and a stack of evidence proving that your spouse or ex-spouse is stalking you. Be prepared, and you are more likely to get the help you need. Don't leave home without it!

Stalking and the Law

If you believe your life is in danger because you are being followed or harassed by your spouse or ex-spouse, you can seek protection not just through an order of protection, but also through new states.

Each state has its own definition of stalking. Most accept the concept that stalking makes a person concerned about their safety.

In 1990, California became the first state to pass a law that made stalking a crime. This law was passed after several people who had gotten orders of protection nonetheless fell victim to their stalker. Since the California law was passed, all 50 states now have anti-stalking laws.

Red Alert

If you suspect that you are being stalked, don't hesitate to get advice and help from local victim specialists to design a plan of action. Your local phone book might have the phone numbers of victim or rape centers listed under *"Community Services Numbers"* or *"Emergency Assistance Numbers."* You can also look for victim assistance programs that are part of local prosecutor's offices or even some law enforcement agencies.

Although the laws in the various states differ, almost all make illegal any action or actions that form a pattern of conduct that seeks to harass and/or threaten the safety of another. Punishment for this crime varies from state-to-state.

Unfortunately, not all law enforcement officials are even aware of these laws. If you believe you are being stalked, it's a good idea to get a copy of your state's law from your public library or local law library and bring it to the police, along with evidence supporting your claim. If you still get no response from the police, you can go directly to your local or state district attorney's office.

More information on stalking can be obtained from the National Center for Victims of Crime, 2111 Wilson Boulevard, Suite 300, Arlington, VA 22201, (703) 276-2880 or (703) 276-2889. Their Web site is http://www.ncvc.org.

In sum, the conflict, anger, and violence that can be a part of some extreme cases during and after divorce are cause for alarm, and must be dealt with swiftly. This is not a time to try to settle your case or work out your problems with a marriage counselor or mediator. Pull out all stops. This situation calls for the intervention of the authorities—your lawyer, the police, the victim specialists, the district attorney's office, and the courts.

The Least You Need to Know

➤ High-conflict divorce can go beyond litigation to harassment or even violence.

➤ Call the police if your spouse is harassing you, even if you do not have an order of protection.

➤ Document whatever you can to help obtain an order of protection.

➤ Always file an order of protection with your local police and keep a copy with you at all times.

➤ All 50 states now have stalking laws. Because many law enforcement officials still don't know about these new laws, bring a copy of your state's statutes with your evidence to the police department.

Chapter 12

Closing the Book on Your Case

In This Chapter

➤ When the divorce decree goes into effect

➤ When you can collect pension, Social Security, and other benefits

➤ How remarriage can affect the divorce decree

➤ When a spouse does not comply with the decree

➤ When your lawyer's job is over

It's finally over, or at least you think it is. You've been to court and had a trial, or you've signed a convoluted (or simple) settlement agreement. You're divorced, right?

Probably not. Depending on where you live, your lawyer (or your spouse's lawyer) most likely must draft a document known as the *judgment of divorce* or *decree of divorce*. If your case has been decided by a judge after trial, the judgment of divorce usually refers to everything the judge wrote in his decision. If you and your spouse settled your case, the judgment of divorce might include provisions on custody, child support, division of property, visitation schedule, or other issues; it might also simply refer to your agreement with the assertion that all its provisions are deemed to be included.

If you and your spouse simply bought a "divorce kit," a collection of printed forms necessary to obtain a divorce, it probably includes a judgment of divorce. You'll need to fill in the relevant information and then submit the judgment to the proper court.

When the Judgment Is Final

After the judge signs the judgment of divorce and any record is made of that signing, the divorce is usually effective. (In some jurisdictions, recording in a record book the date on which the judge signed the judgment of divorce is called *entering the judgment*.) In some states, the judgment of divorce might be deemed effective even before it is entered. Either way—whether the judgment has to be entered or merely signed—for better or worse, you're single again.

You can usually get a copy of the judgment of divorce from the court or from your lawyer. It's a good idea to get a certified copy of the judgment of divorce (a photocopy with a stamp from a court official stating that the document has been compared with the original and is the same). There is usually a fee for this service. Also, depending on where you live, you might need identification to be allowed to look at your divorce file, so be sure to bring some identification to the courthouse.

After the Judgement Has Been Entered

When your lawyer (or your spouse's lawyer) has the judgment of divorce, he'll send it to your spouse's lawyer (or vice versa). This isn't just a courtesy to let him know you're divorced; it starts the clock running during which an appeal can be filed. If you and your spouse settled your case, there won't be an appeal, but your lawyer will send the copy anyway. If a judge tried your case, either one of you could appeal, but the clock doesn't start running until one lawyer sends the judgment of divorce to the other, with notification of when it was entered.

In some jurisdictions, the time to file an appeal begins from the date that the judgment is entered or from the date that the court clerk serves the judgment on the parties or their counsel. It is very important to determine when the clock starts ticking because once that time is up, you cannot ask the court to extend it or relieve you from your default if you did not file your notice of appeal on time.

Divorce Dictionary

Judgment of divorce: The written document that states that a husband and wife are divorced. In some states, this may be called a **decree of dissolution.** Typically, lawyers draft the judgment of divorce for the judge to review and sign.

If you and your spouse handled the case yourselves, make sure that you both get a copy of the judgment of divorce. If you're no longer talking, have a friend mail your spouse a copy of the judgment with notification of when it was entered and ask the friend to sign a notarized statement that he has mailed it. This is your proof that you had the judgment sent to your spouse.

Your Benefits

Your settlement agreement or decision by the judge should include your getting the Social Security, retirement, survivor, or disability benefits to which you are entitled.

When will you receive your benefits? Usually, you receive them when your spouse does or at the earliest possible time your spouse could have received them. For example, some retirement plans allow employees to take out money when they turn 55, even if they are still working. The plan might allow ex-spouses who have been awarded part of the plan to do the same. Every plan is different.

You probably won't get these benefits right after the divorce. To get your benefits, the Social Security administration will usually need a certified copy of your judgment of divorce and any agreement in order to process your claim. In the case of pension benefits, your lawyer (or your husband's lawyer) will usually have to draft an order at the same time he drafts your judgment of divorce. The order explains when you'll get your pension benefits. The judge then signs it, while your case is fresh in everyone's mind, and your lawyer sends a copy to your spouse's pension-plan administrator. Notify the plan administrator if you move, and as the time draws nearer for you to receive your benefit, contact the plan administrator (the address should be in the order) to find out what information it needs to process your claim.

Changing Your Name

In some jurisdictions, the judgment of divorce will include a paragraph giving a wife the right to resume her maiden, or other, name. Government offices usually require that you show them a certified copy of the judgment of divorce before they'll issue documents in your maiden, or other, name.

For the most part, however, you can simply start using the name you now want to be called. For some, it's the maiden name. For others, it might be the name from a prior marriage. Many women who have children retain their ex-husband's family name until their children are out of school. Although divorce is common now, they'd rather not flag their status.

Modifying the Divorce Decree

Modification of a divorce decree is complicated, and you will need your attorney's involvement. As with other issues, it's usually easier to get a decree modified if you had a trial and a judge decided your case than if you and your spouse settled.

When Bobby Kingston was 4 years old, his parents divorced and signed an agreement including all financial issues as they related to Bobby until he turned 21. Unfortunately, no mention was made of who would pay for Bobby's college. When Bobby turned 17, his mother, Irene, tried to get Bobby's father, Joe, to help pay for college. Joe refused to pay. Irene hired an attorney, who made a motion asking the judge to order Joe to pay for college. The judge refused, saying Irene had the chance to ask that Joe pay college tuition when she signed the agreement 13 years earlier. The judge protected the settlement agreement.

If, on the other hand, a judge had decided the case between Bobby's parents after a trial, Irene would have had a good chance of getting the tuition paid by Joe. Because the trial took place when Bobby was only four years old, the judge would probably not have made a decision on college tuition. After all, what if the child doesn't want to go to college? Because tuition might not have been considered by a judge when Bobby was 4, Irene's request would seem reasonable to a judge 13 years later.

What if you notice a mistake in your divorce decree right after you get it? It will probably be easy to modify if the mistake is clerical, such as an incorrect date. It will be harder to modify if there is a dispute between you and your spouse over what is correct.

For example, it is not a clerical error if your lawyer forgot to include in the judgment of divorce your wish to be with your children on Mother's Day. Your lawyer can try to have the decree modified. Judges will usually agree to a modification if both sides agree to it.

How Remarriage Alters Things

If your case was settled, your agreement probably took into account the possibility of remarriage. For example, if your ex is paying you maintenance and the agreement says that stops if you remarry, you can be sure your ex will comply with that part of the agreement! If your ex's lawyer forgot to put in that provision, your ex might have to go to court to be allowed to stop paying maintenance, and he might not win.

If your case was tried by a judge, the law in your state might affect what happens if you remarry. For example, the law might provide that support automatically stops on remarriage. Your ex does not have to go to court to have this change made; the law has made it for him.

Can you keep your remarriage a secret? Of course you can, but that's not a good idea. Most agreements require you to notify your spouse (or your lawyer, who will notify his lawyer) about a change that affects the deal. If you don't have an agreement and you're collecting maintenance, the law probably provides that it stop on remarriage. Eventually, you would have to give back the money you kept. If for some reason your case went back to a judge, your actions would work against you.

When Your Second Marriage Ends

What if you get divorced from your second spouse? Does your first spouse have to resume paying you? Not usually. The same applies to any benefit you gave up when you remarried. A second divorce does not bring your first spouse back into the picture, so be sure that you want to give up your entitlements before you tie the knot a second time.

Remarriage after a divorce has the most impact on the person who was the breadwinner in the first marriage. If you're the breadwinner, suddenly you're contributing to two households, not just to your former household and your own expenses. Your new spouse might resent the money that's going to your ex or your children. Also common is that she might resent the time you spend with your children or the time they spend with the two of you. These are issues to consider before remarriage.

Henry married Eleanor two years after his divorce. Henry, a real-estate broker, earned enough to live comfortably on his own while giving child support to his two children. Eleanor was a nurse. Her income plus Henry's enabled them to live in a small, two-bedroom apartment in Chicago. When Eleanor and Henry had their first child, money got tight. Eleanor, who early in her marriage was very understanding of Henry's supporting his kids from his first marriage, suddenly began resenting Henry for continuing the child support. She began to feel that the support money belonged to their own child. This put a tremendous strain on their relationship.

What If You Lose Your Job?

If your case was settled and not tried and you lose your job, *you might still be obligated to pay whatever you were paying while you were employed*, depending on the laws of your state. Why? You (or your lawyer) had the opportunity to include in your agreement a provision calling for reduction of maintenance or child support should you lose your job.

Might a judge give you a reduction anyway? Possibly, but it would be easier if your case had been decided at trial, where the judge would address only what was before him, not what may or may not happen. In some jurisdictions, unforeseeable events might provide a basis for changing an agreement. Also, in some jurisdictions, if your children's economic needs are not being met, a judge might be more likely to review and possibly change the agreement. It is essential that the paying spouse go to court immediately for the modification. Generally, spousal support continues to accrue unless you obtain an order modifying it.

Red Alert

When negotiating your settlement agreement, if you are the spouse who might pay alimony, consider adding a clause to the agreement stating that you no longer have to pay alimony if your ex-spouse remarries.

When Your Ex Does Not Comply

Enforcement of the decree is difficult, if not impossible, without the help of a lawyer. Some lawyers specialize in collections, and others won't touch it. Before you incur the cost of trying to chase your spouse to collect money, ask yourself:

1. Does my ex-spouse have the money or income for me to collect? If the answer is "no," you'll probably be wasting your time and money trying to collect what he owes you.

2. Are there any other assets that the judge will allow me to collect? A car, home, boat? If so, how much will it cost me to collect against those assets, and how long will it take? Again, it simply might not be worth it.

3. Has my ex-spouse put assets in someone else's name? If so, you might run into serious collection problems.

Silver Linings

If you are having problems collecting the child support ordered by court or put into your settlement agreement, you do have recourse.

Your ex-spouse's wages can be garnished.

You can contact your state's child support enforcement agency.

You can hire a company that will attempt to locate your spouse and help collect support. Some of these companies do not charge a fee, but take a percentage of what they collect, such as Child Support Network (http://www.childsupport.com/index.html), Child Support Enforcement (http://www.supportkids.com/), and the Child Support Assistance Network (http://www.childsupportassistance.net/).

Here are some Web sites that can be of assistance:

Federal Office of Child Support Enforcement (http://www.acf.dhhs.gov/programs/cse/index.html)

SupportKids.Org (http://www.supportkids.org/enforce_agncy.htm)

National Child Support Enforcement Association (http://www.ncsea.org/)

What if money isn't the issue? The problem is that your ex-spouse has custody of the children but refuses to send you their school reports.

If you still have a lawyer, you can ask that she call your ex's lawyer about the problem. Sometimes, a phone call is all it takes. If the lawyers are no longer in the picture, you might want to write a letter to your ex. It might not do any good, but at least you'll be making a record of the problem should you later decide to pursue the issue in court. (First, make a copy of the letter. Unless your agreement requires you to do so, you don't have to send it by certified mail. Some people don't pick up certified letters.)

Of course, some problems with compliance must be handled by a judge. A woman lived in Missouri, but her daughter flew to New York every summer to visit her father, in accordance with the parties' separation agreement. At the end of one summer, the father refused to send the daughter home. He claimed his daughter's stepfather spanked her. The judge ruled that the child should not be spanked by anyone except a parent, but that she should be returned to her mother in Missouri.

Bidding Your Lawyer Adieu

Once the divorce is final, your lawyer is no longer your lawyer. Technically, the case is over, and any new problems that might arise can be addressed by any lawyer you hire to work for you.

Will lawyers help if there are problems after the divorce decree is final? That depends. Some will assist and bill you for the work. Others will tell you they can no longer handle your case. They might be too busy, or they might not like your ex-spouse's lawyer, or they simply do not want to be involved anymore. Still others might take a call or two from you without asking for payment.

In some jurisdictions, a lawyer must take formal steps to withdraw from your representation after the case is completed. Because family-law matters are ongoing because of support payments or later division of assets, someone must be "of record" to receive service of process in the event that there is a reason later to go to court. When your lawyer withdraws, the person of record is you, by default, and your address must be on file with the court.

Breaking Up Is Hard to Do

After months or years of a dependent relationship with your lawyer, some people feel lost once the judgment of divorce is final. Others feel angry that the lawyer who won them a big award is not willing to help them collect it.

It might be hard for you to accept that lawyers are simply in the business of providing legal services. Don't take it personally if your lawyer says goodbye. It is time for you to move on to your own, independent life.

The Least You Need to Know

➤ Be sure that your spouse has received a copy of the final judgment of divorce with the date of its entry. Have a friend mail a copy if need be, and then sign a notarized statement that she mailed it. Include the date of mailing and the address where it was sent.

➤ Entitlement to Social Security, pension plan, and retirement benefits should all be addressed at trial or during negotiations. Don't wait until after the judgment of divorce is final to discuss your ability to collect against your spouse's benefits.

➤ In general, it is more difficult to modify a judgment of divorce that was the result of negotiations than it is to modify one that was the result of a trial.

➤ Before you hire a lawyer to collect unpaid moneys, ask yourself whether you have a reasonable chance of collecting and how much it will cost you to collect.

➤ Your lawyer is technically out of your case once the judgment of divorce is final.

Part 3
The Economics of Divorce

When we're young and idealistic, it's difficult to understand how mere money—or lack of it—could cause conflict in a marriage, let alone destroy it. As we go through life, however, the importance of money looms large. Even in the best of marriages, a lack of money can cause tension as working parents burn the candle at both ends attending to their relationship, their children, and the bills. If money causes such dissension in marriage, it's only natural that during divorce, it can become the white-fanged monster that destroys any remaining civility.

Your hearts, minds, and libidos have diverged, but your finances are still inextricably bound, and that money will help you set sail for your new life: a new car, a home for your children, or tuition for school. In Part 3, we'll help you navigate the financial minefields that can turn even the friendliest of divorces into The War of the Roses. *We explain how to negotiate effectively and protect your interests; how to land on your feet despite the financial hit; and how to mitigate financial fallout such as bankruptcy or credit card debt.*

Chapter 13

Dividing It Up

In This Chapter

➤ Simple, low-conflict techniques for dividing your assets as fairly as possible

➤ How to look out for your interests when dividing money, property, and debt

➤ The difference between community property and equitable distribution: how your state will tend to view your claims

➤ How to divide the cash, the house, and the family business

The unhappy wife hired two movers the weekend her husband was out of town. They hauled away all the furniture and put it in storage. It's not the fairest way to divide the spoils of a marriage, and it's not the most cost-effective, either. She had to pay big bucks to the movers and her lawyer, who faced the unenviable task of explaining to a judge what her imprudent client had done. The woman's actions also placed a significant emotional impediment in the way of settlement.

The Art and Science of Division

If you can't just take the money and run, how should you go about fairly splitting the accumulated possessions of your life together?

Depending on what you have, the job can be easy. You can go around the house and simply take turns choosing what you want. Whoever chooses first during the first round will choose second during the second round and so on. This worked for a friend of ours—until her husband went up to the attic and selected an antique lamp she'd forgotten. But she swallowed her protest and went on with the process, and she's glad she did. This game of round-robin might sound childish, but if it works for you, go for it! It's better than paying your lawyers hundreds of dollars an hour to do the same thing.

Many people divide furnishings and other items in the home, including collectibles, by listing everything and then taking turns choosing from the list. The key is establishing ground rules. If sets (sterling, bedroom, dining room) are not to be broken up, for instance, then you might decide to allow each person to choose three items per turn, not one. Write each person's name after chosen items. Then, when it's time for one or both of you to move out, each one receives the items allocated on the list.

Variations in State Law

What do you need to know and do? First, you must familiarize yourself with your state's law.

The laws governing the division of property vary depending on where you live. Lawyers use the state law, as well as the case law (decisions from cases decided by judges) as a guide to what would happen in your case should you end up in front of a judge. Based on that law, they have a pretty good idea of where the chips would fall if your case went to court. If your lawyer is doing the job, he or she will use that knowledge to work out a fair distribution of what you've acquired.

Arizona, California, Idaho, Louisiana, Nevada, New Mexico, Texas, and Washington are known as *community property states*. Although community property—the idea that property acquired during the marriage belongs to both spouses equally—is based on the theory that marriage is a partnership, only three of the community property states, California, Louisiana, and New Mexico, require that property be divided equally upon divorce. The other community property states, like the rest of the states, use a system of *equitable distribution*—the division of assets based on what is fair.

Fairness Under the Law

Just what is fair? The law might direct judges to consider several different factors when dividing property. In some states, there is a presumption of equality; in other words, if you want more than 50 percent, you have to prove you're entitled to it.

In other states, the court weighs the factors without any presumptions.

What are the factors a court might consider in deciding how to distribute your money and goods? They vary, but in general, they include the length of your marriage, the nature of the property, the responsibilities each of you had in the marriage, whether you have children and who they are going to live with, your health, your education, and your non-economic contribution to the marriage. In a long marriage, the likelihood of a 50-50 division of assets is much stronger than in a short one.

One doctor friend of ours was married for only two years and had no children. His income was easily $200,000 a year. Although his wife had no career and no apparent means of support, the court awarded her a six-month period to get on her feet and ordered that the family condo—acquired during the marriage—be sold, with the assets split. The wife received a Lexus, the family car.

Of course, this was a relatively simple case. The rules and guidelines are not always clear-cut. What about property you had before you got married, which increased in value during the marriage? You need to talk to your attorney. Depending on where you live and what was done to make the property increase in value, part or even all of the property might be subject to distribution.

It might sound frightening, but it's not. Either your case is complicated enough to require help from your attorney, or it's simple enough for you to work out the division of assets yourself.

Re-Learning Long Division

"Four. I don't think I can eat eight."

—Yogi Berra (when asked if he wanted his pizza cut into four or eight slices)

Unfortunately for most people married more than a couple of years, complexity rules. The game of round-robin, described earlier, is a lovely exercise in forgiveness, but most of us own more than furniture, china, and knick-knacks. There's a pension, a savings account, an account for the kids' college tuition, some bonds still left over from the wedding, and some paintings that aren't worth much now, but you never know.

How do you work it out without a legal staff? The first step is, again, a detailed list of the elements you will need to work through.

Taking Inventory

Your master list must include all the assets you have accumulated during the course of your marriage. Include the date the asset was acquired. (If you can't remember but you know it was acquired during the marriage, that's good enough.) Make sure to note the cost (if you can recall) and what you think it's worth now. Also, note to whom it belongs—you, your spouse, or both. Remember, even if one spouse bought it, if it was bought during the marriage, from a marital viewpoint, it probably belongs to both of you, unless it was acquired with funds that are not joint property.

Dividing the Cash

Next, you must divide those assets whose ownership is relatively clear-cut. Generally, the easiest thing to divide is the cash. Before you try to divide savings, figure out what will be needed to run the house for the next several months and set aside any sums needed beyond that which comes from income. For example, if one of you is going to move out, money will be needed for the move. If you plan to maintain two homes rather than one, extra cash will be required there. After you've accounted for this type of expense, you should be able to divide the remaining cash 50-50.

Even-Steven: Furniture, Cars, and the Small Stuff

In the wake of divorce, many people like to start from scratch and leave the furniture. Our friend Lisa, for instance, did not take a single sheet or towel from the family home following her divorce. Her sudden liberation signaled, for her, a chance to reinvent herself. All her new possessions, in the context of her new life, became symbols of her personal growth as well as her release from marital pain.

For others, the possessions accumulated during a lifetime represent luxury and comfort; association with a former spouse presents no problem at all. Fortunately, for those who are amicable, dividing the furniture and cars should present little problem. Just set values for your belongings, and then divide them according to value. If one item, such as the car, is worth more than all the furniture, the spouse who keeps the car will have to pay the difference. Personal assets, such as tools used to repair the house or do gardening, should remain with the one who used them the most.

Who Gets the House?

You and your spouse can also work together to deal with the house. You will, of course, need to have the house appraised. You can each hire a real estate appraiser to value the house and then take the average of the two values. If you both trust and like the same person, you can save money and hire one person. Some couples each choose an appraiser and ask the appraisers to choose a third appraiser, who's valuation will be binding.

You have to subtract the mortgage from the value of the house, of course, to figure out what your home is worth. When you have that number, what then? You need to make some decisions. Do you, as a divorced couple, want to continue to carry the house—and can you afford to? If the answer to both of these questions is "yes," you will have many issues to resolve—but at least in terms of the house, you are set.

If you cannot or will not carry the house, you will have to make the difficult decision to sell. Before you place your home on the market, however, consider these relevant points:

➤ Will your spouse or you be able to find comparable or sufficient housing at a lower monthly cost? Remember, mortgage payments are tax-deductible, and rent is not. You might be better off paying a higher monthly mortgage than a slightly lower rent. However, when insurance and taxes are figured in, renting might be cheaper.

➤ Are you selling at a loss because of the divorce? If you hold onto the house a year or two longer, might you do much better?

➤ Does the house require significant work? Will a renovation make it more marketable, and if so, do you have the funds to pay for the work? If not, you might decide to hold onto the house for now—even if you rent it to someone else—and sell up the road.

➤ Will a move be so disruptive to the children that holding onto the house becomes an option, even in the face of financial sacrifice?

When You Keep the House

If you decide to hold on to the house, how does that work? Say that you've decided to hold on to the house until your youngest child turns 19 and has been out for a year. How, then, will you share in the profit? Because you and your spouse are working this out (rather than letting a judge decide for you), you can make whatever arrangements you both agree to, but here are some ideas:

➤ The spouse who pays the mortgage from the time of the divorce until the house is sold should probably get a credit from the net sale proceeds (gross proceeds less outstanding mortgage, broker's fees, and so on) to the extent the principal of the mortgage was reduced while he or she lived there and paid the mortgage. In the best of all possible worlds, that spouse would also get credit for any improvements made to the house during his or her solo tenure there. The rest of the net proceeds would then be split 50-50. By the same token, the cost of improvements to the home over a minimal amount (say $300) could be shared. But watch out for disputes over whether the repair is needed.

➤ Consider agreeing that if the remaining spouse remarries or has a significant other move into the house, the sale provisions that were going to go into effect when the youngest child turned 19 (or 21, whatever you have agreed) apply after the move or remarriage. For some, having a stranger move into "his" or "her" house is too much to bear.

➤ If your spouse is paying the mortgage with support from you, it might be fairer to simply agree to divide the net proceeds with no credit for mortgage payments.

➤ Decide now how you're going to handle the sale of the house when the time comes. How will you choose the list price and sale price? You might each choose your own real estate agent and then settle on the average of the prices they recommend, or you might have your respective agents choose a third agent, unknown to either of you, who will set the listing and sale price.

Now is the time to consider such strategies as dropping the price by a certain percentage if the house is not sold within a certain number of months from when it is first listed. You can set the percentage now or leave the final figure to the discretion of the agent who handles the sale.

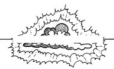

Silver Linings

The person paying the mortgage is the one eligible for the deduction, according to Internal Revenue Service regulations.

Under the new tax law, if the property is held jointly, you can take a one-time $500,000 ($250,000 for each spouse) tax-free profit for sale of your home if you have lived at the location for two of the previous five years. The ex-spouse can still get credit for the residence if the residence sale is delayed but he or she no longer lives there.

Even if the sale of the house seems far in the future, you might also take the time now to devise a "first option," which means that the spouse who stays in the house has the first right to match a bona fide offer on the house and "buy out" the other spouse. If that spouse passes on the right to buy, the spouse who didn't stay in the house then has the same right to buy out the other. (You can also reverse who gets the first option.)

Finally, anyone who's bought or sold real estate understands that the taxes saved or incurred with such a sale can be enormous. Therefore, it goes without saying that if you plan to keep the house "in the family" after the split, you should consult a tax attorney or accountant about the ramifications of leaving your name on the house deed even though you yourself will be gone. The last thing you want to discover, 20 years down the road, is that you're liable for taxes you never dreamed of.

Now is the time to decide how the tax on the profits, if any, will be shared. Fifty-fifty? In the same proportion as the proceeds of the sale? Remember, you might get a larger share of the net proceeds if you made the mortgage payments. You might then have to bear a larger share of the taxes as well.

When negotiating over the house, remember to give credit where credit is due. If the person who keeps the car has not paid the other spouse for half the value of the car at the time of the split, it's reasonable to post that sum as a credit against the car keeper's share of the house.

Do put everything in writing. Ask a lawyer how your signatures should appear to make the agreement legally binding. (Do you need witnesses? Should your signatures be notarized? Find out now, or be sorry later.)

Silver Linings

Remember, if you can agree to agree with your spouse, you can create ground rules that work for both of you. Perhaps you want to agree to a credit equal to only a percentage of the amount of the mortgage paid off. After all, whoever stayed in the house had the benefit of its use. Maybe you want to wait until the youngest child turns 21 before selling the house. Whatever the two of you agree on is okay.

Dividing the Family Business

One of the potentially most contentious tasks facing the divorcing couple is dividing a family business. Some avoid conflict by trading the business for the house; whoever gets the business gives the house—lock, stock, and barrel—to the other spouse. This strategy is not always fair. The only way to know for sure is to have a reputable business appraiser value the business. That step is expensive, but it's probably well worth it.

Depending on what the appraiser says, it might be fine to trade the house for the business. What if the business is worth a lot more? What if the appraiser can't figure out what the business is worth because your soon-to-be ex won't provide access to the ledger?

If your spouse won't cooperate with the appraiser, you need a judge's help. You might have to hire a lawyer who will then ask the judge to order your spouse to cooperate.

If cooperation is in the air—and if the business is worth more than the house—the two of you can agree on a financial settlement to compensate the partner who walks away. Of course, such calculations are complex, and you will probably want a lawyer to help determine the exact amount to be paid, over what time frame, and at what rate of interest.

Here's an example of how the calculations might work: Marty's dental practice is valued at $350,000; the house, which Sue wants, is valued at $200,000. The mortgage is $50,000. If Marty sold his practice, he'd have to pay $100,000 in taxes. If Sue sold the house, she'd have to pay $40,000 in taxes.

Practice		House		Total Assets for Marty and Sue
Value:	$350,000	Value:	$200,000	
Less taxes:	–100,000	Less mortgage:	–50,000	
		Less taxes:	–40,000	
Net:	$250,000	Net:	$110,000	$360,000

Red Alert

Make sure that you consult a lawyer before trading the right to stay in the house for ownership of the family business. Sometimes, the math involved here is simply too complex for ordinary mortals, and an accountant or tax attorney must be called to the scene.

Marty and Sue each get half of the total assets; that's $180,000 each. Marty's net ($250,000) minus his half ($180,000) means that Marty owes Sue $70,000. With the help of a lawyer, the couple decided that Marty would pay Sue $70,000 over four years at 6 percent interest.

Sounds easy, right? It isn't always this simple. Maybe Marty never intends to sell the practice, so why subtract taxes he'll never have to pay? Maybe Sue never intends to part with the house. As you go about crafting your own settlement, you will have to take your personal situation into account.

In some jurisdictions, unless taxes are immediate and specific and can be calculated with certainty, the court will simply ignore the tax issues and divide according to present value.

Leave No Stone Unturned

Make sure, when dividing the spoils of a life spent together, that you account for all the financial elements, including pension funds, taxes, and debt.

In some states, pensions can be divided between you and your spouse, even though only one of you earned it. (Remember, marriage is viewed as a partnership in most states.) Check with an attorney. Pensions are often divided 50-50 from the date of your marriage until the date you separated, started a divorce action, or actually became divorced.

Taxes are a joint responsibility as well. It's fair for spouses to agree that if past filed joint tax returns are audited, and if there is a deficiency, the spouse whose income (or failure to report income or aggressive deduction) caused the trouble pays the tax debt. If it's impossible to figure out who's to blame, you should each pay half the debt. Although the spouse who didn't work might be appalled, the truth is you both enjoyed the money when it was earned, and you were also both responsible for paying Uncle Sam.

Debt is a joint burden as well. Remember the game of hot potato? You might feel like you're playing it again when it comes to determining who walks away from the marriage with the debt. Many people think that just because their spouse paid the bills during the marriage, he or she will continue in that obligation after divorce. Nothing could be further from the truth. Judges will divide debt just as they divide assets. Although the lion's share of the debt might go to the spouse with the significantly larger income, an individual who has managed to avoid paying bills during the marriage can be saddled with large loan payments after divorce, providing that individual has the income or assets to pay.

Therefore, it's imperative that you subtract debt from savings before you divide stocks, bonds, or cash. If the debt is larger than the savings or you don't want to deplete savings, you still need to divide the debt. You can divide it any way that seems fair. If one of you overspent against the wishes of the other (maybe that's part of the reason you're divorcing), it might be fair for the spender to pay the debt, unless he or she spent the money for the family, in which case a 50-50 division of debt might be more fair.

You Can Do It!

Consider paying off all the credit cards with available cash. This will both decrease the amount of dollars owed and secure the credit history of both parties. A late payment by either party on a jointly held card will reflect on the credit history of both. Most credit-card companies won't consider dropping only one of the joint cardholders from the account.

To protect your interests and arrive at a fair solution, make a list of your debt, when it was incurred, who incurred it, and why. Write down the monthly payment due, and then figure out who should and can pay it. If all else fails, ask for legal advice. It will cost you money, but it might save you money, too.

Toward Financial Resolution: A Worksheet Approach

With the help of financial analyst Ted Beecher, we've developed a series of worksheets to help you move toward financial settlement and cut the best deal you can. In the end, whether you plan to settle or litigate, you will have to provide elaborate documentation and a settlement proposal before a resolution can be reached. The sooner you compile these documents, the better off you'll be.

In addition, the very act of compiling your information will help you through the thought process: What is your true financial position? What can you really ask for? What kind of counter-proposal are you likely to get from your spouse?

Remember, by filling out our *Idiot's Guide* worksheets, you will come face to face with the likely gap between your position and that of your spouse. Thus prepared, you will be better able to support your position in settlement negotiations or in court. It's this simple: The more prepared you are, the more likely you will be to come out ahead.

Our worksheets also walk you through gathering the sort of information you will need to present in the financial affidavit most courts require. By organizing this material in advance, you will save time and legal fees.

Getting Started: A Basic List to Get the Ball Rolling

The first list you will make is just a simple one to start the thinking process. As you move through our other worksheets, you will find that we ask for the same information again, but with more detail. You can skip this first list and dive right into the more elaborate forms, or get started here:

	Market	Debt	Net Value	Husband's Share	Wife's Share	Total Value
1. House	_____	_____	_____	_____	_____	_____
2. Business	_____	_____	_____	_____	_____	_____
3. Car	_____	_____	_____	_____	_____	_____
4. Savings	_____	_____	_____	_____	_____	_____
5. Checking	_____	_____	_____	_____	_____	_____
6. Pension	_____	_____	_____	_____	_____	_____
7. IRA	_____	_____	_____	_____	_____	_____
8. CD	_____	_____	_____	_____	_____	_____
9. Furniture	_____	_____	_____	_____	_____	_____
10. Jewelry	_____	_____	_____	_____	_____	_____
11. Other	_____	_____	_____	_____	_____	_____
Total:	_____	_____	_____	_____	_____	_____

Amount Needed to Make Division Equal:

_____	_____	_____	_____	_____	_____

What You Will Need for Your Settlement Proposal

Before you can hope to work out a settlement, both you and your spouse must propose your respective plans. To help you come up with your plan, use the forms provided:

Name: _____

Address: _____

Age: _____

Date of birth: _____

Phone: (day) _____(evening)_____

Date married: _____

Children (names and dates of birth):

_____

_____

_____

Income: _____

Place of work: _____

Spouse's income: _____

Where he or she works _____

Settlement Proposal: Yours (Add Pages as Needed)

Some of the details you might include in your settlement proposal include:

> Split of assets: Create a balance sheet.
>
> Alimony/maintenance/child support: Determine this via computer program, if possible.
>
> Contributions to college expenses.
>
> Support for non-working spouse.
>
> Division of pension.

Settlement Proposal: Your Spouse's (Add Pages as Needed)

Go through the same process for your spouse, envisioning what he or she will ask for.

Residence

Current market value (FMV) _____

Current mortgage amount _____

Monthly payments, including utilities and rent or maintenance) _____

What did you pay for the house? _____

Will the house be sold now or later? _____

If the house is not sold, who will live in it? _____

Asset Checklist

Annuities _____

Checking accounts, bank accounts, certificates of deposit, savings accounts, and so on _____

Stocks, bonds, mutual funds, limited partnerships _____

Real estate (in addition to the primary residence, other rentals, vacation properties, and timeshares) _____

IRAs, 401(k), 403, pension, deferred compensation, and highly compensated employer plan _____

Unpaid bonuses and non-cash compensation such as car and paid lunches _____

Defined benefit plan (you will need details for later) _____

Life insurance cash value _____

Personal possessions _____

Antiques and collectibles _____

Paycheck stubs _____

Debts (credit cards, loans, personal debt, and so on) _____

Gather tax returns for the past three years _____

Financial Affidavit Information

The courts typically require most of the following information before they will consider hearing your case. If you can collect this material in as much detail as possible, you will be far ahead of the game. Remember, if there is a policy, you need the policy number and the backup material. If there is an account, you need the statement.

Job title: _____

Primary employer: _____

Hours per week: _____

Payroll: _____

Monthly gross income: _____

Monthly payroll deductions: _____

Exemptions claimed: _____

Federal income tax: _____

Social Security: _____

Medicare: _____

State income tax: _____

Health insurance premium: _____

Dental insurance premium: _____

Retirement contributions (401[k] and so on): _____

Total deductions: _____

Net monthly income: _____

Other sources of income: _____

Deductions from income, including legitimate business expenses: _____

Net monthly income from other sources: _____

Net monthly income from all sources: _____

Net monthly income of children: _____

Income reported on last federal tax return: _____

Monthly income of other party: _____

Real estate, including location, market value, outstanding mortgage, net equity, and a list of all furniture:

_____

_____

_____

_____

Motor vehicles, including year and make, market value, outstanding loans, and net equity:

_____

_____

_____

_____

Bank accounts, including name of bank and current balance:

_____

_____

_____

_____

Stocks, bonds and mutual funds. (Attach broker statements.) Include stock or bond name, shares or par, and the market value for each position or holding:

_____

_____

_____

_____

Life insurance. List the company name, the policy number, the owner's name, the insured's name, the beneficiary's name, the face value, and the cash surrender value:

_____

_____

_____

_____

Pension, profit sharing, and retirement plans. For each plan, list the plan name, the participant, and the value:

_____

_____

_____

_____

Monthly expenses for ___ adult(s): _____

___ child(ren): _____

Housing: _____

Rent: _____

First mortgage: _____

Second mortgage: _____

Homeowners fee: _____

Total: _____

Utilities: _____

Gas and electric: _____

Telephone: _____

Water and sewer: _____

Trash collection: _____

Cable TV: _____

Total: _____

Food: _____

Grocery items: _____

Restaurant: _____

Total: _____

Medical (after insurance): _____

Doctor: _____

Dentist: _____

Prescriptions: _____

Therapy: _____

Total: _____

Insurance: _____

Life insurance: _____

Health insurance: _____

Dental insurance: _____

Homeowners insurance: _____

Total: _____

Transportation: _____

Vehicle 1: _____

    Payment: _____

    Fuel: _____

    Repair and maintenance: _____

    Insurance: _____

    Parking: _____

Total: _____

Vehicle 2: _____

    Payment: _____

    Fuel: _____

    Repair and maintenance: _____

    Insurance: _____

    Parking: _____

Total: _____

Clothing: _____

Laundry: _____

Childcare: _____

Childcare related: _____

Education: _____

For children: _____

    School: _____

    Lunches: _____

    Sports: _____

For spouse: _____

    Tuition: _____

    Books and fees: _____

Recreation: _____

Entertainment: _____

Hobbies: _____

Membership in clubs: _____

Miscellaneous: _____

Gifts: _____

Hair care/nail: _____

Books/newspapers: _____

Donations: _____

Total: _____

Total of all expenses: _____

The Least You Need to Know

➤ When dividing assets, strive to share fairly with your spouse.

➤ Debt will be allocated based not only on who incurred it, but also on what it was incurred for and who has what income.

➤ Before selling your house, be sure that is the wisest financial course of action.

➤ If one of you is going to have continued use of the house, be sure to spell out the time frame by which such use will stop; do clarify up front a mechanism for selling the house.

➤ Consult with an accountant about the tax consequences of selling your house and keeping your name on the deed.

Spousal Support

Long after the ink is dry on your judgment of divorce, you might still be writing checks to your ex. Whether your state calls the payments alimony, support, or maintenance, you call it blood money. Is there any end in sight?

Maybe the payments haven't begun; you're not divorced yet, but you want some idea of what this breakup is going to cost you. Or perhaps you need to know how much money you can expect to receive so that you can start to rebuild your life.

The Who, When, and How Much of Maintenance

Whatever your situation, you must first understand the maintenance basics—what *maintenance* (or *alimony*) is exactly, when it is appropriate, and how customary guidelines will determine what happens to you.

In a nutshell, maintenance is financial support that one spouse provides to the other in the event of divorce. Maintenance is determined, in large measure, by the laws of the state where you live. Some basic rules, however, are virtually universal:

➤ A wife can pay her husband alimony and vice versa. Gone are the days when only husbands paid wives support.

➤ Most payments stop when the recipient remarries or dies, although there can be cases where payments are "for life."

➤ Although you can negotiate otherwise, the payments are usually tax-deductible to the person who pays them and considered taxable income by the recipient. Stated another way, what you receive might be reduced by virtue of taxes, whereas your payments might cost you less when the tax deduction is figured in.

Safety Net for the Homemaker

It's understandable that maintenance can be a key cause of resentment following divorce, especially when it must be sustained for years. Except for the very wealthy, helping to support not just one household, but two, is an extraordinary burden. For the one receiving the payments, meanwhile, the reality of a restricted lifestyle and dependency on an ex-spouse can be onerous, indeed.

Divorce Dictionary

Maintenance, or alimony: Refers to payments made by one spouse to the other to assist with the support of the recipient spouse. Payments usually terminate upon the death of either spouse or a date decided by a judge or agreed upon by the husband and wife. They may also terminate upon remarriage of the supported spouse. Payments received are usually taxable for the recipient spouse and tax-deductible for the paying spouse.

Take the case of Patty and John. When they married, both were teachers. Three years later, when Vivian was born, Patty stopped working. Patty and John decided she would go back to work in four years, but then, they had two more children, and four years became eight years. When all three children were finally in school, Patty no longer wanted to go back to work. During the school year, John took some coaching positions to make ends meet while Patty took care of the kids. In the summer, John did construction work while Patty took the kids to the beach. John resented Patty's refusal to work but went along with it.

Now, Patty and John are getting divorced. Patty would like to work, but there are no jobs. Besides, she hasn't taught in more than eight years. She needs to take some refresher courses. John is panicking. He could barely pay the bills when he was supporting one household. Now, he'll have to support two. It just doesn't seem fair that he's done all the work, and now he'll have to do even more.

Patty is upset, meanwhile, because the family cannot afford to carry the house. Of course, if she had known they were going to divorce, she would have kept working. She's angry about the position she's in.

Could this nightmare happen to you? Remember, just because you are divorcing does not mean you can ignore decisions you and your spouse made about how you wanted to live your married life. You might be able to eventually change those decisions, but in the beginning of a divorce, they are the realities you have to address.

Rules of Thumb

The basic rule is simple: The breadwinner spouse pays, and the non-breadwinner cashes the checks. If you both worked or both have the ability to work and could easily get jobs, the chances are good that neither of you will have to pay the other. If one spouse earns vastly more than the other, a certain amount of maintenance may be required as well.

In one case we've followed, a couple—a lawyer and a doctor—were divorcing. The husband was a partner at a large law firm, and his wife worked in the emergency room at the local hospital two days a week for $1,000 a day. Neither had to pay spousal support to the other.

Child support, which we cover in the next chapter, is a different matter. The doctor-wife had custody of the parties' two children, and she was entitled to support from her husband for the children. Most states have a system whereby child support is determined based on a percentage of the parents' income and the number of children, upon the children's needs, or a combination of the two. Check with your lawyer.

What's Fair? Coming Up with a Number

How do you know how much maintenance to pay or to demand? There are specific guidelines. In general, courts look at the following factors to determine the size of the support check. It follows, of course, that lawyers who try to settle a case out of court (or you and your spouse if you're trying to do it yourselves) also need to look at these factors:

➤ **Your income**   Is there sufficient money to enable both of you to enjoy the same lifestyle, or are you both going to have to cut back?

➤ **The length of the marriage**   The longer the marriage, the stronger the claim for support.

➤ **Your ages**   Younger people are thought to be better able to find work. Older people nearing retirement might be unable to pay support for a long period of time.

Social Security might be an issue if either of you is close to retirement age. In a marriage of more than 10 years, if the non-working spouse does not remarry, he or she might be eligible for half of the Social Security payment of the former spouse, depending on the state.

➤ **Your health**   Is one of you ill and unable to work? That could affect how much will be paid and how long it will be paid.

➤ **Job sacrifices you made during the marriage**   Did you give up a good position because your spouse had to relocate for her job? Maybe you never used your degree because you worked as a bookkeeper in your husband's business. Whether your sacrifice was obvious or more subtle, it could impact the duration of your support award.

➤ **Education and job skills**   The easier you can find work, the shorter the duration of your support.

➤ **Who the children are going to live with**   If they're going to live with you and that shortens the time you can spend working each day, you might be entitled to more support than if the children were living with your spouse or if you had no children.

➤ **Independent income sources**   Maybe you have a trust or other source of income. You never touched it during the marriage because you planned to leave it all to your children. Now, its existence could affect the amount of support you'll receive or have to pay.

➤ **Distribution of other assets**   If you and your spouse accumulated a lot during the marriage that will be split, you might not be entitled to maintenance at all. Let's say your wife built up her medical practice while you were married, and now she has to pay you half its value of $350,000. Depending on where you live, the receipt of that lump sum could reduce additional support payments.

➤ **Marital fault**   In some jurisdictions, the reason for the breakup of your marriage could affect the duration and amount of support.

➤ **The tax implications of the payment**   If you have to pay taxes on what you receive, you might need a larger amount than if you do not have to pay taxes on the payment.

➤ **The past standard of living, assuming that it was based on fully reported income**   In some states, the idea of maintaining the same lifestyle is part of the statute and is a goal, although it is not often reached.

Judges and lawyers look at these factors to determine how much maintenance one of you should pay the other. The single most important factor, is, of course, how much money there is to go around.

You Can't Always Get What You Want, but You'll Get What You Need

We've all heard the notion, bandied about on TV and in the movies, that maintenance should enable the receiving spouse to continue to live "in the style to which he or she has become accustomed." Well, forget it! That's just a Hollywood fabrication.

It sounds nice, but you'll notice that it's not in the top-12 considerations just listed. Although many vital factors figure into the award, the "style to which you have become accustomed" doesn't weigh that heavily. In almost all cases, that style was based on an intact family unit that's no longer a reality. (And sad to say, in too many cases, luxurious lifestyles are fueled by a failure to pay appropriate taxes or "loans from the family store." Such dirty little secrets often come to light during a divorce action, limiting the available funds for everyone.)

It is, in short, impossible to state any rule about how much you should expect to pay or receive. Unless you are wealthy, you should expect to cut back, create and stick to a budget, and consider going to work or working more.

Getting the Best Deal

When negotiating for maintenance, be sure to look at the big picture. For instance, Ann Parsons did not want to sell her house under any circumstances. Her lawyer told her that if her case were decided by a judge, the judge would order the house sold and would order her husband to pay her support. Ann's husband had a checkered job history, although he was well paid when he did work. Ann decided that rather than take any support, she would keep the house and get a job to pay the bills.

It wouldn't have been the right deal for everyone, but for her, it was. She decided what she really wanted and looked at the big picture. She couldn't rely on her husband to pay her support, and the house would give her income when and if she was ever ready to sell it.

You Can Do It!

Here's a word to the wise: Take that job. Don't turn down a job for fear it will lower your maintenance settlement. If it's a good job with the possibility of advancement, you'll be better off taking it than depending on maintenance payments that are likely to fall short of your needs. In fact, a judge will look at your lack of employment and, instead of increasing payments to you, simply declare you "underemployed."

You Can Do It!

When negotiating, start by asking for more than you either need or expect to get. Then, during negotiations, be willing to give up what you don't mind losing.

All situations are different, of course, and negotiating the terms of maintenance will vary from one couple to the next. However, as you go about cutting your own deal, make sure to follow these general guidelines:

1. The deft negotiator will first figure out what he or she really wants and will cast a cold eye on the reality of the situation. Do you want to stay home with the kids

or go back to work? Do you want the house or your share of the cash from its sale? Will your spouse be responsible enough to meet his or her obligations? Don't hold out for promises you know your spouse probably will not live up to.

2. If you decide you want support above all else, you must determine your expenses, including recurring expenses and one-time costs due to the divorce. Will you have to move and have cable, telephone, and electricity installed? Or are you staying put, but you need some replacement furniture?

   Make a detailed list of these one-time and recurring expenses. Then, make a list of all income and savings. Try using checks and credit-card bills for 12 months and get an average of your monthly expenses. You should, by the way, come to terms with the fact that you might need to use some of the savings for your one-time expenses.

   After you determine the monthly expenses, calculate your shortfall. Is the shortfall a sum you can realistically expect to receive from your spouse? If so, great. (Remember, you might have to pay taxes on the money, so subtract that from your spouse's payments.)

   If you know your spouse can't pay that much, look at your list again. Is there any place where you can compromise? Is there any way you can add to your income?

3. You don't have to be Donald Trump to know that, when making a deal, you never present your bottom-line figure right away. Maybe you've played enough mind games with your spouse to last a lifetime, but you *must* play one more to get a fair shake. Start high (or low if you're the one who has to pay), and gradually move down (or up).

4. If you're going to pay, avoid a deal that requires you to reveal your income every year. It's pretty common for a deal to include an increase if the paying spouse's income goes up, but do you really want to have to reveal your income to your ex every year? You're better off using a set increase, such as a percentage of the current amount of support or an increase equal to the annual increase in the cost of living where you live. (The downside of this approach, of course, is that if your income does not go up, you'll still have to pay the increase.)

5. If you're going to receive the support, ask that you not be held responsible for paying taxes on it. If you're paying the support, say that you want the tax deduction. (Maybe you can compromise on this by agreeing that each of you will take one of the children as dependents.) Remember the general rule: Spousal support is usually taxed to the person who receives it unless you agree otherwise.

6. Make sure that the duration of the support depends on a fixed event if you're the spouse making the payments. "Payments until my wife graduates from college" is not such a good idea because she might never do that. "Payment for five years" is much better.

7. Make sure that you can afford to pay or accept what you're about to agree to. However guilty, angry, or in love with someone else you might be, do not agree to something you cannot afford.

8. Consider using a lawyer to negotiate support. Even if you and your spouse have worked out everything, this area is usually so fraught with emotion that it is not a bad idea to let someone else handle it.

Make sure that spousal support payments are not crafted to end when a child comes of age. In general, the Internal Revenue Service will view such payments as disguised child support and might disallow the tax deduction for them. (That is because child support is not tax-deductible to the paying spouse, and the recipient spouse does not have to include that money in income.) Although this might be good for the recipient (who now won't be taxed on the support), it is bad for the paying partner (who will now be unable to deduct the payments from his or her income), and it can wreak havoc on a deal.

You Can Do It!

If possible, arrange spousal support through mediation or settlement, not litigation. This will provide both parties with the most flexibility in getting what they deem most important from the arrangement.

In addition, reworking the agreement can present a sticky problem because the IRS might go back to recharacterize what is taxable and what is not taxable. Presumably, the receiving spouse has been paying the taxes. You will now have to amend and seek a refund. It is better to draft your agreement correctly the first time and stay away from contingencies that reduce support at or about an event concerning the child such as, for example, reaching the age of 18.

When Circumstances Change

We all know that life is a roller-coaster. One moment, you're flying high, on top of the world; the next, your world has been shattered to a thousand bits. Economies can crumble; companies can fold; real estate values can soar or plummet based on world events or the fates.

The roller-coaster is one reason why it might be best to see a judge when negotiating support. In general, if a judge decides your case, you will have an easier time changing a support award than if you and your spouse sign off on the payment in a separate agreement.

Why is that? When you sign an agreement, judges assume that you thought of all the possible things that might happen in the future and that you accounted for them in the agreement. For example, if you were to pay support at the rate of $300 a week for five years, the agreement could have provided that if you lost your job, you would no longer have to make payments. If you didn't provide for that and you do lose your job, you can ask a judge to allow you to stop making the payments—but the judge might point out that you had your chance to include that in the agreement and now it's just too late.

When a judge decides your case after a trial, on the other hand, he or she does not account for future possibilities. The decision is based solely upon what the judge has heard in court. Therefore, if you or your spouse lose a job some years down the road, you'll have an easier time convincing the judge to make a change than if you had signed an agreement.

Bottom line? Make sure that you account for all possibilities when you sign an agreement, and always consult with an attorney.

Silver Linings

Despite the security of those monthly support checks, it may be best thing for the receiving spouse when the period of support is over and the maintenance ends. At that point, both partners are economically independent and, with the umbilical cord cut, can go their own ways. Such separation affords a true sense of closure—often not possible, even after divorce, when financial strings persist.

The Least You Need to Know

➤ Spousal support is based on a number of factors, whereas child support is usually based on a percentage of your income, the children's needs, or a combination of the two.

➤ Spousal support is usually included in the receiving spouse's income and tax-deductible from the paying spouse's income.

➤ When negotiating, never reveal your bottom line in the beginning. Figure out what you really want before you start.

➤ It is easier to change support that a judge ordered than it is to change an amount you agreed to pay or accept, so be sure that you think of all possibilities before you sign an agreement. Better still, consult an attorney.

Child Support

If you're the noncustodial parent, you will be expected to contribute to your children's economic needs. This money, paid to the custodial parent on behalf of the children, is child support. The following chapter takes a comprehensive look at this system and helps you come to terms with the nitty-gritty of your own case, including who pays, how much, and for how long. We help you investigate the ever-changing legal code, and, in case you or your children have not been getting their due, we provide some tips on how to collect.

Understanding Child Support

Child support comes in two varieties—direct and indirect. When the noncustodial parent sends money directly to the custodial parent on a regular basis—every week, every other week, or every month—the child support is direct. Indirect child support, on the other hand, involves payments made to third parties for expenses such as school tuition, camp, lessons, after-school activities, and healthcare costs.

If you are the custodial parent, you might wonder whether you're better off receiving a larger amount of direct support and paying the third parties yourself or letting your former spouse make those payments and getting less direct support. Conceptually, it is nearly always better for the custodial parent to receive sufficient funds from the noncustodial parent to pay tuition, school activities, or camp. It is more than simply the money; it is a question of control. Consider the pros and cons of direct versus indirect child support:

Custodial Parent

Pros	Cons
If your former spouse pays the third party directly and those expenses increase, he or she will pay the increase.	If what you receive includes amounts to be paid to the third parties, and the costs of those third-party expenses rise, you might have to bear the increase.
Some former spouses will be more reliable if they are paying third-party expenses directly because they feel more involved in their children's lives.	Some spouses will be less reliable if they are obligated to pay the third-party expenses. You will have to chase your former spouse for payment while the third parties are hounding *you*.

Noncustodial Parent

Pros	Cons
If you're obligated to figure third-party expenses into your payments, your former spouse will probably bear the cost of the increase.	If you pay the third parties, you'll bear the cost of any direct increases.
You might feel more in control and more directly involved with your children if you pay third-party expenses.	If you give your former spouse money to pay third parties and he or she doesn't make the payments, the third parties might chase *you*.

What are you to do? If a judge decides your case after a trial, you'll have no choice; whatever the judge decides goes. If you're settling your case, on the other hand, you can compromise. If your former spouse is the noncustodial parent and is reliable, you're probably better off having him or her pay the expenses directly to the third party to avoid responsibility for increases in big-ticket items, such as school tuition. If your former spouse is unreliable or disagrees with you about signing up your child for an activity, you're better off receiving more child support and paying these extra costs yourself. The point of child support is to enable the child to enjoy the lifestyle of the wealthier parent. If that has a benefit to the ex, so be it.

One of the most frequent questions lawyers get from their noncustodial clients is "Why can't I pay child support directly to my child?" (So what if the child is two!) "Why can't I set up an account so I know the money is being used for the kids?" The real question being asked is, "Isn't my spouse the one benefiting from the child support?"

Divorce Dictionary

Child support: A sum of money to be paid by one parent to the other to assist with the support of the couple's children. Child support is sometimes paid directly to a third party, such as a college, or a health care provider, rather than to a parent. In some jurisdictions, child support is paid to a state support collection unit which in turn pays it to the recipient spouse. Child support usually terminates upon a child's emancipation.

The truth is, your ex *is* benefiting, to a degree. If your former spouse pays the rent with child support, of course, he or she is also benefiting. The same goes for the phone, electricity, cable TV, and even food. Let's face it, your ex isn't going to buy steak for the kids and hamburger for himself or herself.

Silver Linings

You can negotiate a smaller amount of maintenance, also known as *spousal support*, in return for a larger child support payment. Bear in mind, however, that your child support obligation, depending on the ages of your children, can last for many more years than maintenance. In addition, there's no tax deduction for child support, whereas maintenance is usually tax-deductible. (See Chapter 14 for details on spousal support.)

What if your children spend equal amounts of time with each parent? Usually, each of you will be responsible for those expenses incurred while the child is with you. However, you still have to work out how to pay for other costs, such as clothing (there's no point in having two entire wardrobes) or education. If your incomes are about the same, those expenses can be split. If there is a disparity in your incomes, the expenses can be divided according to the percent of the total each one earns.

For example, if your combined income is $100,000, and you earn $40,000 but your former spouse earns $60,000, the $1,000 tuition payment would be split 40/60.

Obviously, this kind of expense sharing takes a lot of goodwill and planning, but so does negotiating an arrangement whereby the children spend equal amounts of time with each of you. If you can't work it out and a judge has to decide this issue, it is unlikely he or she will agree to a 50/50 living arrangement for the children, nor will the judge allow you to decide how the expenses should be divided.

A Review of the Law

Every state has its own formula for deriving child support. Each state also has exceptions to the formula and exceptions to the exceptions, so it is critical to check the law of your state before you make a deal.

You Can Do It!

No matter what your differences regarding child support, you must negotiate out of the presence of your children. If you are expecting payment, make sure it is delivered directly to you. If you are protective of your children, you will keep them out of financial negotiations between you and your ex.

Usually, the formulas are based on the ratio of the parties' incomes, although the definition of income varies by state. Income can be defined in the very broadest way—to include not only wages, but also assets such as stocks or a pension or regular, annual gifts from family members—or it can be defined in a narrow way, limited only to earned income.

The law usually provides for deductions to be taken from the income, and those deductions vary from state to state, too. Federal, state, and local taxes and payments already being made on behalf of other children from prior relationships are among the common deductions.

A percentage of your share of what's left then becomes your annual child support obligation. Different states use different percentages, and the percentage usually increases depending on the number of children you have.

In some states, a ceiling is placed on the income used to calculate child support, such as a combined parental income of $80,000. All income above $80,000 might be subject to a different percentage from the first $80,000 of income. A cap might apply to the amount of income above the $80,000 for the purposes of calculating child support.

Most states have developed a statutory formula that is used to calculate child support.

Mark's income as a bank manager was $90,000. Nancy's as a paralegal was $50,000. Their combined income was $140,000. For the purposes of child support, their one child was entitled to 20 percent of the combined parental income up to $70,000 in their state. The child support was to be paid in the ratio of the parents' incomes to their combined income. Because the combined income was double the amount used for the purposes of the base calculation—$140,000—the law in their state allowed the judge to decide how to use the extra $70,000 of income. The judge decided to cap the income to be considered for support at $110,000. He then calculated that 20 percent of $110,000 was $22,000—the total amount of child support. Nancy had to pay 36 percent of this amount, or $7,920, and Mark had to pay 64 percent, or $14,080.

Red Alert

Child support laws are often changing, both because state legislatures modify existing statutes and because judges decide cases that might alter the interpretation of the law. You must always check your state's law before agreeing to accept or pay child support.

Although there are hardship provisions, judges are usually reluctant to lower the percentage without good reason.

George was paying the mortgage on the marital residence to keep it from foreclosure. His wife, Margaret, and son, Ben, lived there while he lived in a boarding house. He asked the judge to lower his child support payment because his income was too low to pay the mortgage and the court-ordered child support. The judge refused his request, and the family had to sell their home at a loss.

Had George and Margaret been able to negotiate the child support during this time of decreased income for George, they might have been able to keep the house until they could sell it at market value.

What's Fair?

If you and your spouse believe you can reach a settlement, how do you know what's in your child's best interest but also fair to both of you?

To Settle or Not to Settle? That Is the Question

Now that most states have formulas for determining child support, there is little mystery about the outcome if you were to have a judge decide instead of settle out of court. If you are the custodial parent and your spouse is not willing to meet the state's guidelines during negotiation, why should you settle? Most of the time, of course, you shouldn't. But there are exceptions. The following are some important reasons for agreeing to less support than the state's guidelines might otherwise allow:

➤ **More certainty that you can collect the support** Most parents will pay what they can afford and especially what they have agreed to pay. In contrast, when they fall hopelessly behind or a judge orders them to pay more than they can afford, they often default, and it's a lot harder to collect.

➤ **Add-ons** If you agree to a child support figure that is less than the formula, you might be able to get your spouse to add on other items. Maybe the law of your state doesn't obligate a parent to pay for after-school activities, camp, or even college. You might be willing to accept less child support than the formula provides if your spouse will pick up some of these items.

➤ **Ease of modification** If a judge decides your case and a year later your former spouse gets a big raise, you would have to go back to court to get an increase in child support, and you might not win. Also, you might have to pay legal fees. On the other hand, if you negotiate, you can include a provision in your agreement that obligates your spouse to increase the child support if he or she gets a raise. You've saved yourself legal fees and headaches. It might be worth it to take a little less than the formula for one or two years, knowing you'll get an increase down the road without the hassle of returning to court.

➤ **Exception to the formula** Remember, hardship provisions to the law usually make the formula inapplicable. If your spouse demonstrates to a judge that hardships exist, the judge might not apply the formula. If that situation is a possibility for you, negotiation might be in your best interest.

Likewise, if you are the noncustodial parent, negotiating might be best for you because

➤ Your spouse might agree to less than the guidelines allow.

➤ You have more say over what your financial needs are and can tailor the agreement to your situation.

➤ You can modify the agreement to state that if your income decreases by a certain amount, your child support payments can be reduced accordingly.

Duration of Child Support

Child support should terminate at the age your child is considered emancipated under your state's laws. In some states, that means age 18; in others, age 21.

Other events can terminate child support as well: the child's entry into the military or assumption of full-time employment or marriage before the age of emancipation. If the child moves in with the noncustodial parent on a permanent basis, child support should stop. (You might want to negotiate a sum the former custodial parent will have to pay in that case.)

In some states, your child's right to obtain support from you continues after your death; that is, your estate is liable for the court-ordered payments made before your death. Your estate becomes a party in the action where your support obligation was ordered, and it can be enforced or modified just as it could have been before your death. In some jurisdictions, it is insufficient that you and your spouse agree to a modification of child support. You must go to court to obtain an order modifying the amount of support. Otherwise, your support obligation continues to accrue and is enforceable as any other judgment, even though your child might be living with you. Get an order modifying support even if you and your spouse have agreed.

If you and your spouse agree, child support can extend beyond the age of emancipation. For example, if in your state the emancipation age is 18, but you want your spouse to continue to pay child support until your child graduates from college, you would try to negotiate a provision stating that child support continue for as long as the child is a full-time undergraduate student but in no event beyond the age of 21.

What Should the Child Support Figure Be?

How do you go about determining exactly how much child support *you* should pay or receive?

First, before you even begin your calculations, bear in mind that child support payments cannot be deducted on your taxes unless you and your spouse agree otherwise and write that into the settlement agreement. Therefore, under most circumstances, you will have to earn, on average, from $115 to $140 (depending on your tax bracket) to be able to pay $100 in child support. By the same token, the parent who receives child support does not have to pay taxes on it, so he or she is getting the full amount paid.

To ascertain a fair amount of child support without using your state's formula, it is best to figure out a monthly budget for the children. Household expenses, such as rent, food, mortgage, and utilities, can be allocated one half to the children and one half to the parent or allocated one part each among all the children in the household and the parent. Clothing costs for the year should be added up and divided by 12, as should camp, extracurricular activities, birthday party gifts, and similar items that are paid only once or twice a year.

Once you and your spouse have worked out a budget, you can determine the total contribution for each of you. There should, of course, be a

Red Alert

If your child support agreement includes a mechanism to increase child support without returning to court, consider a similar mechanism to decrease child support in the event of a financial setback, such as a job loss or a reduction in income of, for example, 25 percent or greater. If you are the parent paying child support, you might want a provision that reduces it by, say, a third or half, when the children are in camp or away at college, particularly if you are also contributing to camp or college. Why not a 100 percent reduction? Your former spouse still has to maintain the home for your child after camp or during college vacations (assuming that your state is one of the few in which the age of majority is 21).

mechanism for calculating cost-of-living increases for this payment into the future. You can base your formula on the cost-of-living increase as determined by your state's Department of Agriculture or other indices, or if you prefer, you can base it on increases in your incomes. Because most people prefer not to reveal income each year, most people base such payment increases on outside, objective criteria.

Don't Miss a Beat: Taking All Your Expenses into Account

If your child is a toddler, it's difficult to think about what college will cost or who will pay for it years down the road. If a judge is going to try your case and you have young children, you'll probably have to return to court when the child is a junior or senior in high school to have the judge address the issue of who will pay for college. If you want to settle all the issues now, however, a provision that often works is this: You and your spouse simply agree now to pay half of what it would cost to send your child to the most expensive school in your state's college system. Any excess amounts (say your child gets into Harvard) will be paid by the parent or parents who can afford it. This way, both parents have a minimum obligation.

What about the Bar Mitzvah, the First Communion, the sweet-16 party, the first car? If you negotiate an agreement, anything goes. If your case goes to court, judges may not address those types of expenses.

If you want to be ready for anything, you want to figure some of the following expenses into your agreement now:

➤ Babysitter and day care

➤ Birthday parties

➤ Camp

➤ First Communion

➤ Bar/Bat Mitzvah

➤ Sweet-16 party

➤ Application fees for colleges

➤ Travel costs to visit prospective colleges

➤ SAT, achievement test fees, and tutoring costs

➤ Other tutors as needed

➤ Orthodontia

➤ Psychotherapy

➤ After-school activities

➤ Sports activities, uniforms, equipment, and fees

➤ Boy Scouts or Girl Scouts

➤ Car, driving lessons

➤ Wedding

Wait a minute, you might be thinking; if all those items are extras, what am I paying child support for? Answer: Food, shelter, clothing, telephone, utilities, and so on. Of course, depending on the amount of child support you are paying, your spouse may use some of the support for these extras.

Be careful, though. Anything you sign might come back to haunt you. Harvey, for instance, felt so guilty about leaving his wife, Jessie, that he agreed in writing to pay for each of their four daughters' weddings at the Waldorf-Astoria or someplace comparable. The daughters were only teenagers at the time. Unfortunately, Harvey's business took a turn for the worse. Although he could not afford the expensive weddings, he was obligated to pay for them. He went into debt to do so.

If you have a breakdown in negotiations, you can fall back on your state's child support formula. Beyond that, seek help from your lawyers or a mediator.

When a Parent Is in Default

You got a terrific deal from either a judge or a negotiated settlement agreement. But you have a problem: Your former spouse won't pay.

What to do? Each state has its own enforcement procedures, so it's best to consult with an attorney about how to enforce your award. In some states, all you or your attorney need do is notify your former spouse that you intend to have his or her wages *garnished* and then proceed by filing the required notice with his or her employer.

Garnishment means that the child support will go directly from your ex-spouse's employer to you, but there are usually limits on how much can be garnished per paycheck, and those limits might be less than the amount you're supposed to receive. It is important to seek legal advice about how to proceed because a mistake might mean that you have to negotiate the child support payments all over again and collection will be delayed. What's more, you'll need legal help in collecting amounts above and beyond what may be garnished.

When Garnishment Fails

Usually, when your ex is in default and you have collected all you can through garnishment, you will have to go to court to ask the judge for a money judgment. Then, you have to try to collect against your former spouse's assets, such as a bank account.

Be Aware of the Law

In 1992, the federal government passed the Child Support Recovery Act. That law punishes people who willfully fail to pay a past-due support obligation to a child who resides in another state. A judge can fine and imprison (for up to six months) first-time offenders. Repeat offenders can be fined and imprisoned for up to two years.

The law does have teeth, but with these caveats:

➤ Your ex-spouse and your child cannot reside in the same state. If they do, the law does not apply.

➤ A judge must determine the amount of child support due. The law does not apply if you have not been before a judge who decided how much is due.

➤ If the amount due is $5,000 or less, your former spouse must have owed it for more than a year for the law to apply.

➤ If the amount due is more than $5,000, there is no minimum time period.

➤ Your spouse's failure to pay must be "willful." If he or she can show that circumstances made it difficult or impossible to pay, the law might not apply.

This law is rather new but is gaining in popularity and publicity as the crackdown against "deadbeat" parents grows. It remains to be seen, however, whether it will be a cost-efficient way for parents to collect child support.

When You Think You're Paying Too Much

If you and your ex-spouse are on friendly terms and you have been laid off from your job or have had a reduction in your pay, the first person to talk to is your former spouse. If you're lucky, she or he will be willing to reduce the amount of child support for a period of time until you get back on your feet or make a trade, such as less child support now but more later.

If talking to your ex is not realistic and if a judge decided your case, you can appeal his decision, provided you do so within your state's time deadlines. Consult with an attorney who is knowledgeable about how the appeals courts have ruled in such cases. In some jurisdictions, the higher courts tend to defer to the lower court in child support matters, on the theory that the lower court judge had the opportunity to observe you and your spouse in court and may have reached a decision based on what he or she saw. Stated more directly, if the judge thought you were lying about your income, the appeals court might be inclined to go along with that judge's decision.

You can also return to court after a period of time—at least a year—if the situation has changed or if you were unable to prove something at trial that can be substantiated now. Peter testified that he could not afford the full percentage of child support because he suspected he was going to lose his job. The judge would not consider the *possibility* of Peter's losing his job as sufficient to warrant his paying a lower percentage of child support. Six months later, Peter did, in fact, lose his job. He went back to court and was able to get a reduction in his child support obligation.

Silver Linings

Even if your ex-spouse remarries into wealth, most courts will not require the stepparent to shoulder the expenses for someone else's child. However, if there is a gross disparity between your income and your spouse's resources—including those derived from the new spouse—you might be able to get a reduction, particularly if you can show that your ex has access to the money or is living with the children in a lavish lifestyle.

When You're Not Receiving Enough

What if the child support you are receiving no longer pays for your growing child's food, let alone clothing, shelter, and after-school activities?

See an attorney. Your ability to increase the payments depends in large part on whether a judge decided your case or you and your spouse negotiated the deal. In general, if a judge decided your case after a trial and you can show that your children's economic needs are not being met, you probably have a good chance of getting an increase. If you and your spouse negotiated your deal, it's harder to get a judge to change it but not impossible if your children's reasonable economic needs are unmet.

Insurance and Healthcare for Your Children

If a judge is trying your case, health insurance will be one of the items he or she will direct you or your spouse to maintain. If you are negotiating a settlement, here are some things to consider:

➤ If you have health insurance through your employer, keep your children covered. If neither you nor your spouse has health insurance through an employer, agree to allocate the cost of the premiums between you.

Red Alert

A problem often arises when one spouse pays healthcare costs, and the other pockets the reimbursement. You can avoid this problem up front in your settlement agreement: Simply ask that your spouse reimburse you within 10 days of receipt of the doctor's bill, not when the insurance comes through. If you are not engaged in settlement discussions, ask the judge to include this time limit in her decision.

➤ Be sure to allocate the uninsured healthcare costs. Allocation can be in the same proportion that your individual incomes bear to your total income. If one of you is not working, then the other should pay all these costs.

If you and your spouse are negotiating, you should both agree to provide life insurance for the benefit of your children (assuming child support otherwise ceases upon the paying spouse's death). The parent who is paying child support should provide enough to cover his or her support obligation, which means that each year, he or she can reduce the proceeds. (Remember, child support usually ends when the child turns 18 or 21.) The amount should include the paying parent's share of college as well.

The parent who is not paying child support should also maintain coverage, if he or she can afford to do so, to help with college.

Who should the beneficiary of the life insurance be? This is an emotionally charged issue, but it doesn't have to be. Some people set up convoluted trusts, whereas others insist on leaving the proceeds to their three-year-old. Neither solution is usually satisfactory.

There are two sensible solutions. If your children are young, name your former spouse as beneficiary and hope he or she will use the money to care for your child. If the children are older, you can make them the beneficiaries, but you still have to hope that the children are taken care of. You can, of course, name a relative, but we don't recommend that. Your ex-spouse may justifiably express doubt as to whether the relative will ever use the money for the children at all.

For the very rich, trusts and trustees may be warranted. For the rest of us, just plain trust—in the other spouse—is best.

The Least You Need to Know

➤ It is difficult to modify—up or down—child support that you and your spouse have agreed to, so don't leave out any important points in your agreement. It is easier to modify child support a judge ordered you to pay.

➤ Unless you and your spouse agree otherwise, child support payments are not tax-deductible and are not reportable as taxable income.

➤ Each state has its own rules for how much child support should be paid and has its exceptions to those rules. It is best to consult with an attorney before entering into a deal where you might be paying too much or receiving too little.

➤ Don't forget the items that add to the expense of raising children—parties, gifts, activities—when you negotiate child support.

➤ Don't make the children messengers. They should not carry support checks.

Chapter 16

Managing Your Money Solo

In This Chapter

➤ The big picture: your financial profile then and now

➤ Reestablishing yourself financially

➤ Divorce and bankruptcy

➤ Selling your house, business, stocks, or other holdings to make ends meet

➤ Creating a budget you can live with

If you have been married for a short time, divorce will have a minor impact on your finances. Before you married, you probably lived on your own, worked, and got along pretty well. You are fortunate that it will be easy for you to get back on your feet—financially, at least.

If you've been married for years, however, the lifestyle changes brought on by your new circumstances—and your new finances—can be devastating. You'll find yourself far ahead of the game if you know what to expect. In this chapter, we present a guide to money management for the newly divorced.

Expect Your Financial Situation to Change

There was a time—it might seem like centuries ago—when you spent weekends at the country home, casually went out to eat, bought any book that caught your eye, shopped at Saks; it goes without saying that your children had the latest toys and computers and wore 100 percent cotton, nothing less. Now, you count every penny you spend. You hunt for sales at K-Mart and Filene's Basement, let your hair grow "fashionably long," and swallow your pride when accepting hand-me-downs for your kids. Dinner is, more often than not, pasta. (So what? It's healthy.) And a night out on the town means renting a video from the New Release rack at the local video store. In short, your former life seems so impossibly extravagant you can't imagine how you ever spent money in so cavalier a fashion. You wonder if you will ever again be able to enjoy what you now consider the luxuries of a distant past.

Unless you are wealthy, if you have been married for a long time, and especially if you have children, you are likely to inhabit a different financial planet after the divorce.

For one thing, you and your ex-spouse each need a home. If there are children, one parent—the residential parent—will be sustaining a home on less money than before. That parent might need to go out and get a job, even if he or she has not previously worked.

The nonresidential parent, meanwhile, will be helping to support the children according to his or her state's guidelines or a separation agreement, while at the same time maintaining a separate household. This nonresidential parent might be required to provide support he or she can little afford. If the residential parent does not work outside the home, the courts might instruct the working partner to provide spousal maintenance as well. Following divorce, some people start new families and must also help support them.

Sharing the Responsibilities of Your Former Life

In many instances, especially for those who have children, divorce will change your relationship but not sever it. As much as you might wish otherwise, you might still be bound by finances and responsibilities for years to come.

Even after you have left the matrimonial home, your children will need your financial support and so might your nonworking ex-spouse. What's more, although your support burden will probably be fixed, your earning power can always take a turn for the worse. If you don't get a cost-of-living increase, if you're laid off, or if your expenses are too high, you might have a difficult time making ends meet.

Here's a tale of woe: One evening, after the children had been tucked in and fallen soundly asleep, Helen informed her husband, Henry, that she had lost all feeling for him. No, she hadn't met anyone else, but she wanted to try. The long and the short of it: Their marriage was at an end.

Helen told Henry that she wanted him to move out. Shocked and dazed, he began looking for an apartment nearby.

A computer programmer, Henry had had a hard enough time paying the mortgage and bills when his family was intact. Adding a second household to his expenses forced him to moonlight, and his life became nothing but work.

Maintaining the Homestead

Not that it's any consolation, but things were difficult for Helen, too. Indeed, any parent who maintains a home for young children assumes responsibility for their needs, including all the extra expenses that implies. You might receive a certain amount of help in meeting these responsibilities from your ex-spouse, but more and more, these days, a large part of the financial burden will fall on you. There's no getting around it. On the first of the month, you face a stack of bills that you must pay no matter what your income is.

Helen, for instance, had to go out and work. Her new job, as a cashier in a Caldor's department store, was tiring and didn't pay much. But she did earn enough to contribute to the mortgage. She and the children had to cut their expenses precipitously and had far less time together, to boot.

If, like Helen, you have children living with you, you'll find yourself protective not just of your pennies, but also of your time as you juggle school, work, and single parenting. You are no longer just the "chief cook and bottle washer": You are also the breadwinner, even if that is a role you have not assumed before.

Taking Stock of Your Finances

As soon as you're faced with the prospect of going it alone financially, call your accountant, if you have one. Your accountant, who is familiar with your family's financial situation, is in the best position to help you develop a plan to get back on your feet.

If you don't have an accountant or your accountant is no longer willing to work for you because he or she is working for your spouse, see the manager at your bank. Bank officers are very helpful. Don't overlook this important resource. They act as private financial consultants during a time when you can use all the support you can get.

You Can Do It!

Juggling finances on a tighter budget requires looking for better prices on purchases, something you may find difficult as you have increasingly less time. But there are solutions: Many people we know have joined discount consumer clubs and buy purchases in bulk. Others now buy selected items over the Internet. You can save money, even if your time is limited.

Red Alert

One friend of ours has refused job after job because she feels the entry level positions are not commensurate with her age. We have continually suggested she get in touch with reality. While many of her friends from college have been in the workplace for 20 years, she has spent 20 years at home. She is 45, but she has no more work experience than recent college graduates. She will need to start where they do in order to get ahead, and the sooner she accepts that the sooner she will be able to take care of herself. (Our friend is currently living off her savings, refusing to give in.) Please don't make this mistake yourself.

Carmen Carrozza, a bank manager in Chappaqua, New York, has seen many people in the midst of divorce come through the door. The most uncertain are often women whose spouses have been the sole providers while they have been caring for the children. They have been steeped in the joys and burdens of their children's lives and waited each evening for the 8:30 train to arrive to see their spouses for an hour or two before retiring.

Even though they worked for a few years before having children, they have been out of the workforce too long to reenter at the same level, or the work they used to do has changed dramatically.

In most instances, Carrozza tells such customers, the most important first step is finding a means of earning money for themselves; in other words, they must find a job.

Looking for Work

If you haven't worked for a number of years, getting back into the workforce will take some time and getting used to. But it is not impossible and can ultimately reward you with far more than financial security. You will begin to feel self-reliant. You will meet new people. And you will find you are distracted from the problems related to your divorce.

Discover the person you have not yet become. You probably have more resources and talent than you give yourself credit for. To help you identify your natural aptitude, we suggest you list your special interests and abilities in detail. Use the list to help you focus your studies, your job search, and your goals.

You Can Do It!

Before you start looking for a job, make sure that you're heading in the right direction. Rank your special interests in such areas as art, teaching, organizing, cooking, or childcare. Then, if possible, follow these interests as you seek work or build a career. And remember, with adult education courses at your local high school or community college, you should be able to increase your skills and credentials.

Developing a Credit History

According to bank manager Carrozza, one of the most common concerns for those in the midst of divorce involves building personal credit. The task is far easier, of course, for people who can show they have income, often by documenting a job.

The credit issue is vital. These days, it seems, we can hardly exist in America unless we pull out a credit card to pay the tab. If you have been working all along, your credit rating will not be affected by your divorce. If you have been relying on your spouse's income, on the other hand, you will have to establish your own credit history. Although the prospect seems intimidating, it's not as formidable as it sounds.

First, you must be able to identify your sources of income, including salary, interest, and, of course, maintenance. Because banks are seeking good credit risks, they will be looking not just at your income, but also at debts, credit history, collateral, and stability (how long you've been living in the same place). There's a formula to this, and it's not mysterious: If your income-to-debt ratio is 30 to 40 percent (you use no more than 30 or 40 percent of your income to pay mortgage, car loans, and the like), banks will consider issuing you a bank credit card.

If you don't have a viable personal credit history, you can start to build one by shopping at stores that give instant credit; department stores, gas stations, and local stores are all good candidates. Begin by making small purchases on credit, and pay your bills promptly. Then, get a Visa or MasterCard. Pay your debts on these cards right away, too. If you've done things right, you should have your own positive credit history in about a year.

Handling Your Debts

In addition to generating income and establishing credit, you will have to come to terms with your debt. You and your spouse most likely have joint debts. These would include a tax debt, a mortgage, a car loan, and credit cards. If you are the non-moneyed spouse, you might have your name on the mortgage or car loan statement anyway; this means you are in debt—even though you have no income to offset the debt.

Third parties, such as the IRS and banks, don't care whether you are getting maintenance or child support. They don't care if you are divorced. They just care about the money you owe them and how they will get it back. They are not bound by the divorce settlement. They will hold both you and your spouse liable for payment.

Jim, for instance, owned a construction company. One year, he hid income by simply not mentioning it on his income tax statement. His wife, June, was shocked to learn that the IRS held her as well as her husband liable for his income tax evasion. She was not protected by their divorce settlement because the income tax statement was filed jointly.

Silver Linings

If you've been held responsible for a spouse's debt, you may seek recourse in the "Innocent Spouse Rule," a provision in the Internal Revenue Code. Under this rule, if you can show that you are completely ignorant of your spouse's wrong-doing, you might not be held liable. Check with your accountant to see whether you fall into this category.

Devious Ways a Divorcing Spouse Might Hide Assets

When it comes to money, greed is, unfortunately, a common trait. If someone has been planning a divorce for a while, and if that person is so constituted, he or she might devise numerous strategies for hiding money from a spouse and children. With the right legal help, however, wronged spouses can often come away with much of what is rightfully theirs.

Bankruptcy

As a strategy, it's more common than you might think: To avoid payment to an ex, some people will go as far as declaring *bankruptcy* in the middle of their case. If this happens to you, you must hire a bankruptcy lawyer, who will ask the judge to exclude you from the list of "creditors" who will not be paid. The spouse declaring bankruptcy might find he or she has gained an advantage when it comes to distribution of your worldly goods, but if you take the action you should, maintenance and child support will not be affected by the bankruptcy action.

During the bankruptcy process, creditors, including a spouse, can challenge the bankruptcy declaration. Some people file a petition for bankruptcy in the middle of the divorce case to lessen their obligation to their spouses.

Illegal Transfers: How to Catch Your Spouse in the Act

Another devious way the moneyed spouse might try to reduce the amount of assets declared during a divorce action is to transfer assets to a friend or family member. She will then claim that she no longer has these assets. The lawyer for the recipient spouse has to then prove that the transfer was made to deprive that spouse. If the transfer is about to happen, the recipient's lawyer can go to court to try to block the transfer. To substantiate this claim, the lawyer has to prove to the judge why he thinks the property is about to be transferred and what property or money is involved.

Marion Dupont came from a wealthy family, who gave her several properties after she married Andrew Billings. After three years of marriage, Marion met a man with "more intelligence and energy than Andrew could ever hope to have." After she broke the news to Andrew and filed for divorce, she began transferring the titles of her property to her sister. Andrew was clever enough to suspect Marion would do something sneaky, so he hired a private investigator. The PI did his homework and was able to provide proof that Marion was in the process of transferring the titles. Andrew's lawyer then brought this to the attention of their judge and was able to block the transfer.

Up for Sale: Divesting Your Assets to Make Ends Meet

If your living situation and financial status have changed for the worse because of your divorce, you might consider liquidating some assets or selling the house that was awarded to you to help with your cash flow. Before you make this decision, speak with your accountant or a financial planner.

Selling Your House

You should consider many factors if you are thinking about selling your house:

1. Your house is an asset as well as a home. If you have children, their emotional needs must be considered. At this time of turmoil and change in their lives, the house should not be sold for a few years, if possible.

2. If you receive the house through a divorce settlement or judge's decree while your spouse gets the liquid assets, think carefully about whether you have enough cash to live comfortably in the house or whether you should move into less expensive living quarters. If the monthly payments on the house are small, you might as well stay where you are.

3. As explained in Chapter 13, if you are careful, you might gain some tax benefits, depending on when you sell your house and how old you are when you sell it. If you buy a new home *within two years* of selling your house and if the new home costs at least half the sale price of your current house, you will not have to pay capital gains taxes on the profit. (The original purchase price of your home plus the cost of improvements are compared to the sale price to determine the profit or loss and the capital gains tax that will result.)

Silver Linings

The law holds that once in your life, you may sell a residence and not pay capital gains tax on up to $125,000 of the profit, provided you are 55 years of age or older. If you are 53 years old, it's better to keep the house for two more years to get this tax break. Caveat: You must have lived in the house for the previous three out of five years to qualify. Check with your accountant!

Living Within Your Means

You have already created a budget in preparation for your divorce settlement. But now that reality is settling in and your financial status has actually changed, it's a good idea to sit down with pen and paper (or keyboard and monitor—there *is* software that can help you with this) and parse things out anew.

As you did before, compare income and expenses, including such occasional items as tax payments, Christmas gifts, and savings.

Now, as you did before, put these two lists side by side. Add each column. How do they match up? Are you ahead or behind? If you're behind, put a star next to the expenses that are optional or that can be reduced. By how much can they be reduced? Is there any way you can eliminate or reduce expenses that are not starred? If you need help with this, consult your accountant or bank manager.

Sample Income/Expense Statement

Income Source	Amount	Expenses	Amount
Salary, net	$2,000	Housing	$1,500
Child support	2,500	Groceries	800
Babysitting	800	Clothing	300
Interest	200	Entertainment	150
TOTAL	$5,500	House repairs	150
		Car	100
		Heat, elec., water	500
		Children's extra-curricular	100
		Childcare	800
		Toys, gifts	40

Income Source	Amount	Expenses	Amount
		Misc. tax	50
		Haircuts	60
		Adult education	100
		Vacation	170
		Misc.	50
		Savings	100
		TOTAL	$4,970

Managing your money is, these days, a requirement for managing your life. The sooner you assess you situation and come to terms with your true financial means, the sooner you will be able to take care of yourself in a realistic and healthy way.

The Least You Need to Know

➤ Divorce means more expenses on the same income. If you are being supported by your spouse, you face the challenge of entering the job market.

➤ Establishing yourself financially means getting an income and developing a good credit history.

➤ If you are considering selling your house, check with your accountant to determine if and when the house should be put up for sale.

➤ Creating a new budget will give you a sense of control over your finances.

Part 4
Focus on the Children

Divorce is a time when you are necessarily focused on your own feelings. It is often difficult to think about anything but what is happening to you: Whether you are surprised to find your marriage coming to an end or you've been contemplating a separation for months, severing this relationship is all-encompassing.

If you have children, however, you have a dual responsibility: to yourself, and most important, to your kids. Your children know only the security and love they have had with the parents who have nurtured and guided them throughout their short lives. The thought of losing one or even both parents is frightening. The other life changes your children might experience—from changing residences to adjusting to a step-family—would disorient even the strongest, most experienced adult. In the chapters that follow, you will learn how to help your children understand and cope with the changes their family is about to undergo.

Chapter 17

MINE!

What Does Custody Really Mean?

In This Chapter

➤ Toward a definition of custody: Custody is not ownership

➤ The difference between physical custody and legal custody

➤ How to decide the children's primary residence

➤ Mothers who choose to forego custody

➤ Special considerations in high-conflict divorce

Once upon a time and long ago, you and your spouse lived together under the same roof as a family. You slept together, ate together, vacationed together, and, most important, raised your children together. One, or perhaps both of you, worked outside the home. Sure, you were overburdened by household chores; sure, you were tired from too many hours at the office or on the train. But there were the compensations: the thrill and sheer idyllic pleasure of weekend soccer or basketball games, the gentle intimacy of an afternoon at the park, the dance recitals, class plays, and rounds of Monopoly or Scrabble on rainy afternoons. You also had some treasured time alone while your spouse went off with the kids for an afternoon.

Now that you are divorcing, things have changed. For many men, this means a move to another residence and the encroaching realization that you will not be seeing the kids as often as before. Perhaps you now realize that you might have been taking your kids for granted; the thought of leaving them may well be painful—perhaps far more painful than the split from your spouse.

Many women, on the other hand, are struck with the sudden realization that they must manage alone. An at-home mother may now be going back to work. The hours and days they devoted to their children will now be spent at some office while a babysitter fills in at home.

Before you make these changes, of course, you and your spouse must, if at all possible, put your differences aside to talk about how you will divide your responsibilities and arrange for the custody of your children.

Negotiating Custody

At first, the very concept of negotiating custody might seem alien. While you were all a family unit, you both had custody—although you probably never thought of it that way. You were just your children's parents, nothing more, nothing less. Together, you decided where they went to school, what religion they practiced, and whether they would go through the ritual of getting braces or attending camp. It was natural in your family—as in most intact families—for you and your spouse to discuss these things and come to an agreement about what was best.

Once you and your spouse no longer live under the same roof, things will change. Now, you will have to decide how these decisions are made. Will one parent have the final say? What role will the other parent—the one no longer living with the children most of the time—assume? Will one parent feel overburdened with responsibility or restricted in making decisions that are, after all, best made by the person actually living with the children? (For the parent who might be doing most of the child-rearing, the thought of getting approval from an ex before taking a child for psychological or academic help, for instance, can be frustrating, indeed.) Meanwhile, will the other parent feel cut off from his or her children, painfully disenfranchised from their lives?

You must ask yourselves these questions up front. If you can put your personal animosity aside for the moment, you might be able to arrive at a practical, workable custody arrangement together. If you can't, court battles—sometimes lasting until your children are finally emancipated—can ensue.

Custody Is Not Ownership

Any negotiation, of course, is based on the assumption that you understand precisely what custody is—and what it is not. In a way, it's unfortunate that we ever coined the term *custody* for parents who no longer live together. The term has so many negative implications: A criminal is taken into custody; a mentally ill or cocaine-ridden mother loses custody of her child because of child abuse.

Yet here we have two parents who have been living with their children, and, unless one parent has been abusive or is a drug or alcohol addict, both have been involved in raising the children; both have been supportive, responsible, loving, and kind. Because the parents' relationship broke down, in many jurisdictions one parent will probably get custody of the children unless it is decided otherwise.

Parents should understand that custody does not mean ownership. Children cannot be owned like a car or a house. What custody does mean is that one (or both) parents have the final say in the decision-making for major issues in child rearing (*legal custody*). Custody usually also determines with whom the children primarily reside (*physical custody*).

When You Lose Custody

When Barry and June divorced, Barry could not imagine relinquishing custody of his children. Barry's children embodied his personal hopes and dreams; he identified much of his success in life with his kids. When the judge decided that custody of the children should go to June, Barry went into a deep depression.

Barry needed to understand that losing custody did not mean losing his children. The custody battle was over, but Barry still had years of co-parenting ahead.

Divorce Dictionary

Custody: The legal right and responsibility to raise a minor child and to make decisions.

Physical custody: In this arrangement the children live primarily with one parent who has "physical custody."

Sole custody: One parent has the right to make all major decisions regarding the children, and the children reside primarily with that parent. The parent who does not have sole custody has "visitation rights."

Joint custody: Joint physical custody means the children reside with each parent for an equal length of time. Joint legal custody means the children reside primarily with one parent, but both parents have an equal right to make major decisions about the children's lives.

Custody is a legal term. But if you are the noncustodial parent, your relationship with your children goes on, no matter what the official custody decision might be. You can continue to be involved with your children. If it's important to you, you will continue to share great times and impart the values you embrace. Whether you officially have "custody" does not have to change your relationship with your children. You can still be heavily involved in your children's lives.

Silver Linings

We can't state strongly enough that custody is a legal term and has no bearing on how deep your relationship is with your children. How your time is spent with your children and the quality of your relationship with them is the primary factor in determining their well-being and the continuation of a close relationship with them—*not* whether or not you have legal custody.

Andrea, a producer of television commercials, was a career-oriented woman. Although she had three children, she decided to move from Pennsylvania to California after her divorce because she was given a unique opportunity to be a producer in Hollywood. Andrea called her kids once a week and saw them once every two months for one week. Andrea insisted on having joint decision-making after she moved to California. She claimed that if she didn't, she would feel uninvolved with her children. To prove to the judge that she was an involved parent, she wrote long letters to her children's court-appointed law guardian, berating her husband for trying to cut her out of the picture.

Andrea conveniently forgot that she was the one who had moved away from her children. More to the point, if she had spent as much time writing letters to her children as she spent writing to their law guardian, her relationship with them would have been much closer, in reality, than anything formal decision-making rights would have given her.

Divorce Dictionary

Joint custody: Sharing the raising of children despite a divorce. Joint custody can mean the children will live with one parent most of the time, but both parents will make major decisions. It can also mean the children will divide their time equally between the two parents' homes.

What's important in the final analysis is your relationship with your children, over which you *should* have significant control.

Joint Versus Sole Custody

For the sake of the children, the goals of divorcing parents should be the same: involvement of both parents in the lives of the children and elimination of conflict between the parents. These two factors should dominate all others when thinking about custody.

In the 1980s, there was a trend in many states toward *joint custody,* where both parents jointly decide on major issues regarding their children. Sometimes, joint custody includes an equal, or close to equal, living arrangement with each parent. Even if there is joint physical custody, the actual time spent with each parent can vary widely.

With *sole custody,* one parent has the final say in the decision-making for the children and the children primarily reside with the parent who has sole custody.

In the last 15 years, psychologists have had enough time to do long-term studies on the outcome for families in joint custody and sole custody arrangements. Here are three of the most important findings of these studies:

1. Joint custody is a viable option only if the parents have an amicable relationship with each other, communicate well, and live in close proximity. Parents in this situation feel more involved in their children's lives than the noncustodial parent in the sole custody arrangement. In a family where one parent says "black" and the other parent says "white," the children are better off with a sole custody arrangement to reduce the possibility that their parents will fight over every decision that must be made on their behalf.

2. For parents not on friendly terms, joint custody and joint decision-making mean more room for disagreement and continuation of the conflict. These parents are more likely to return to court than the parents who have one decision-maker (sole custody).

3. Children who tend to be easy-going by nature can adapt well to joint physical custody. Children who do poorly with constant change, have difficulty adjusting to new situations, and seem to need a great deal of stability and security in their lives do poorly with joint physical custody.

Determining the Primary Residence

The parent who has been most involved in the daily care of the children should provide their primary home. Traditionally, this has been the mother. In growing numbers, although still small, some fathers have been providing most of the care either by choice or by default.

Following is a checklist of routine caregiving tasks that will help you decide which parent should maintain the primary residence for the children. Be honest with yourself when filling out the checklist. Your children will benefit, and you will be more comfortable with the outcome.

Red Alert

While joint custody can work well for parents who get along, those parents who are embattled in divorce or are mutually hostile after the divorce should have as little contact with each other as possible. Joint custody means joint decision making. For parents who fight, the more interaction, the more opportunity to fan the flames. This is a prescription for disaster for the children. Conflict in front of the children or using the children as part of the conflict should be avoided at all cost.

Task	Mother	Father
1. Provides meals	❑	❑
2. Holds and comforts children	❑	❑
3. Changes diapers	❑	❑
4. Dresses the children	❑	❑
5. Bathes the children	❑	❑
6. Plays with the children	❑	❑
7. Takes children to the doctor	❑	❑
8. Stays home with sick children	❑	❑
9. Reads stories to children	❑	❑
10. Takes children to school or activities	❑	❑
11. Puts children to sleep	❑	❑
12. Communicates more closely with children	❑	❑
13. Attends more school events	❑	❑
14. Disciplines children	❑	❑
15. Is called by children when they awaken during the night	❑	❑
16. Children seek comfort from whom?	❑	❑
17. Arranges playtime with friends	❑	❑

Adapted from Baris, M.A. and Garrity, C.B.: Children of Divorce: A Developmental Approach to Residence and Visitation. Psytec; DeKalb, IL; 1988.

When a Mother Decides to Give Up Custody

Our society, rife with double standards, puts women in a bind when it comes to family. Women fought to be able to earn as much as men for the same work and to be able to have childcare paid by their companies so that they might work. Some gains have been made for women in their quest for equal economic status with men. Many women who enjoyed interesting careers before they had children decide to spend more time—or full time—with their children when they finally start their families. Others need or want to continue their careers.

However, if their marriages break down, custody is less likely to automatically go to the mother because both parents are working. Even if the mother tries to better herself by going to school and putting her child in day care, she might lose custody of her children, as happened in a recent highly publicized case in Michigan. This mother, a college student, lost custody of her child when a judge decided the father's home was more stable because he lived with his parents; the child would have Grandma during the day, as opposed to day care. Fortunately for the mom, the Michigan Supreme Court overturned the judgment on appeal.

Of course, a mother might choose a career or an alternative lifestyle over remaining with her children as the custodial parent. Society is invariably shocked when mothers relinquish this "natural attachment." Yet for some, it is the best choice.

Sometimes, it's difficult for very young people—male or female—to handle the overwhelming burden of parenting young children alone as they work to earn a living. Some women, for the sake of their own personal growth, need the time and space that primary custody would simply preclude. A woman who is frustrated about her own life will not be as effective a mother as a woman who is fulfilled. Deciding to relinquish much of the daily childcare responsibilities will benefit the children if they have a happy, self-assured mother and a father who can fulfill the primary nurturing role.

Doreen got married in her freshman year of college. She had wanted to be a biologist, but she fell in love with her classmate, Brian. Within a year of getting married, she was pregnant with her first child. She loved the role of mother and left school. Doreen then had another child and for the next five years devoted her time to caring for her children. When the children were spending long days at school and at after-school activities, her marriage to Brian began to deteriorate. Doreen was itching to do something different with her life.

Meanwhile, Brian, an accountant, had moved his practice into their home. When Doreen's unhappiness finally reached the breaking point, she decided to go back to school and renew the life she had abandoned at the age of 19. She and Brian agreed that Brian would remain in their home with the children and that she would move to a local condominium. Brian had primary custody, but the children lived with Doreen on the weekends. She was able to pursue her new life and still have a close relationship with her children.

Silver Linings

Just because a woman is not primary custodian in no way implies that she has given up her role as mother. No one would ever suggest that a father who doesn't have primary custody has given up being a father! What's important is maintaining the relationship with the children. As always, it's the relationship that counts, not the legal custody arrangement.

Custody Issues When Conflict Is Out of Control

What could be worse for children than their parents going through a divorce? They're parents in a heated conflict—both during the marriage, throughout the divorce, and after the divorce. The type of custody arrangement that is best for the children depends on the quality of their parents' relationship. Here's a case in point.

Harriet and Bill had been snapping at each other for years, the fire of passion that characterized their early romance long extinguished by the mundane realities of life. Harriet and Bill had two children, Gwen, 14, and Martin, 12.

Bill, manager of a healthcare facility, couldn't keep his eyes off Marion, a lab technician 10 years his junior. After so many years of squelched sexuality in his marriage, Bill couldn't pass up the opportunity to engage Marion in conversation. What started out as a flirtation ended up as a passionate romance.

A year later, Bill decided he wanted a permanent relationship with Marion. After much anguished decision-making about leaving his family, he decided to tell Harriet that he wanted a divorce.

Of course, Harriet was shocked. Despite the fact that she was dissatisfied with her relationship with Bill, she had grown used to the same old arguments they had about sharing responsibilities around the house, Bill's watching too much TV, and their lack of communication. Yet the thought of his moving out—to marry someone else!—made her heart race with anxiety.

A few weeks later, Bill decided it was time to work out the details of the divorce. He said he wanted joint custody of the children. The thought of giving up his role as decision-maker was too much to bear. Needless to say, Harriet, who had lost her husband to a younger woman and never wanted to speak to him again, could not imagine ever being able to sit down with Bill and make a mutual decision regarding the children.

In this situation, Harriet was probably right. As long as the animosity between Harriet and Bill was so great, it would not be possible to come to an agreement, and decisions had to be made. If Harriet's and Bill's situation was like most other divorced parents whose conflict is ongoing, joint custody would result in more fighting and perennial visits to court.

Custody is probably the most sensitive issue for parents going through a divorce (unless, of course, they are in agreement on that issue). In most cases, both parents have been putting their greatest effort into their children, so how can one parent be given custody, seemingly relegating the other parent to second place? The legal system by its nature has to define as precisely as possible the legal status of the people involved. Unfortunately, the term "custody" strips the profound meaning of "parent" down to its bare bones.

That's why it is so important to emphasize that custody is simply a legal term. Difficult though it is to absorb, it does not have to mean a change in the relationship of parent and child.

Divorce raises intense emotional issues in most cases. When children are involved, it's natural to want to maintain as much control as possible of the lives of the children.

That's one reason for custody battles. There are others—in some cases, unfortunately, one parent is not as interested in raising the children as in reducing monetary obligations to the family. In this scenario, a parent might threaten to ask the court for sole custody in order to scare the other parent into reducing child support or other monetary obligations.

When parents separate amicably, some form of joint custody is possible. While the children still have the task of adjusting to living in two homes, as long as the parents get along, the children usually fare well.

The Least You Need to Know

➤ Custody is not ownership. No one can "own" your children. Both parents will always be parents, and the relationship with their children is completely under their own control.

➤ Joint custody, where both parents share in the decision-making necessary in the children's lives, has been shown to be feasible only with parents who are cooperative with each other and live in close proximity.

➤ Sole custody, where one parent makes all the decisions and the children live primarily with that parent with liberal visitation with the other parent, has been traditionally recommended.

➤ The primary residence should be with the parent who has up until the divorce been the primary caretaker of the children.

➤ Mothers who choose not to be the custodial parent are usually not abandoning their children. They recognize their own personal limitations and need for growth.

➤ In high-conflict divorce, sole custody is the only workable arrangement because it reduces the need to go back to court to make decisions on behalf of the children.

Chapter 18

Breaking the News

In This Chapter

➤ When to tell your child about your separation

➤ What to say

➤ Helping your child deal with grief, anger, and rejection

➤ Dealing with real abandonment by a parent

If you have children and you haven't yet told them about your intention to separate or divorce, this is the moment you're probably dreading. How can you break the news to your children, who look to their parents for love and security? What will go through their minds as you begin your discussion with them? How can you ease their fears while being realistic about the enormous changes about to occur?

No matter how old your children are, they must be told of the impending separation as soon as possible. Even a toddler can understand, if addressed at his or her level. It is far more injurious to wake up one day with Mommy or Daddy gone than to be told in advance—preferably by both parents together—that one of you is moving out.

When to Tell Your Children

As soon as you and your spouse have made the decision to separate, it's time to tell your children. Telling your children sooner rather than later will ensure that they don't hear the news from another source or overhear you talking to someone about this disturbing news. Deception can promote fantasies about what is really going on, fears of abandonment, wondering about whether they will ever see their departing parent again, and a lack of understanding of the new realities they are about to face. If your children suspect information is being held back, a breach of trust might develop, becoming difficult, if not impossible, to repair.

How to Tell Your Children

Setting the stage for open, honest communication with your children is your most important job. Ideally, both parents should be present when your children are told. Presenting a united front will help your kids by easing their fears of abandonment and will reduce a loyalty conflict: It's all Mom's fault; Dad is the innocent victim.

If you have more than one child, gather them together for a family meeting to break the news. Let the children know that both of you are available to talk to each of them individually or together again after the meeting. Having all the children together will give each child support from his or her siblings. Be prepared for an avalanche of questions regarding the logistics of the divorce, custody, and visitation. Even money may be of concern to the children.

What to Tell Your Children

As always, your aim is to be open and honest with your children. That doesn't mean you have to go into all the gory details, but children who are told nothing about the reasons for their parents' divorce are unnecessarily frustrated and have a more difficult time working things through.

Red Alert

It can be emotionally disastrous to withhold the news from your children. "I never heard my parents fight, so I was shocked when my father called me into his room to tell me he and Mom were separating," says Jeremy, age 12. "It took a long time for it to sink in. I wish they had let me know sooner. I feel like they've been lying to me."

Some children, especially older ones, might not be particularly surprised. Alicia, a 13-year-old, recently had this to say: "My parents had been cold to each other for a long time. Sometimes, they would scream at each other, and all I wanted to do was run away. It came as no surprise when they sat me down and told me they were getting a divorce."

For children who have not been exposed to fighting, a simple explanation will go a long way toward helping to digest the news. Depending on the age of your youngest child, say as much as possible about why the marriage is ending. When speaking to your children in a group, use language that even the youngest can understand.

Telling the children that you are going to divorce and why is the toughest part of the family meeting. But it is only the beginning. Because children are appropriately centered in their own world, they need to have precise and concrete information about how their lives will change. By the end of the discussion with your kids, they should know

➤ As much as possible about the reasons for the divorce

➤ When the separation will take place

➤ Where the parent who is leaving will live

➤ With which parent they will live

➤ When and under what circumstances they will see their other parent

➤ Whether they will be moving into a new house or apartment

➤ That he or she will have open telephone communication with the parent who is leaving

Divorce Dictionary

With **sole custody,** one parent makes the primary decisions regarding the child and the child lives with that parent.

Each parent should cover one or two points and then give the other a turn. To see how it works, review the following successful scenario. (Of course, you should modify the specifics in accordance with your own situation.)

Dad: As you may know, your Mom and I have not been getting along for a while now. Although we were once happy together, we've grown apart. We tried to work things out and have been seeing a marriage counselor for quite a while, but we've reached an impasse.

We think we'll be happier if we live separately, so we've decided to get a divorce. You have done nothing to cause us to divorce. It is not your fault. This is between your mother and me.

Mom: I'm sure you know that we both love you very much. Just because your Dad and I don't want to be together anymore doesn't mean that we don't want to be with you. Parents can divorce each other but can't and don't want to divorce their kids. We will be your Mom and Dad forever. We will always be there for you just as before. You will always be taken care of. You will always have a home. Each of us will be with you, but not at the same time.

Dad: I have rented an apartment a few blocks away, and I'll be moving there next Saturday. You'll be living with your Mom and coming over to live with me every other weekend. We'll also get together once a week for dinner and homework help. We'll be sharing each holiday. I'll call you every night after school, and you can call me anytime. You'll have your own room at my apartment, and you can decorate it any way you want. (If the living arrangement is not yet settled, you can say, "The details haven't been worked out yet, but we'll let you know as soon as they are.")

Mom: Your family will always be your family, even though Dad and I aren't going to be in the same house. Your grandparents, aunts, uncles, and cousins will still be your grandparents, aunts, uncles, and cousins.

If you have any questions, you can ask them now, or you can talk to Dad or me later at any time. Remember, we'll always be there for you, and we love you very much.

Silver Linings

Not all children will be surprised that their parents are divorcing. In some cases, when there have been nightly battles, children are actually happier knowing that they'll never have to hear the shouting and name-calling again.

You Can Do It!

If you and your spouse can agree on living arrangements and visitation, it is so much better for the children. It is also very important that you and your spouse decide on these arrangements so the children are not asked to choose sides. If visitation details are at issue, and both parents agree, it's okay to get a feeling from your children—especially the younger ones—as to what arrangements would make them feel most comfortable.

If you and your spouse are in a heated battle, or if your spouse has left suddenly, a family meeting with both parents will probably not be possible. You might not know all the details of the living arrangements, but your children should be informed of whatever information you have, to give them a handle on the changes in their lives.

For the purpose of telling your children, set aside your anger. Blaming one parent will only cause confusion. Because your children are emotionally attached to the other parent, they will feel conflicting loyalty. Not only will your child feel torn between his parents, but also eventually, he might react against *you* to defend his relationship with the other parent.

When 12-year-old Michelle was told by her mother that her Dad had moved out after a final blow-up the night before, Michelle was devastated. Her mother was so angry at her Dad that she blamed him for all the ills of her marriage: She had to do all the housework, even though she worked; he would come home late at night; they never went out because he was too "cheap"; and other complaints.

At first, Michelle was sympathetic to her mother and understood her unhappiness. She felt angry at her Dad for not being more considerate of her mother's feelings. But after a week had passed, Michelle started to feel guilty for having bad thoughts about her father. She missed him. She began to wonder whether her mother had told her the whole truth and even started developing feelings of resentment toward her mother; had her mother, she wondered, been instrumental in driving her father out of the house? The more her mother spoke against her father, the more difficult it was for Michelle to sustain a warm relationship with her mother.

When a Parent Moves Far Away

If one parent chooses to move far away, enormous stress is placed on the children. While sometimes necessary for employment circumstances, it's always better for both parents to stay within reasonable driving distance to the children. Once a parent moves far away, the children will not see that parent often, and they will probably have an erratic visitation schedule—long summers away from the custodial parent with little contact during the school year. Added to that, they will usually have to travel long distances to see their parent. (See Chapter 19 for more details.)

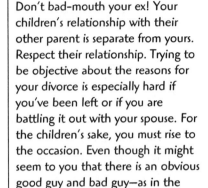

Red Alert

Don't bad-mouth your ex! Your children's relationship with their other parent is separate from yours. Respect their relationship. Trying to be objective about the reasons for your divorce is especially hard if you've been left or if you are battling it out with your spouse. For the children's sake, you must rise to the occasion. Even though it might seem to you that there is an obvious good guy and bad guy—as in the case of the infidelity of one parent—the reality is almost never that clear-cut.

Helping Children Deal with Intense Emotion and Pain

No matter how "correctly" you explain things to your children, they will still experience a range of emotions, including disbelief, fear, anger, rejection, and grief. The only thing worse for parents than seeing their children suffer is being the cause of that suffering. And parents in the throes of divorce often find themselves in that situation.

As a parent, you are no doubt familiar with the difficult job of comforting your child during sickness, injury, insults by classmates, lost friendships or betrayals by friends, or embarrassing moments in class. It is impossible to shield your children from all the hurt that life brings. However, the breakup of a family and possibly the loss of one parent is surely one of the toughest hurdles for any child to overcome. This moment and the next year or two will test your emotional strength and your parenting skills to the limit. You think you're not up to the task? You are. You have no choice.

That doesn't mean you have to go it alone. Friends, family, psychologists, teachers, ministers and rabbis, your lawyer, and books are all there to help you manage this transition. Use whatever resources you need to acquire the knowledge and support necessary to help your children get through the initial shock, adjust to the changes about to begin, and adapt to their new way of living.

No matter how troubled your children might seem in the wake of your divorce, you can help them heal by viewing the world through their eyes. Karen Breunig, co-author (with psychologists Mitchell Baris, Carla Garrity, and Janet R. Johnston) of *Through the Eyes of Children: Healing Stories for Children of Divorce* (August 1997, Free Press) notes that parents must be aware of three overriding issues and deal with them up front:

1. **Children fear that they will not be allowed to love both parents without interference.** To address this concern, says Breunig, parents must remember that loving the other parent is a child's birthright. A child is partly like each parent, she notes, and "when you tear down your ex-spouse in front of your child, you're tearing down a part of your child."

2. **Children harbor the fantasy that their parents will reunite.** Parents must acknowledge that the child has these feelings, Breunig states, at the same time making it clear that reuniting is out of the question. "You must support your child in the grief," she notes, "so that he or she understands it's safe to talk about feelings without fear of rejection. You must listen to the feelings while, at the same time, telling the child that you and your ex will both be there to parent them, but that you cannot promise a reconciliation will ever take place."

3. **Children may be emotionally damaged if exposed to too much anger and rage, even if those feelings are not directed at them.** "Emotions run so high in a divorce," says Breunig, "that it takes tremendous adult responsibility to shield children from all the things it would be damaging for them to hear. People can't often control their feelings in the midst of an emotionally damaging divorce, but they can control how they act out those feelings in front of their children. If you've just found out that your spouse has been unfaithful and wants a divorce, it would be very difficult to hide the situation from a child, depending upon age. In such situations, it is not necessarily unhealthy for them to see your grief and sadness. But it can be quite damaging for them to see your rage or hear you lambaste the other parent. Children must be spared the pain of adult emotional business, as much as possible."

Dealing with Fears

Children of divorce are usually most fearful of abandonment and loss of parental love. It is crucial, therefore, that you take every opportunity to reassure your children that their parents love them and will always be there for them. According to psychologist Mitchell Baris, Ph.D., "What differentiates a parent-child relationship from any other kind of relationship is loyalty. Mom will always be Mom, and Dad will always be Dad, and nobody else will ever replace them. Even if the parents remarry, even if they'll be living in two houses, or even if one parent will be living far away, Dad will always be Dad, and Mom will always be Mom."

Let them know (assuming that one parent is not *actually* abandoning the family) that they will have a continuing relationship with both parents—even if, for the moment, you wish you would never see your spouse again! (If you have trouble saying things that you know are in the children's best interests but that stick in your throat, try viewing your spouse as their parent rather than your archenemy. Just for now, put yourself in his or her shoes.)

Dealing with Blame

Children are likely to blame one or both parents for the divorce. Sometimes—and of more concern—children blame themselves. Reassure your children repeatedly that the separation has nothing to do with them. Assure them that although parents can divorce each other, they cannot divorce their children—nor would they ever want to.

Dealing with Anger

Your children might not evidence or express anger until after the shock of the announcement has worn off. Anger, if not constructively channeled, can become destructive or self-destructive. Hidden feelings can fester and manifest in ways that seem unconnected to the separation.

Eric, for instance, had a close friend, Alex. They saw each other at school every day and often went over to each other's house after school. After Eric's parents announced their separation, he fought with Alex over everything. It seemed that Alex couldn't do anything right. Because Eric kept the news about his parents' divorce to himself, Alex didn't have a clue about what was going wrong. Alex stopped seeing Eric. Eric lost a best friend at a time he needed one the most.

To help your children work through this anger, make yourself available. Children need to know that their feelings count. Listen attentively when your children want to talk. Answer questions as honestly as you can according to the child's age. The more they can express their feelings, the easier the adjustment will be.

When a Child Is Abandoned

What if, in the worst-case scenario, your spouse announces that he or she plans to abandon the family and have absolutely nothing to do with the children after the divorce?

If possible, it behooves you to convince your partner that the children need him or her in their lives, no matter what. Communicating this urgent message to a spouse who is threatening abandonment might be your best weapon against the devastation of parental loss. Ironically, some parents abandon their children because they, themselves, lack self-esteem. They think their children would do better without them. If your spouse harbors such feelings, you must do your best to explain how crucial he or she is to your child's well-being.

What if, despite your urgings or completely to your surprise, your spouse actually just up and leaves? If this was a surprise to you, your own shock will make it monumentally more difficult to tell your children. You know intuitively that your children's self-esteem will be affected by your spouse's decision to cut them off. No matter how hard it is for you, it is far more damaging to your children because children don't have an adult's perspective on life or the inner resources to handle such extraordinary rejection and hurt. Your children might experience self-doubt, depression, and regression.

It is your job to pick up the pieces. If you are the parent who has remained, you must be there with all your love and support, making sure your children understand that there's nothing wrong with them. *They* are worthwhile and cherished by you. Instead, it is the parent who left who has the problems that must be worked through.

Remind your children that the flight of their other parent has nothing to do with them; they bear absolutely no blame. Also remind them that they still possess your undying love, as well as the love and support of other family and friends. Be cautioned that it is unfair to give the children hope that someday their parent might return.

As the remaining parent, it is also your job to be on the lookout for the psychological side effects of abandonment. Your children might very well experience strong feelings of rejection, a longing for the departed parent, and eventually anger. If there are any signs of depression after a three-month period, consult a psychologist.

The Least You Need to Know

➤ Telling your children that your marriage is ending is difficult but not insurmountable. If you and your spouse can manage to share this task, your children will benefit.

➤ Trust can be achieved by being as open and honest with your children as is appropriate for their age.

➤ Your children's sense of security will be enhanced if you and your spouse can assure them of a continued relationship with both parents.

➤ Try to work out the children's future living arrangements before you announce your plans to separate or divorce. Tell the children about these plans when you announce the divorce itself.

➤ Helping your children handle their grief, anger, and feelings of rejection will be your most important job in the coming months. If you are overwhelmed, seek professional help during this crisis period.

➤ Actual abandonment by one parent is a difficult scenario for children. Do what you can to prevent it, but if that's not possible, assure your children of your love for them.

Coparenting and Visitation

Unless parents have agreed or the court has ordered joint custody, the children officially "live" with the custodial parent and "visit" the noncustodial parent. This unfortunate term can make the noncustodial parent feel less than a parent. The terms "time-sharing" and "coparenting" have now become popular with psychologists working in the field of divorce and with many divorced people. The new phraseology emphasizes that both parents are still parents—a crucial concept for making life work after that cataclysm of divorce.

When Parents Live Apart

Aside from the trauma of a once-intact family's splitting up, children of divorce must adapt to the stress of moving back and forth between two parental homes. Some adjust well to this lifestyle; some have a harder time. In either case, each parent is important in the children's lives, and the children miss the absent parent. Having both parents in the picture—even if they are not living together—is best for your kids.

To make this lifestyle work, each parent must be tuned in to his or her children. Parents must strive to lessen the stress children may feel and to stay in touch with their individual and developmental needs.

Here are some tips for making coparenting work:

➤ Cooperate with the other parent as much as possible.

➤ Both parents are entitled to know what's going on when it comes to a child's schooling, medical care, and social life.

➤ Establish a polite business relationship with the other parent.

➤ Be responsible in maintaining the visitation schedule. If a change must be made, work it out with the other parent in advance.

➤ Respect the rules of the other parent's household, just as you respect the rules of school and other public institutions.

➤ Don't send messages to the other parent via your children. Business should be conducted only between parents.

Silver Linings

You have a great deal of control over the way your children handle life after divorce. By cooperating with the other parent, you are establishing a life pattern your children can carry into the future. Most of the time, children of divorce can do very well (after a period of adjustment, of course) if their parents maintain a cooperative relationship.

All About Attitude

To coparent successfully, a positive attitude on your part is a must. If you see your ex as your children's parent, rather than as your archenemy, you stand a better chance of making coparenting work.

For example, don't criticize the parenting skills of the other parent. Seven-year-old Melissa's father never failed to comment to Melissa about how wrinkled her clothes were and how messy her hair was when he picked her up from her mother's home. These negative comments about her mom's parenting skills always got the weekend with her dad off to a bad start.

Don't focus on every negative comment your children make about the other parent when they're with you. Check your attitude: Do you secretly relish these comments because you can't stand your ex and hope your kids support your view? Are you in competition with your ex for the kids' loyalty? Unless your children are saying something *very* disturbing about the other parent (physical or mental abuse, alcohol or drug abuse), any negative comments your children might make are often best taken with a grain of salt. Don't blow such comments out of proportion, and remember, your children will resent and distrust you if you cheer them on.

On the other hand, be realistic. Don't overcompensate for your negative feelings toward your ex by bending over backwards to paint him or her as perfect. Nothing in life is all good or all bad, so how could it be for your children's experience at either home? Children should understand that there will be fun times and boring times, happy times and angry times, at either home. In any case, portraying your ex as all good will have a false ring to your kids. ("If you like my dad/mom so much, why did you two split up?")

Any angry feelings you have towards your ex-spouse are best kept between you, your therapist if you have one, and your friends or family. Try to put a lid on your anger when you're with your kids. Sometimes, anger comes out not directly, but through a negative attitude towards things related to your ex-spouse. This negative attitude is also confusing and potentially damaging to your kids. It's important to identify unconscious attitudes that get expressed in ways you might not recognize, but your kids' radar will pick them up.

What's your attitude toward your ex? Here's a quick quiz to find out. If you answer "Yes" to two or more of the following items, you need an attitude change!

1. I hate my ex so much, I can't stand the thought of my kids being with him (her). _____Yes _____No

2. When my kids come back from seeing their other parent, I tell them to take a shower or bath to wash my ex's presence away. _____Yes _____No

3. When my kids tell me they had a good time with their other parent, it ties my stomach in knots. _____Yes _____No

4. Whenever my kids say nice things about their other parent, my lips start to purse, and I'm silent, or I get the urge to say something really bad. _____Yes _____No

5. If my kids report that their other parent is doing well and is happy, I get a sinking feeling in my stomach. _____Yes _____No

6. I "accidentally" say things against my ex to friends or family within earshot of my kids. _____Yes _____No

7. If asked, I can't come up with one good thing to say about my ex. _____Yes _____No

191

We hope this little quiz will tune you in to your feelings and bring them to the surface. Not only will this be beneficial to your children, but it might help you get rid of some of the anger that is boiling inside you.

Age-Appropriate Visitation

It's a famous story: Two women were fighting over a baby each claimed as her own. Wise King Solomon had the women brought before him. To be fair, he ruled that the baby be cut in half, with one half given to each woman. The pretender agreed. The real mother screamed, "No! Give the baby to her!" King Solomon then knew that *she* was the real mother.

Although it's important for both parents to maintain a relationship with their children, visitation schedules based simply on dividing up the number of days in a calendar year without regard for the age of the children, the psychological needs unique to the children, or the temperament of the children can cause unnecessary stress; for very young children, ignoring these factors can cause permanent psychological harm.

It's obvious, of course, that children are individuals. Each child can tolerate more or less disruption and more or less time away from the security of a primary home. It's also clear that, for most children, the ability to make transitions from place to place increases with age. For time-sharing to work, both parents must be attuned to their children's unique requirements and needs, as well as the general developmental pattern that most children follow from birth through the teen years.

Infancy to Two-and-a-Half Years

Infancy, psychologists agree, is a time for building an attachment to the primary caretaker. The infant's developmental task is to form trust in the environment. Long separations from the primary caretaker can result in symptoms of depression and regression and later may result in problems with separation and the ability to form relationships.

Toddlers are beginning to develop a sense of independence. They are becoming aware of themselves and begin to speak and walk. They can use symbols to comfort themselves, such as a picture of Mom or a toy she gave them.

Teddy was 18 months when his dad decided his marriage was not worth the effort. He loved Teddy, but had grown distant from his wife and was looking for a change. When Teddy's parents separated, they went to a child psychologist to get advice about an appropriate visitation schedule for Teddy with his father and to ask for ways to make the separation from Teddy's mother easier. The psychologist suggested that Teddy be allowed to take his favorite blanket with him when he was with his Dad. This blanket allowed Teddy to have a connection to his life with Mom and gave him great comfort.

Because the successful attainment of these developmental tasks lays the foundation for secure and healthy children, parents should design a schedule that works within the confines of the children's needs at this stage. The best schedule, say the experts, is short but frequent time with the noncustodial parent: *short* because infants and toddlers can't maintain the image of their primary caretaker for long and *frequent* to enable them to bond with the noncustodial parent. Most psychologists agree there should be no overnight visitation for these very young children.

Jonathan was a five-month-old baby when his parents separated. His father left the house and moved into a nearby apartment. He saw his son regularly at his former home. Jonathan was just at the age in his growth when separation from his mother for any reason causes an infant separation anxiety. All parents are familiar with this stage in an infant's life; no one but Mommy will do. As with any other infant of this age, whenever Jonathan's dad held him, he would start to scream.

Jonathan's father would not accept the fact that this was normal behavior. Angry at his estranged wife, Jonathan's father refused to cooperate with the recommendations of a child psychologist.

Red Alert

If your child is grieving for the other parent, he will not be able to focus on his relationship with you. Give your child the time he needs to adjust to separation from his primary caregiver.

The child, the expert said, should be returned to his mother's arms during these anxious moments. As a result of the father's insensitivity to Jonathan's genuine developmental needs, Jonathan eventually developed an aversion to his father. Jonathan's dad thus laid the groundwork for his son's resistance to visitation.

Two-and-a-Half to Five Years

This is a time of continued growth and individuality. These young children can now hold the absent parent in mind for comfort for longer periods of time. Language is developed enough to enable these youngsters to express feelings and needs. Feelings and bodily functions are now more in their control. There is also a growing identification with the same-sex parent at this age.

Time away from the primary caretaker can increase, and overnights can be introduced, depending on the temperament of the individual child. If the child resists long periods away from her primary caretaker, short but frequent visits should continue until the child is more able to withstand longer separations.

Six to Eight Years

The hallmark of this period is development of peer and community relationships, a moral sense, empathy, and better self-regulation of impulses. Children develop a concept of themselves as they gain competence and master skills.

For children to develop normally, it's important during this age for the noncustodial parent to participate in the activities within the community in which the children live.

At this stage, children thrive on consistent contact with friends, school, and extra-curricular activities. Although the length of time away from home can be increased for those aged six to eight, if a child is homesick, most child development experts recommend that the time away should be decreased to a tolerable level.

You Can Do It!

Teenagers often feel displaced in the wake of divorce, and the experts say that support groups of peers can often be particularly helpful. Do look to get your adolescent involved in a well-run support activity to help with the transition.

You Can Do It!

Adopt an attitude of sensitivity and flexibility when it comes to the visitation schedule you establish for your children. If your children are nearing adolescence, their social agenda becomes paramount to them. Although spending time with their parents is very important (and sacred for the noncustodial parent), parents who respect their children's needs to develop a social life of their own will be helping them to grow normally and will score points with their kids.

Nine to Twelve Years

During these years, children develop their academic, athletic, and artistic skills. They become more involved in community activity. There is an increased desire to maintain friendships and seek approval of peers, as well as growing self-awareness as they begin to evaluate their own strengths and weaknesses against the larger arena of the world.

As before, the noncustodial parent is advised to schedule visits, as much as possible, within the orbit of the child's home base. The closer children feel to the noncustodial parent, the more agreeable they will be to segments of time away from community activities and friends.

Thirteen to Eighteen Years

This period marks the beginning of psychological emancipation as children establish their personal identity more strongly than ever before. There is a mourning of the loss of childhood as children relinquish dependency and the protection of the family circle to venture out on their own. Kids at this age are dealing with their sexual feelings. They are also beginning to see how to work within the rules and regulations of society.

At this age, children have generally come to count on a fairly established visitation schedule and routine. Nonetheless, that may change as these teenage children seek to have input into the schedule so that it dovetails with their increasingly complex academic and social lives. Remember: It is difficult to force an adolescent into a schedule he or she did not help to create.

Scheduled for Success

There are many variations on a workable schedule. Regularity and predictability are key to assuring your children's feelings of security. The degree of closeness of the relationship with the noncustodial parent and physical proximity to the children are also important considerations.

As the years pass, it is normal to revise a schedule so that children spend increasingly more time away from the primary home. As these revisions are made, however, parents must be sensitive to any signs that a child is being pushed beyond his or her capabilities. Remember that your relationship does not depend on the actual number of hours or days you spend with your children but on the degree of your involvement, concern, and openness to your children's emotional and developmental needs. Pushing your children beyond their temperament and capabilities can backfire.

Parents across the country have designed time-sharing schedules that range from one week at each parent's home to rotating every other weekend, with the kids living primarily at one parent's home. You know your kids best, so think about what would work for them. Here is just one example of a visitation schedule based on children's ages:

Age	Time with Noncustodial Parent	Vacation Time
Infant to 1 year	2 hours, 4–5 days per week; later, 4 hours 1 weekend day, no visit second weekend day; visits in the residential home	No change
1 to 2 ½ years	2 hours per day, 2 days per week if custodial parent works or 3 days per week if custodial parent doesn't work; 5 hours one weekend day, no visit second weekend day in the custodial home until 2 years and then in the noncustodial home	No change
2 ½ to 5 years	2 hours per day, 2 days per week; 7 hours 1 weekend day at noncustodial parent's home; between 4 and 5 years old, depending on child's temperament, 1 overnight per weekend every other weekend, plus one or two 2-hour visits per week can be phased in	Start with 2 days and 1 overnight working toward 2 overnights by 5 years old, 4 times a year
6 to 8 years	Phase in two overnights every other weekend plus one or two 2-hour visits per week	Start with three 4-day overnights per year working toward 1 week winter or spring holiday and one 1-week plus one 2-week summer vacation

continues

195

continued

Age	Time with Noncustodial Parent	Vacation Time
9 to 12 years	Every other weekend (or if parents live close, 3-day weekend) plus 1 midweek visit; community contact should be maintained	Share holidays equally; child may spend up to 4 weeks in one block in the summer toward the later part of this period
13 to 18 years	Schedule can be worked out with children's input; home base with specific evenings, weekends, and activities at the other home must be scheduled for predictability; or equal basis with each parent	Depending on child's summer plans, time with each parent should be divided equally up to 2 weeks in each residence; children's input should have easy access to school, involvement from both peers, extra-curricular, and community homes

If at First You Don't Succeed ...

Alice and Dan agreed their marriage had reached an impasse. When they decided to end it, they were both in the same place. They had a 6-year-old son, Jake, and a 10-year-old daughter, Allison. Alice and Dan made an appointment with a child therapist recommended to them by their marriage counselor. The therapist was experienced in working with children from divorced families, so she was able to provide guidance to Alice and Dan in working out a time-sharing arrangement. Because the parents seemed to get along well, she recommended that they be open-minded about how the plan was working. If it didn't work, she advised, they should meet with her again to modify the plan.

Alice and Dan agreed. They decided that the children would live with Alice during the week but have dinner with Dan twice during the week. At first, Allison and Jake would live with their father from Saturday morning until Sunday evening. After three months, Friday night at Dad's was to be phased in for Allison, but because Jake was still very young, he wouldn't begin sleeping over on Friday nights for another eight months. Allison and Jake liked this arrangement, and there was no need to change.

Arnold and Melissa weren't as lucky. They had one daughter, Nicole, age four. Arnold wanted Nicole to live with him every other weekend from Friday night until Sunday night. Melissa agreed, but Nicole did not do well with that schedule. She didn't want to leave her mother and would cry incessantly when her father came to pick her up.

Even after she spent some time with her father, she was moody and complained that she missed her mother. Bedtime was even worse. Arnold and Melissa tried a few more weekends with this schedule, but Nicole did not feel more comfortable. Arnold agreed to wait a few months and then start with one overnight for a while until Nicole got used to being away from her mother and then work up to the entire weekend when Nicole turned six.

Michael and Anita had a teenage boy, John, who was not happy about the divorce. After his parents told him they were separating, John withdrew from both of them in sadness and anger. He just wanted to hang out with his friends and even arranged to stay at his best friend's house every chance he got. Michael and Anita had worked out a schedule where John would live with Michael for two weeks and then Anita for two weeks, but John didn't like the schedule. At first, Michael insisted that John follow the schedule to the letter, but John would not budge.

Michael and Anita consulted an experienced therapist who worked with divorcing families. He suggested that John be included in the decision-making process about where he wanted to live. Michael and Anita talked with John, who by now was getting used to the idea that his parents weren't going to be together any more. John said he wanted to stay mostly in the house where he had grown up, but that he would see his dad on the weekends, as long as he could also hang out with his friends. Michael and Anita agreed to this, and John's new lifestyle eventually became routine.

Silver Linings

According to Dr. Janet Johnston of the Center for the Family in Transition, if a verbal 6-year-old expresses a clear preference about the schedule, parents should try to accommodate those wishes with these caveats: Make sure the child is not just trying to please a parent, and don't let him know it was his idea! Children of this age can't handle the power of making the decision themselves. It's too frightening. Parents should listen to children from ages 9 through 12 and their views should be given consideration. By the time children are teenagers, they can be given more say in determining their visitation schedule, but it is up to the parents to make the final decision.

Keeping the Joy in Holidays Despite the Divorce

Sharing time with the children during vacation can be worked out equitably or it can be fraught with emotion. If both parents follow the same religion, inevitably, no one will want to pass up Christmas, Easter, Rosh Hashanah, or Passover. These are precious times of the year, bound up with lifelong memories, and you'll want to be with your children on these occasions most of all.

Harrison and Susan managed to work things out. They agreed to alternate Christmas Day and Christmas Eve each year. That way, each parent could share gift-giving and a Christmas tree with their children. The kids didn't mind; they got twice as many presents!

David and Vivian shared the Jewish holidays by splitting them up and alternating them. The parent who was not with children for Rosh Hashanah was with them on Yom Kippur. Hanukkah was divided in half, as was Passover. All other holidays were divided up and alternated.

Marion and Will were not very religious, so for them, sharing school vacations was more important than celebrating the religious holidays that fell into those school breaks. They each took one school break and alternated winter and spring break each year.

Long-Distance Parenting

If, for some reason, one parent moves to another state or even another country, continual contact with children can still occur. Steve moved from New York to Dallas because of a job opportunity he couldn't pass up. But he still wanted to stay close to his children, Tim, 5, and Alex, 9. Steve called them every night before they went to bed. He also wrote a letter once a week and sent pictures of his new neighborhood. He even sent a video of himself taken by a friend. Steve also came up with some clever ideas for relating to his children while he was not with them. He told them to pick a television program they liked, and he would watch it at the same time. That night, they would talk about the show. He sent puzzles and riddles that the children could finish, and he would ask them how they did. Every six weeks, Steve spent a four-day weekend with Tim and Alex in their town. He also alternated school holidays with his ex-wife, Sharon. In this way, Tim and Alex maintained a pretty close relationship with their dad, even though he lived a couple of thousand miles away.

Managing Visitation in High-Conflict Situations

Evan: I can't take it anymore! Every time I get ready to go over to my dad's, Mom tells me to make sure to tell Dad he owes her two months' support! Then, Dad tells me to bring a message to my mom that he's paying her too much! I just feel like running away from both of them.

Kate: I know what you mean. I can't stand the way my dad always asks me who Mom's been seeing. Then, he asks me to find out more about her dates and tell him.

Matthew: My mom and dad can't keep from making snide remarks to each other when my dad comes to pick me up. Why was I so unlucky to get parents who hate each other?

Amy: I always feel pressured to take sides. Why don't they understand I need and love both of them? I don't want to side with one against the other!

Divorce is generally born of conflict. But when extreme conflict persists even after the couple has parted ways, the children of that marriage may find it difficult, if not impossible, to heal. Indeed, when parents cannot put their mutual anger aside and when they sweep their young children into the conflict, they have ceased to protect those children and irreparable damage may result.

These children of high-conflict divorce, torn between the two most important people in their lives, are often emotionally damaged by the struggle. According to psychologists, such children are often depressed and aggressive. Later, as adults, they will usually have difficulty with intimate relationships. They are far more likely to divorce than adults who come from intact families or even divorced families at peace.

Because open conflict is most likely to take place at the time the children go from one home to the other, many psychologists specializing in divorced families now recommend that the number of transition times be reduced in high-conflict situations. Here are some specific recommendations for visitation schedules when open warfare rages:

➤ **For moderate conflict:** When parents function well on their own but fight when they are in contact with their ex-spouse, psychologists Mitchell Baris and Carla Garrity note that other creative solutions are necessary. Some of these may be minimizing transitions—packaging visitation into one block per week. For very young children, the midweek visits might be eliminated. For older children, the visits might be consolidated each week. These may need to be handled by a neutral third party or take place in neutral places.

➤ **For moderately severe conflict:** When there is constant litigation and sometimes even physical threats or abuse between parents, children suffer extreme emotional scars. In such cases, Baris and Garrity recommend caution. Mental health evaluation is mandatory, and supervised visitation may be recommended if the safety of a child is a concern.

➤ **For severe conflict:** In this situation, when children are at immediate risk of physical or sexual abuse, visitation should be supervised and a full mental health evaluation conducted.

Children of divorce are often hit hardest, even when they seem sanguine on the outside. Parents who fail to notice the warning signs of a child in emotional trouble will pay a high price later. When does your child need help? New York psychologist Michelle Gersten, Ph.D., provides the following guidelines:

➤ **Maladaptive personality changes of extreme intensity or duration:** If your child has changed in any major way since the separation, trouble may be afoot. Characteristics to examine include inattentiveness, overactivity, aggression, shyness, or fearfulness. Maladaptive behaviors, of course, should set off the alarms. Remember, all children involved in divorce will show minor difficulties, including eating and sleeping problems. But if these symptoms are short-lived, you need not be concerned. On the other hand, if a school-aged child who had healthy relations with her peers starts withdrawing from social activities, be on the lookout for trouble.

➤ **Regression:** If your child has regressed to behaviors from earlier stages of development, seek psychotherapy. Examples might include a 4-year-old who now has frequent accidents, despite successful toilet training previously, or an 8-year-old who speaks in baby talk.

➤ **Extreme parental conflict:** If the parents continue to fight in front of the child after the initial breakup, therapy may be required. If one parent is manipulative or continually undermines the other, psychotherapy for the child is indicated as well. In one case, a mother consistently failed to inform the father of plans and then told the child the father had simply failed to show. The father, in turn, told the child that the mother "just forgot." The stress of the situation was arduous for the 5-year-old boy, who became confused about his alliances and ultimately needed therapy to successfully relate to his mom and his dad.

The Role of the Parenting Coordinator

Researchers and practitioners such as Mitchell Baris, Carla Garrity, and Janet Johnston, who work with families in high-conflict divorce situations, have developed the concept of the *parenting coordinator*. The parenting coordinator, who must be familiar with family law, conflict resolution, mediation, family therapy, and child development, is not a mediator or a therapist. Instead, this third party works within the confines of the divorce decree to settle disagreements between parents as they pertain to the children. The parenting coordinator may report regularly to the court. He can speak to the children's therapist and to the court. The therapist, however, is protected from litigation so that she can work with the children without being pressured or manipulated by either parent.

The parenting coordinator can also be a facilitator between parents in high conflict. If one parent wants to send something to the children, he or she can send it to the parenting coordinator to make sure that the children receive it. The parenting coordinator may at times determine when the children are ready for increased visitation, which may have been shortened or curtailed because of the conflict. The parenting coordinator maps out a detailed parenting plan, which is agreed to by all parties. The more detailed the plan, the less room for conflict.

Some points covered in the parenting plan include

1. **Visitation plan**   Sets a drop-off and pick-up time and place, designates a means for transporting children between households, institutes a set plan for handling a refusal to visit, and decides who is responsible when children are sick.

2. **Schedule change requests**   A set protocol for trading days or making last-minute changes.

3. **Phone calls**   Should they be regulated? Should children be able to initiate phone calls in private at any time?

4. **Toys and belongings**   Provides guidelines for moving things between two households.

5. **Boundaries or rules at other household** Neither parent can tell the other parent what rules to set; if abuse is suspected or concerns about parental judgment persist, the parenting coordinator must be contacted.

6. **Pets**   Establishes rules for moving them back and forth between homes with the children.

Divorce Dictionary

Parenting coordinator: A person, perhaps a psychologist familiar with matrimonial law, who works with both parents to iron out any problems that may arise after the divorce decree is in effect. The parenting coordinator is a relatively new concept. Some judges are using the concept for post-divorce families. In some places, parents voluntarily choose to enlist the aid of a parenting coordinator.

Children of divorce have strong feelings and thoughts about how children should be treated by their parents. A word to the wise—heed the wisdom of the children.

Here are some recommendations to parents from veteran children of divorce:

1. Recognize that we love and need both parents.

2. Don't turn us into messengers. Mom and Dad should talk to each other directly.

3. Don't say bad things about our other parent.

4. Don't grill us about what is going on at our other parent's home.

5. Don't ask us to take sides.

6. Don't make us feel as if we're being disloyal to you if we enjoy being with our other parent.

7. If you have something angry to say to our other parent, don't say it around us.

8. Don't purposely forget important clothing or gear when we are going to our other parent's place.

How your children fare in the aftermath of divorce in large part depends on the degree of sensitivity the parents have towards the needs of their children. If parents put their children's needs first and are able to take a step back from their own emotional turmoil, the stress on their children will be greatly reduced. It's difficult enough for children to deal with the division of their family, much less their own lifestyle changes. Any help you can give will go a long way.

The Least You Need to Know

➤ One of the most difficult lifestyle changes children undergo as a result of their parents' divorce is moving back and forth between homes instead of living securely in one stable environment.

➤ Establish a polite business relationship with the other parent. Share important information about the children's academic, social, and health news.

➤ Visitation schedules should take the age and temperament of the children into account. The schedule should provide regular and predictable times for the children to be with each parent.

➤ Monitor your children's progress with the visitation schedule. If they are not adjusting, modify the schedule.

➤ If you and your ex-spouse cannot stop fighting, have a third-party professional—a parenting coordinator—act as an intermediary and modify the visitation schedule as needed.

➤ Never put your children in the middle of the fighting. Don't ask them to ally with you against their other parent.

Chapter 20

Two Parents, Two Homes

In This Chapter

➤ What transitions look like through the eyes of your children

➤ Coping skills for children making the transition

➤ Making a smooth exchange

➤ How your attitude can help your children

➤ Steps for reducing conflict

➤ What to do if your children refuse to go

Through the Eyes of a Child

Jimmy: I hate going back and forth. I feel like a Ping-Pong ball. I just want to stay in one place, in my own room with my own things.

Anna: I'm glad I get to spend time with my Dad *and* with my Mom. It's a hassle to go back and forth, but it's more important to me to see both my parents.

Transitions are difficult for children, especially young children. (This is also true for many adults, depending on their temperament.) Try to remember what it feels like when you first go on vacation and you're in a new hotel room. You may have mixed feelings—a little excitement along with some unease because you're in a new place. Remember what it feels like when you stay at a friend's house; there's the strange bed and bathroom, the likes and dislikes of the individual you're visiting, the different routines. The first night you might feel uncomfortable. You miss your own bed, your carpet, your morning coffee; you long to be free to look really grungy until you've completed your morning routine. Imagine this scenario, and you will begin to understand what your child's back-and-forth experience is like.

To your advantage, you are an adult with an adult's perspective. Children, on the other hand, have little life experience and also often experience time differently. What might be just a weekend to you feels more like a month to a child. What might be a two-week summer vacation to you seems like a lifetime to a child.

Children can have difficulty thinking about leaving their custodial parent and their primary home even for the weekend. Although your children love their other parent, the transition might still be hard because it is a major change in your children's reality. For children, every reunion is also a separation; every transition is bittersweet. Every "hello" is also a "goodbye."

If you are the noncustodial parent, when your children get adjusted to being at your home, it might be difficult to think about leaving you again, even though they're glad to see their custodial parent.

For a time after returning to their original home, there is another adjustment period. They might miss the parent they just left and act rebellious, be unusually quiet, or just want to be alone for a while. Each "new" parent should give the children time to adjust and not get overly concerned with behaviors that seem unusual during this period. Be sensitive to your children. Read a book or do some other quiet activity with them. If they seem to need some space, finish what you were doing before they came back. In time, things will get back to normal.

Silver Linings

A child will probably get more one-on-one attention from his parents after the divorce than before the divorce. The working parent who did not spend much time with the children pre-separation might now spend much more time with them. The custodial parent may feel that this is just a ploy to reduce child support (more time spent might reduce support), but this may be the best news for the children. The noncustodial parent will usually bend over backwards to be with the children at the appointed times.

Transitional Tool Kit

Every child has a different temperament and therefore handles transitions more or less easily. Going off to school, camp, or to a friend's house are other examples of transitions that might be difficult for some children. As in all these situations, the more routine, the better. This is especially true for very young children.

To find ways to help your children detach from one home and ease into their new environment, think about some of the things that would make *you* more comfortable if you had to uproot yourself regularly.

Ashley always brings her favorite slippers and a book she's been reading when she travels. Dave takes his laptop and works on the same projects wherever he goes. Karen has a traveling bag that always has the same travel items, so when she opens it up, she's got her home away from home.

To get you started thinking about things you do to feel comfortable when traveling or away from home, make a list of your own.

Six Strategies for Helping Your Kids with Change

Here are some ideas for helping your kids handle the transition from one parent to the other. You know your children best, so think hard about what makes sense for your family:

1. Make a calendar with your children. The calendar should include the highlights of their schedule, including all major activities and especially those times when they will be with the other parent.

2. Remind your children that they are leaving the day prior to the visit.

3. Depending on the age of your children, help them pack their traveling bags the day before they leave. If they are school-aged, make sure that their homework is included. Have a very young child choose a cute traveling bag that is fun. His input into this symbol of his transition will help give him a feeling of involvement and control.

4. Anything that they can keep at their other home (toothbrush, comb, pajamas, and so on) to ease the packing and make them feel more comfortable when they are with the other parent will help.

5. For very young children, a traveling bear or other stuffed toy can help provide a sense of security. If your child expresses worry that his bear might be left behind, get a few traveling friends that can stay behind or be easily replaced.

6. A picture of the absent parent can accompany the child.

Making the Exchange Smoothly

If you and your spouse or ex-spouse have a working relationship, the transition from one home to the other is easier on both the parents and the children. Children sense their parents' tacit approval and take with them the good wishes of the parent they are leaving. Even though the sudden change is stressful, knowing that the parent being left supports the departure and will be fine during the absence gives the children the foundation they need to cope.

Seeing Your Ex as Your Child's Parent

To lessen the uncomfortable feelings you might have when you face your ex-spouse during the exchange, see him or her through your children's eyes. Keep your feelings about your *ex-spouse* separate from those you have about your *children's parent*. This technique will help keep your attitude positive during the exchange, which in turn will allow your children to feel okay about leaving you. And you really want your children to feel okay about leaving you. (Don't worry; they'll come back!)

If you're having a hard time being pleasant with your ex in front of the children, use the time-tested psychological technique of imaging. In the sci-fi flick *Village of the Damned*, the hero protected the earth from psychic extraterrestrials by imagining a brick wall while a time-bomb he devised ticked away. Although it was hard for him to sustain the image of the wall, he was able to do so long enough for the bomb to blow up the aliens. In the same way, you can use imaging to view your ex-spouse as your children's parent, rather than the Nazi in *Sophie's Choice* (as long as we're talking about movies).

Shielding Your Children from Conflict

If the divorce has embittered you and your ex-spouse, you must be especially vigilant about keeping your children out of the storm. Protect your children from conflict at all costs. If you think you're delivering your children to the enemy, they will sense your tension. Glares and averted eyes are missed—and just barely—*only* by the toddler.

Follow these 16 steps for reducing parental conflict:

1. Communicate only when necessary.
2. Keep a mental image of your spouse as your children's parent.
3. Think of your parenting relationship as a business relationship.
4. Don't get hooked into old patterns of fighting or being goaded into a nasty retort.
5. Use clear and simple language without taking a judgmental or accusatory stance.
6. Make the conversation as brief as possible.
7. End any communication that looks as if it might escalate into a shouting match.

8. When face-to-face with your ex-spouse during your children's transition from one home to the other, bury your feelings and exchange polite greetings. Keep it short.

9. Don't discuss arrangements or other business with your ex-spouse during transitions.

10. Turn the other cheek to any sarcastic or accusatory comments. Excuse yourself as quickly and politely as possible.

11. Don't exchange checks and money in front of your children.

12. Don't use children as messengers or delivery people.

13. Have a positive attitude.

14. Don't discuss anything with your spouse about the divorce at the exchange, including schedule changes.

15. Give a hug and a kiss goodbye to your children; wish them a good time.

16. Smile. A happy parent makes for secure children.

Red Alert

If tension is very high, as it might be at the beginning of the separation, it is better to have a third party make the exchange or have one parent drop off the children at school or an after-school activity and the other parent pick them up.

Children Who Fight Visitation

In some cases, children will refuse to leave to be with the noncustodial parent. There are several reasons why this might happen:

1. A parent is not tuned into the children's interests or is not actively involved with the children during their time together.

2. Your children may be very young and anxious about separation from the parent who does the majority of caretaking.

3. Open conflict is causing the children to appear to be aligned temporarily with one parent.

4. In rare cases, there may be child abuse (which we discuss a little later in the chapter).

If your children don't want to leave their primary home to be with their other parent, having a good heart-to-heart is the first step. The problem may be one that can be easily resolved, such as more attention given the children by the noncustodial parent, a change in discipline style, or having more toys or other entertainment.

Either or both parents may unknowingly be causing the children's refusal to go. Following are two checklists, one for the custodial parent and the other for the non-custodial parent. Be honest. You're the only one looking at this.

Custodial Parent Q&A

1. I have done my best to encourage my children's visits with their other parent.
   ____Yes ____No

2. I do not give double messages to my children about seeing their other parent.
   ____Yes ____No

3. I make sure my children know that, although I miss them, I know they will be well taken care of. ____Yes ____No

4. I tell my children I am fine when they're away. ____Yes ____No

5. I make sure to pack everything my children need so their time with their other parent goes smoothly. ____Yes ____No

Noncustodial Parent Q&A

1. I understand it takes a while for my children to adjust to different surroundings, household rules, and customs. I don't pressure them to forget about their other parent when they're with me. ____Yes ____No

2. I make a mental note if, after a reasonable amount of time with me, my children are not adjusting. ____Yes ____No

3. I allow my children to speak to their other parent on the phone. ____Yes ____No

4. I don't do my work when my children are with me and are awake.
   ____Yes ____No

5. To stay involved with my children, I participate as much as possible in activities that center on *their* lives (Little League, dance class, play dates, and so on) instead of dragging them to things that are important to *me* but of no interest to them.
   ____Yes ____No

Go with the Flow

Sara, who was 12 years old, called her father to tell him that she didn't want to go to his house that weekend. She said her girlfriends were having a slumber party, and she didn't want to miss it. Her father insisted that she not go to the party because that was his time to be with her.

This wasn't the first time Sara had to miss a social event because that was her weekend to see her father. She felt misunderstood and resented her father for keeping her from her friends. Ultimately, she started feeling as if she didn't want to be with him at all.

If her father and mother had been more flexible with the visitation schedule, on the other hand, Sara could have had her social life and would have felt that her father really understood and cared about her emotional and social needs.

Six months after his parents divorced, nine-year-old Allen began refusing to go to his father's place for the weekend. When asked on several occasions, he wouldn't say why. Finally, he admitted that he was bored because his father would spend most of his time finishing reports for work, and Allen had no one to play with. When Allen opened up about his feelings, his father made sure to do his work after Allen went to sleep and devoted his time to Allen. After that, Allen looked forward to his weekends with his dad.

What's your scenario? If your children are resisting visitation, scrutinize the situation. Perhaps a simple change will turn things around for you, too.

The Anxiety of Transition for the Littlest Children

Refusal to leave the custodial parent is most common in very young children because they are too young to carry a mental image of the parent to whom they are most attached (usually their mother) and fear abandonment.

For these young children, the transition from one parent to the other can set off anxiety about safety and survival. According to Janet Johnston, a foremost researcher in children and high-conflict divorce, children up to six years old may continue to have difficulty if they have had "repeated distressing separations and maintain an anxious attachment to the parent. It is also possible that children under the ages of four or five do not have a sufficient understanding of the concept of time and, for this reason, are confused about the particular visitation schedule. Consequently, they are anxious about when they will be reunited with the primary or custodial parent."

If you and your ex-spouse get along, and your children are very young, the cause of your children's refusal to leave their residential home is likely normal, age-related separation anxiety. The noncustodial parent's recognition of this and willingness to work with the custodial parent to ease his or her children's anxiety will go a long way toward building trust and bonding with that parent. Insensitivity on the part of the noncustodial parent, on the other hand, can result in continual resistance to seeing him (or her) and the eventual failure of that children-parent relationship.

When a Parent Is Maligned

If you think your ex has begun to wage a campaign against you, suggest that your children see a mental health professional to aid their adjustment to visitation. If your ex refuses to seek help, you might be justified in seeing your attorney to request that the court mandate a mental health intervention. The problem is complex. This situation calls for psychological help for the entire family.

Silver Linings

If you have a good relationship with your children, they're not going to buy the hard line that you're awful if you're really not. If you've been a caring parent, the children know it no matter what your ex-spouse says. As long as you're totally tuned in to your children, empathetic with their emotional needs, and helping to build their self-esteem, the children can't be alienated from you by your ex. If you think your children are being "brainwashed," you might discuss your suspicions calmly with them. You'll get a better feel for the true situation at their other home, and you'll be able to address any confusion on your children's parts.

If you are the custodial parent in a heavily litigated case and your children refuse to visit their other parent, make sure that you are not bad-mouthing your ex-spouse in front of your children or sending them negative messages. If you want what's best for your children, you must put aside your feelings toward your ex-spouse and encourage your children to develop or maintain a relationship with their other parent. If your children lose their other parent, their self-esteem will take a nose-dive, and they'll suffer feelings of abandonment—even if it now seems that they don't want to be with that parent.

Red Alert

Participating in open conflict—whether it is screaming at each other or making snide remarks—is the single most damaging thing you can do to your children. Although you have no control over your ex, you do have control over yourself. Don't get dragged into a fight. Stay cool.

Rebecca's parents separated because her father was seeing another woman. Rebecca was eight years old when her father moved out. Her mother was in shock. When the shock wore off, her mother was filled with rage. She did not hide her feelings from Rebecca. Instead, she told Rebecca that her father couldn't be trusted and that he was insensitive and even cruel.

Rebecca couldn't bear to see her mother so distressed. She aligned herself with her mother against her father. Even though she had been close to her father before the divorce, her angry feelings prevented her from relating to him. She didn't even want to see him.

Rebecca's father accused her mother of brainwashing Rebecca against him. He went to court to try to gain custody. The litigation was heated and drawn out. Rebecca suffered terribly from the fighting and the insecurity of not knowing where she would be living. She continued to refuse to see her father.

Eventually, her father, who lost the custody battle, became less and less interested in fighting Rebecca's rejections of him. He and his girlfriend married and started a family of their own. As far as Rebecca was concerned, he found it easiest to just drift away.

What could Rebecca's father have done in this situation instead of giving up? For one thing, he might have realized that despite her current feelings, Rebecca needed his involvement to have healthy and happy relationships as an adult. Given this realization, he might have stayed around for the long haul. He could have been careful to let Rebecca know the door was always open for her. For instance, he might have continued to send regular postcards or letters, even if Rebecca did not respond. If she was like most children in this situation, she would have asked to see him again—in her own time.

When your ex maligns you to your child, it puts your relationship at risk. Yet psychologists note that a hurt, angry ex-spouse cannot always control the expression of powerful, negative emotions. Moreover, they may be unaware of just how much they are damaging the child they love.

How do you handle this situation without drawing the child into the conflict more than he or she already is? According to psychologist Karen Breunig, co-author of *Through the Eyes of a Child,* "the best thing that I would advise is to appeal to the better graces of the offending parent. Explain how damaging this is for the child since the child identifies with *both* parents." It might also be useful for the offending parent to seek therapy.

If your ex remains closed to such suggestions, Breunig says you should discuss the situation with your child. Explain that you are going to work the situation out with the other parent and, if appropriate, assure the child that the statements made about you are not true. "Leave the lines of communication open so that your child can feel comfortable about checking these accusations with you, personally," says Breunig.

"Whatever you do," she concludes, "do not fight fire with fire. You will just be turning up the flames on your kid."

If You Suspect Abuse

If your children seem fearful or refuse to visit the other parent on a regular basis, you might have a genuine concern about safety and even abuse. If this is the case, speak to your lawyer and a mental health professional before making any accusations to your ex-spouse.

The courts have been inundated with child abuse charges in divorce cases. The judges are leery of the parent who makes such charges if there is no hard evidence. False allegations can even result in a change of custody.

On the other hand, if your children are victims of abuse, there must be immediate intervention, generally in the form of supervised visitation. Despite the fact that judges frown on the accuser, statistics reveal about half of abuse charges turn out to be true.

If you feel stuck between a rock and a hard place, you are. Make certain that you have grounds for your belief before you make any accusations against your ex-spouse.

The Least You Need to Know

➤ Children who switch households regularly—different place, different people, different rules—carry a heavy burden. It takes time for them to adjust.

➤ Prepare your children well in advance of leaving your residence.

➤ Check your attitude! Your children need a relationship with both parents.

➤ Never engage in conflict with your ex-spouse in front of your children.

➤ If your children refuse to see their other parent, speak to your children if they're old enough. If necessary, consult with a mental health professional. If you are on good terms with your ex, discuss the problem with him or her. If you are at war, talk to your lawyer.

Single Parenting

After the shock of your divorce has dulled ever so slightly, you face the realization that you and your children will be a slightly smaller family. Whether your children are living primarily with you, or whether you live with them three days each week or every other weekend with midweek visits, you will still be experiencing your family with one less member—the other parent. This definitely takes a bit of getting used to. In time, new patterns of living will start to feel normal, and the fresh wounds of the family's division will begin to heal for everyone.

A New Beginning: Just You and the Kids

At first, being a single parent might seem overwhelming. Remember how you felt when your first child was born? You were scared but excited. You didn't know what to expect. You were exhausted and awed by your responsibility for this new life. Yet you rose to the occasion.

Single parenting is once again a time for reorientation. This time, it's just you and the kids.

If You Are the Custodial Parent

If you are the *custodial parent*, you will be spending more time than your ex-spouse does getting the kids off to school; buying their clothes; and taking them to the doctor and dentist, after-school activities, and friends' houses. But, hey, weren't you doing all that before?

Divorce Dictionary

Custodial parent: The parent with whom the children live most of the time and who has the unilateral right to make decisions concerning the children without having to consult the other parent. Even in situations where sole custody exists, the other parent may have to be consulted before incurring major expenses, such as college or health-care, for which that parent may be responsible.

What's really different for you now? There are some differences with regard to the children. You will not have backup for discipline. You might be the one helping the kids with their homework all the time. If you haven't so far, you will be the one pitching them balls or shooting baskets with them after school. You will be alone with them at dinner time.

With the exception of the last item, this is not all bad. Your relationship with your children will get even closer than before, when you might have shunted them off to their other parent to play his or her role as "mother" or "father." Now, you can explore the other world of parenting.

"But when will I get a break?" you might ask. Your break comes when your kids are with their other parent. That's a nice, solid break. Enjoy it!

Eat, Drink, and Be Merry

It will take some adjustment to having meals with one parent missing. Not only will it remind you of your new marital state, but, after a while, you might crave the company of other adults. What to do? Invite friends or neighbors over for dinner once or twice a week. Take your children out to restaurants so that you can be surrounded by people, or just enjoy catching up with your kids' daily activities. Don't park them in front of the TV while they're eating. Have your meals together. That will give all of you a stronger sense of family.

Working Single Parents and the "Latch-Key" Kids

Divorce, out of necessity, adds to the single-parent workforce. Custodial parents who used to stay home to raise the children now usually have to get a job. This leads to the increase in the number of "latch-key kids"—children who come home from school to an empty home. Of course, the number of families in which both parents work has increased, so it is not just the children of single parents who let themselves into the house or apartment to fend for themselves until a parent gets home. There have been whole books written on this phenomenon and its impact on society. We don't have the space for such analysis here, but would like to present some basic guidelines:

➤ Common sense dictates that very young children should never be left alone. Beyond the obvious danger, it's illegal.

➤ Many states allow children of 11 and older to stay home alone, but laws differ from state to state. If you are unsure of the laws in your area, contact your local District Attorney's office.

➤ Even if leaving your child home alone is legal, you must make sure the circumstances are secure. Do you live in an apartment building with a doorman the children can call on should there be a problem? Are there adult neighbors your children may contact? As a general rule, children need the security and experience of an adult nearby through the early teen years, especially if the parent will be away for an extended period of time.

➤ Finally, if you plan to leave your older children home alone, make sure they are armed with emergency phone numbers and strategies for dealing with an array of situations, from physical injury to prank phone calls.

An Issue of Discipline

Studies have shown that children do best with firm discipline combined with a lot of communication and affection. You may be tempted to overindulge your children to make up for the pain they are going through because of your divorce. This approach has been shown to have the worst outcome for children. Even a very strict, authoritarian approach (no hitting, please!) seems to help children and teenagers more than a permissive style. At this unsettled time, children need boundaries and limits combined with a lot of patience and understanding.

> **You Can Do It!**
>
> As an experienced parent, you have probably checked out the range of organized activities available to your child during after-school hours. If you haven't found anything that works, be sure to check the local Y or Boys and Girls Clubs, your church or synagogue, and your child's school, which may well offer enrichment activities, intramural sports, or clubs. For older children, volunteer activities organized by youth organizations can be ideal.

Caring for Yourself

Taking care of your own needs is one of the most important things you can do to support your kids. If you are an unhappy parent, it will have a major impact on your children. They look to you for strength and support. It's frightening to children of any age to see a parent lost to depression and thus removed from them emotionally; for many, the situation provokes anxious feelings of losing that parent as well, something especially painful at the time of divorce. To help them, help yourself:

➤ Get enough rest and exercise, and eat healthy.

➤ Put yourself in places where you can meet new people.

➤ Get busy with renovating your new life; start with renovating your house or apartment!

➤ Take an adult education class.

➤ If necessary, go into psychotherapy for a while.

As the custodial parent, you have a lot on your plate. As long as your ex-spouse is in the picture, however, you are not entirely alone in raising your children.

Silver Linings

If you and your spouse have been battling it out for custody and visitation, be grateful now that the other spouse wants to be active in your children's lives. While you might fear the times when your children are away from you and you are denied access to them, you will come to realize that the time they spend with their other parent gives you a much-needed break, allows your children to have both parents in their lives, and gives you help with the monumental tasks of parenting. After the war is over and custody is finally determined, we've actually heard some custodial parents admit that they've been "sentenced to sole custody."

If You Are the Noncustodial Parent

The noncustodial parent will also be facing new challenges. Much of what is true for the custodial parent is also true for the noncustodial parent. The good news is that you have time for entertainment and your errands when the kids are not around. Then, when the kids are with you, you can really devote that solid block of time to them. If you used to give short shrift to your children because you were too tired when you came home from work, you might not have developed the kind of fulfilling relationship you can now enjoy.

The noncustodial parent, often the dad, must make a special effort to maintain a close and loving relationship with children. Jack Feuer, a journalist, a divorced father, and the author of several books for divorced dads, has some winning strategies for forging bonds when a parent is not in daily contact with the kids:

➤ Put a phone line in his or her room so you can call without going through your ex-spouse.

➤ Send them photos of your time together.

➤ Volunteer to coach your child's youth sports team.

➤ Baby-sit when your spouse must go out.

➤ Avoid the "Disney Dad" syndrome—the tendency of noncustodial dads to make every second special. These fathers take them places, buy them things, and make the visit into one big playtime, Feuer says. Yet children want everything to be normal, and you must establish a normal post-divorce life with your child.

➤ Share discipline with your spouse. Noncustodial dads are often reluctant to share in the discipline, Feuer notes. But it is important that dads participate in the discipline process and that they develop, with their ex-spouse, a style of discipline that is consistent in both homes. "My son goes to bed 30 minutes later on school nights at my house than he does at his mom's," says Feuer, "but if he misbehaves at school, the punishment is the same at both houses. And if she says he cannot see videos because he misbehaved at school, he does not see them at my house, either."

➤ Give your children a sense of possibilities, establish horizons, and teach values.

➤ Come to terms with your divorce so you don't communicate feelings of anger to your children. If you are having trouble dealing with your emotions, seek counseling. "Because many men do not know how to experience strong emotions when they feel them," Feuer says, "they might have the impulse to flee, removing themselves from the emotional lives of their children in the process." Because this is the worst mistake a divorced father can make, Feuer suggests therapy as a viable alternative.

➤ Treat your ex-wife as a business partner. "Be civil and courteous," Feuer says. "The research on the impact of divorce on children is often ambiguous, but there is one thing on which everyone agrees: The degree of hostility and amount of conflict between parents has a direct impact on how children will grow up. Do not ever fight with your ex-wife in front of the kids for any reason."

You Can Do It!

Spending quality time with your children is the greatest gift you can give them. Communicating in a genuine way—really listening to them—will not only solidify your relationship, but also will help them get through this tough time.

"Your job as a parent is the most important you will ever have," says Feuer, "and you must live up to your end of the responsibility. Be a dependable parenting partner, and remember, the kids come first."

Don't Overdo It

You've probably heard the cliché about "weekend dads" (or moms) who spoil their kids by entertaining them at expensive places and buying more toys and gifts than they could ever hope to see at their other parent's home. This is a mistake. Your children need *you*, not amusement parks, shows, toy stores, and other places that might assuage your guilt or show them what a great parent you are. Occasional trips are fine, but your children will appreciate "hanging out" time much more.

Your Enormous Responsibilities

What are your practical responsibilities as a noncustodial parent? You don't have to buy the clothes for your children, but if you can afford it (even if you are paying your ex-spouse support), it might be a good idea to have a spare outfit or two at your place. Some toys for the younger kids is a must. If you cook, do be the provider of home-cooked meals. If not, try to learn. If you can't see yourself in that role at all, or you think you're hopeless, then order in or go out.

Red Alert

It's best if both parents can agree on a single disciplinary policy. But the reality is often different. If you've punished or docked your children at your residence, don't expect the other parent to uphold your disciplinary measures at his or her home. Do continue with your punishment when your children return, if that's the deal.

Regarding discipline, the same is true at your home as for the primary residence: Firm discipline with a loving touch yields the best results.

What if your very young children are having a hard time being away from their custodial parent? If you can't comfort your small children after a reasonable amount of time, be flexible and hope your ex-spouse will be as well. Bring your children back and try again soon, maybe for a shorter time but more often. In the end, you will have earned your children's trust in you and you won't have risked their emotional well-being.

The Ultimate Balancing Act: Parenting, Work, and a Life of Your Own

Being a single parent is, indeed, a juggling act. If you have not been working, you will most likely have to revamp your entire world view and put major time and effort into developing your career. You will also need help with the kids when you aren't home. Depending on their ages and your financial situation, you might need a full- or part-time babysitter and day care or nursery school. For older children, if you can afford it, having someone at home for their arrival will give them a feeling of security. Even young teenagers—although they won't admit it—feel more at ease if they know someone is looking after them.

Especially if you have primary custody of your children, you'll have to shop whenever you have a spare moment and have dinner ready for your hungry brood. For both parents, spending time with your kids after dinner playing games, reading, and doing homework is the rewarding part of parenting. This is especially true for single parents, whose time with their children is limited to the hours and days that the children live with you.

You Need Friends, Too

Unless the reason for your divorce was that you had a new love in your life, at some point during the healing process you will be ready to meet new people. Dating again can be scary or exciting, depending on your temperament and state of mind and how badly you've been burned. (Read more about this in Chapter 26.) The question here is how to fit a social life into your busy schedule and how it will impact your children.

The best time to become socially active is when your kids are with their other parent. First, you will be free to be you, not your kids' parent. Second, your children will need time to think about your being romantically involved with another person.

The Importance of Optimism

We know you might not believe it, but eventually, you will get your life together. In our most optimistic moments, we love to point to Lori—a recently divorced friend of ours who has done an admirable job.

Lori, the mother of a 7-year-old boy, Ari, and a 10-year-old boy, Jesse, had recently divorced. Her main occupation had been raising her two sons, although she had begun a singing career before she had her first son. After the divorce, she decided to go back to music school so that she could become a teacher. She had some savings to live on but had to work part-time as well.

Red Alert

Children whose parents have divorced may be skittish about new romantic involvement for Mom and Dad. Many children fantasize that Mom and Dad will reconcile, or they might see your new "friend" as taking time away from them. Finally, if children become attached to your new friend and it doesn't work out, they will experience another loss. The bottom line: Never introduce a new romantic relationship to your children until you're ready to make a permanent commitment to that person.

Her children went to school on an early bus every morning. Lori had one class in the morning, did some shopping after the class, and went to her job selling designer eyewear. A classmate of hers agreed to be at her home at 3:00 p.m. when her children got home from school. When Lori got home, she made dinner, worked with her kids on their homework, and read to them before bed. After they were asleep, she did her own homework. Sometimes, she fell asleep before she put on her pajamas.

When Ari and Jesse were with their father, Lori did more school work, ran all her errands, and took in dinner and a movie with a friend. A year after the divorce, she forced herself to go on a date. She made it a point to fit one singles event into her schedule every month. She also joined a fitness club and worked out on her free weekends.

Lori is still single, but today, she's a success. Ari and Jesse, now in the 9th and 12th grades, are top students as well as athletes. They both have an abundance of friends. And Lori is a music teacher who feels pride in her children, her ability to earn a living, and her new circle of friends.

Needs Water and Sunlight: Nurturing Your Kids

Byron's daughter, six-year-old Michelle, lived with him three days each week, every other weekend, and one evening each week. Michelle was more important to him than any other part of his life. He was lucky to have a job as a bank teller, where he could be home at 5:30 p.m. every day with no take-home work. When he picked up Michelle on Friday evening, he always took her to her favorite Japanese restaurant. She could count on it. Michelle ordered the same dish, tempura, every time. When they got to Byron's home, it was time for Michelle's bath and a story. Before Michelle went to sleep, Byron would help her call her mother to wish her a good night.

The rest of the weekend was always spent on activities together both indoors and out. Sometimes, Byron would invite some friends of his who had children, and Michelle would play with them for a while. But mostly, because Byron's time with Michelle was precious to him, he was one-on-one with Michelle. On Monday, Byron took Michelle to her kindergarten class. Because he was still at work when she was finished, he had a standing arrangement with a neighbor's 17-year-old daughter to pick up Michelle and stay with her until he got home from work. Then, Byron cooked dinner and put Michelle to bed. The next morning, Byron took Michelle to school. After school, her mother picked up Michelle and took her home.

Whether you're the custodial or noncustodial parent, your children need nurturing. As single parents, both you and your ex-spouse have to be both mother and father when with your children. Each of you is responsible for the health and well-being of your children when they are with you—including giving hugs and kisses (number one on the list), goofing around, feeding them, making sure that they brush their teeth twice a day, and taking care of them when they're sick.

Once the wounds of the divorce process have healed and you have gotten used to the new family arrangement, everything will fall into place and become less overwhelming. More than half the anxiety you have felt during this trying time will disappear after the legal issues are settled. Working out your new daily life will become easier as time goes on, until it becomes routine. Then…who knows what new and exciting people and adventures await you.

The Least You Need to Know

➤ Single parenting is a challenge, but with good organization and support, you can make it a successful routine.

➤ Single parents are both mother and father to the children.

➤ The most successful disciplinary approach is firmness and consistency, with a lot of communication and affection.

➤ If you are dating, do so when you are not with your children. Don't introduce your new significant other to the children unless you are ready to make a commitment.

➤ To get the most out of your time with your children, focus on *them.* Do activities you both enjoy, take care of their physical needs, keep the communication lines open, and give them a lot of affection.

Redefining the Family

Children whose parents are divorced will, more likely than not, be living in both of their parents' homes. Children will be dealing with more than the usual number of authority figures, different lifestyles, different rules, and different personalities. Sometimes, one or both parents will remarry. They might marry someone who already has children. They might have another child with their new partner. For children, the impact of parents divided and remarried with new families is profound. At a minimum, the situation takes a lot of adjusting.

In the best of all worlds, the two families will be supportive and nurturing to the children, opening up new vistas of experience, providing more interaction, and adding significant people to the children's lives.

No matter how well-intentioned everyone is, some do's and don'ts can help the process of adjustment and integration.

Math for Kids of Divorce: When Two Is Less Than One (Home)

Children handle life better when they are faced with predictable situations and environments, although occasional disruptions are tolerated, and some stress is actually beneficial for children. Your children have been through, or are about to go through, a severe disruption in their lives—your divorce and the division of their family. Now, they need a period of calm and time to adjust to their new family rearrangement.

You Can Do It!

An intact family correctly defines the parents as the authority figures and last word in the house. If children are undergoing the split-up of their family, some of the reigns of decision making can be loosened: Listen to the children, and, within reason, try to accommodate their need to be emotionally at ease.

The goal is for the children to feel at home and comfortable whether they are with their mom or dad. The parent who moved out of the marital home should do everything possible to create another home for the children. Everyone needs his or her own space. A room of the children's own decorated with their input will give them a sense of home. Even if you can't afford an extra room, an area carved out of your one-room apartment will do.

Jack went to his local Home Depot after he moved out of the house in anticipation of his kids' first time at his new apartment. He bought three blue cardboard dressers that worked just fine for temporary furniture for his kids. He bought Winnie-the-Pooh wall stickers for Jeremy and Mickey Mouse wall stickers for Katie. He had already purchased bunk beds that would go in the room where they would sleep. A round night table and lamps to match the stickers were the finishing touch. Jack was handy, so he built shelves for books and toys. When the kids came over for the first time, they were thrilled to see their favorite characters on the walls. They all baked cookies together after dinner. After a call to their mom, Jack read them stories and put them to bed.

Helping Your Kids Accept Your New Spouse

What if, after you are divorced, you plan to marry someone who already has children? In this case, your children have to accept the fact that you and your ex-spouse will never be reunited, that you have a new spouse, and that they will have new stepbrothers or stepsisters. That is a lot to digest! Go slowly and proceed with caution.

Phasing in are the key words here. As we mentioned in Chapter 21, your children should not be introduced to your new partner until you have made a commitment to that person. Assuming that you have decided to remarry, it is now time to introduce your children to your prospective spouse.

Going to a neutral place, such as the movies, a restaurant, the playground, or an amusement park, might be the best way to ease into this difficult introduction. Telling your kids this person, whom they have never met, is going to be their stepparent is moving too fast. Let your kids gradually get to know your new partner over a period of time. When it feels right, open a discussion. Your kids might even initiate the discussion.

Don't expect them to welcome this new presence with open arms. All is not lost if their reaction continues to be negative for quite a while. Accepting your new partner will take time. The more relaxed you are about it, the easier it will be for your kids to adjust.

At some point after your children get to know your new partner, the time will be right to introduce his or her children to your children. You and your new partner can be the judge.

If you are the custodial parent and you have married someone with children whose primary residence is with their other parent, you are now the stepparent to those children, and you and your children will be welcoming those children to your home. If you are the noncustodial parent, you will be helping your children adjust to your new home, a new stepparent, and new stepbrothers and stepsisters.

Silver Linings

Take your time to carefully integrate the new addition(s) to your children's lives. Realize that from their perspective, they have not only witnessed the dissolution of the only family they have known, but are being asked to accept that a stranger is going to receive the love of their parent in lieu of their other parent. If you put yourself in your children's place, you will understand how to handle this difficult adjustment.

The Dynamics of the Stepfamily

There was a time when being part of a stepfamily set you apart. According to Jeannette Lofas of the Stepfamily Foundation, that is no longer the case. Instead, the "new family"—consisting of divorced parents, their new partners, and their children—make up some 70 percent of the population. Today, the stepfamily is the norm!

The statistics are jarring: Half of all children under age 13, or some 30 million youngsters, live with a biological parent and that parent's current significant other. These family systems, adds Lofas, fail at the rate of 66 percent.

How do these families work? "They cannot and will not function as an intact, or biologically connected, family," Lofas states. One reason is "the rejection of non-self tissue—rejection of non-blood. You are not my mother or father, yet you are where they should be, so I don't like you."

Another dynamic, she notes, includes the conflicting pulls of sex and blood. "In an intact family, the couple comes together and has the kid, and they are all going in the same direction. But in the stepfamily, those who are sexually involved—the couple—are torn between sex and blood. Who do I put first, my spouse or my child?" As a result, she notes, "the perception is often that the children are pulling the relationship apart," and very often, this is true.

Finally, children feel a conflict of loyalties. "If I love you, my stepmother, I can't love my mom. Therefore, I do not like you."

In this complex picture, where ex-spouses bad-mouth each other and feelings of guilt are high, everyone feels like an outsider, because, Lofas explains, "no one knows what their role or position is. Just when you think you found your seat, someone else is sitting in it. For instance, a 15-year-old girl might be used to sitting in the front seat of the car with Daddy, but when Daddy has a girlfriend, where should the girl sit? She will try to protect her territory."

You Can Do It!

You can't force a new stepparent or stepfamily down your kids' throats. Especially around this sensitive issue, pay attention to your children's cues—if they are subtle. (They may not be subtle at all!)

But Lofas, who was born into a stepfamily and also married into a stepfamily, sees hope. She imparts some of her most valuable tips:

➤ Go slowly. Learn to partner with a new husband and wife through the creation of structure and discipline and the accumulation of couple strength. For instance, when a man has parented alone, he might allow the kids to stay up late or order dinner in. The new wife might not feel these things are appropriate, but if she tries to change things, the stepchildren will simply ignore her. She can easily slip into the role of "the bad guy," even if she states her point of view as gently as possible.

➤ The stepfather or stepmother should not attempt to be parents to their stepchildren, even if the biological parent has died. Nor should they assume the role of friend. Instead, they should be seen as male or female head of household and a partner to the biological parent.

➤ The stepparent must not discipline on his or her own without the support of the biological parent. To do so always creates dissention, rendering the stepparent "the bad guy" in a flash.

➤ Stepparents should attempt to bond with stepchildren by filling in where the biological parent cannot. For instance, a stepfather might play one-on-one basketball with a stepson or take stepchildren to see a movie; these are activities one can share without filling the parental role.

How to Make Your Children Feel Welcome in Your New Family

Let's summarize some of the things you can do to help your kids adjust to their new family structure.

➤ Be sensitive to your children's feelings about your having a new partner. To understand how your children might feel, imagine this: One night, you had a terrible nightmare. You were back at age 12, and you visited your parents' bedroom and poked your mother. Your dad was snoring loudly beside her. When she awoke and sat up in bed, you discovered it was not your mother at all, but a woman you had never seen before. You were frightened. Who was this woman? Where was your own mother? You woke up from your dream with your heart pounding.

The feelings you would have in our scenario will be close to the real feelings children with new stepparents will have until they have completely adjusted to their parents being with a different partner. This scenario will be less harsh if you or your spouse take a good deal of time introducing your new partner to your children.

➤ If your children feel that their importance to you has been overshadowed by your new family, reassure them that their relationship with you is special and that nothing and no one can replace them. Tell them that they're number one with you. *The capacity for your children to build future relationships depends on how you treat them and deal with them now.* This is not true for your new spouse. He or she is an adult and should understand that the needs of your children come first.

➤ The relationship between your children and their stepparent must grow naturally. Expecting too much too soon is bound to ruffle feathers. Over time, with patience and understanding, and by being there for the children without being pushy, a relationship will grow and take its own course.

In the incisive story "Another Cinderella," writer Norman Stiles creates a fractured fairy tale. Here, Cinderella lives with a good stepmother and great stepsiblings. They can't do enough for her. They don't let her lift a finger around the house, and they even do her homework for her. (She was called "Cinderella" because she watched her stepfamily clean the cinders from the fireplace.) Her stepmother buys her a beautiful gown and glass slippers for the Prince's ball and rents her a coach and white steeds and two coachmen to boot.

But with all this support and care, no matter what her stepfamily did for Cinderella, they could not stop her from crying. She cried day and night. Finally, Cinderella's Fairy Godmother appeared with her magic wand. She turned all the beautiful things Cinderella had into ordinary things, including her gown and her glass slippers. She turned the coach into a pumpkin and the coachmen into mice. Cinderella's stepfamily didn't understand why the Fairy Godmother was undoing all the beautiful things they had provided.

The Fairy Godmother then helped Cinderella's stepmother make a list of things Cinderella had to do to get her things back. Cinderella had to complete the entire list to go to the Prince's ball. Cinderella agreed, and as she completed the list of chores, including her book report for school, she felt better and better until she felt so good about herself she stopped crying. She accomplished all her tasks, and as promised, the Fairy Godmother restored all her beautiful things so she could go to the ball. To make a long story short, she ended up with the Prince.

The moral for stepparents: Don't go to the other extreme. Your stepchildren will, just like all children, reap more benefits from gaining self-esteem through their own accomplishments.

Shifting Sands: Different Homes, Different Rules

When you and your spouse were living together with your children, you each might have had your own parenting styles. *You* might have run your household like a tight ship. Every meal had to be at the same time. Each child had to be responsible for cleaning up his space. Hands had to be washed before each meal. Teeth had to be brushed after every meal. Bedtime was the same time every night. Your spouse, on the other hand, might have been more laid back. When you weren't around, meals could be whenever someone was hungry. It was okay to fall asleep in front of the TV. Neatness was not especially important. Who cares if you're dirty?

Silver Linings

If one of the reasons for the breakup of your marriage was a difference in disciplinary style, divorce should ease that conflict and release your children from the fray. They are already used to the style of each parent, so the fact that their parents are now able to implement their own discipline preference without the interference of the other parent can be a plus for your children.

The children adapted to their parents' temperament and parenting styles and knew what to expect from each. When the whole family was together, one or the other parent would tend to dominate. Maybe this was one of the areas of contention that led to your divorce. Whatever the situation, now that you and your spouse have separate homes, each parent has the opportunity to run the ship any way he or she wants.

Your children will still be familiar with your respective parenting styles, but going from hot water to cold where discipline is concerned adds to the problem of adjusting to commuting from one home to the other. If you and your ex-spouse are not antagonistic, children will adapt and know what to expect. If you and your ex-spouse complain about each other's parenting style, on the other hand, your children will be caught in the middle of the conflict.

To help your children handle the different rules and styles in each home, follow these tips:

➤ **Don't expect your ex-spouse to maintain your rules in his or her home** Explain to your children that every home or public place has its own rules. Those rules may differ from one place to the other, but they still must be respected. If they go to Grandma's house, they might not be allowed to put their shoes on the couch. At your house, on the other hand, your sofa has so many stains it doesn't matter.

➤ **Don't expect your ex-spouse to carry out the punishment you administered two days before your kids left to be with him or her** Maybe the kids were throwing balls in the house and your favorite glass lamp broke. They broke your household rule about not throwing balls in the house. You told them "No candy, cookies, or ice cream for a week." Now, they're at Dad's. Dad should not be expected to dock them from sweets. When they are back with you, your punishment can continue.

➤ **Bedtimes that maintain the children's schedules are important for their health** If you are the noncustodial parent, this is the one area that, if at all possible, you should try to honor across households. It's one thing to have different expectations for behavior and another thing to force the body into different sleep patterns.

➤ **Television time can also be treated differently at each home** The amount of time your kids spend in front of the TV should be decided by each parent for their own home. Don't fall prey to the kids pleading, "Mom lets us watch three shows a night." If you want to spend time with your kids, by all means, turn off the tube!

How Stepparents See It

Judy, a 48-year-old social worker who had never been married, was introduced to Arthur, a 55-year-old divorced man who was the owner of a clothing manufacturing company. He had two adult children—Alice, 22, and Michael, 25. Arthur was still very close to his children even though they were grown. His children enjoyed their time with their father. They would see him every other weekend for dinner and enjoy summer vacations with him at his lake house.

Judy and Arthur were getting along very well and quickly became serious about their relationship. Alice sensed this and began to develop resentful feelings towards Judy for the attention Judy was getting from her father. Alice became "clingy" for a 22-year-old. She asked her father if she could stay in his apartment on some weekends. It was hard for Arthur to say "No." After a few months, Arthur asked Judy to move in with him. She agreed.

Judy found life with her new companion more complicated than she had anticipated. Alice made frequent visits to her father's home while Judy was there. Judy was uncomfortable occupying the same space as Alice in Arthur's apartment, and more often than not, she felt as if she and Alice were competing for his attention and time.

Both Arthur and Judy have to preserve the integrity and growth of their relationship while still understanding Alice's feelings. It is up to Arthur—not Judy—to set the boundaries for his daughter. Although Alice is also an adult, she is still Arthur's child and is in a parent/child relationship. But because she is an adult, she should be able to understand more readily than a child that her parent is entitled to make decisions for his own life. Judy is in an intimate adult relationship with Arthur. She is *not* Alice's parent. But because she is an older adult, she will have to be patient while Alice adjusts to her father's new relationship.

Judy's frustration and anger are real. They are not uncommon for new stepparents. Open communication between the new couple and between parent and child is the best way to navigate these rough waters. The stepparent will have to take a back seat temporarily.

Half-Siblings, Stepsiblings, and the New Baby

It is no longer unusual for children of divorce to have many new relations when their parents remarry. Although getting used to being part of a "blended family" is not easy, there are many positives. If parents have the right attitude, and sibling and stepsibling rivalries are worked out, having additional close relationships can be enriching to your children.

Half-siblings, where one parent is the biological parent of children living in each home, have closer ties than stepsiblings, where the children are not biologically related. That doesn't mean that the stepsiblings can't develop close relationships with your children. Age, sex, and temperament have a lot to do with the way the new family interacts.

Some specific issues come up with half-siblings and stepsiblings in a blended family:

➤ **Jealousy over parents**   Whose dad/mom is it, anyway?

➤ **Sharing space—children's need for their own space and privacy**   Whose home is it, anyway? Whose room is it, anyway? Whose drawers are they, anyway? Whose bathroom is it, anyway?

Every other weekend, Sharon's bedroom was "invaded" by Angela, when it was Angela's weekend to live with her Dad. Angela had no dressing table of her own, so she was told by her father and stepmother to share Sharon's. One night while Sharon was washing up, Angela spotted Sharon's diary. She tried to resist opening it up, but the temptation was too great. While she was reading the diary, Sharon walked in. It took many months and a lot of talking to reestablish the frail trust they once had. Sharon's parents had to find other sleeping arrangements for Angela.

➤ **Need for respect**   Children's individuality should be respected. They should not be taken for granted, such as assuming older children will baby-sit for younger children. Children's wishes should be considered when making plans, and they should be told when plans are changed. Children should sense that you trust them.

➤ **Sexuality between your older children and their older stepsiblings**   Because stepsiblings are not related biologically, sometimes issues of intimacy can arise for adolescents and teenagers.

➤ **A new baby**   Children in a stepfamily are often challenged by the arrival of a new baby—the product of one of their parents and their stepparent. This can be met with excitement or jealousy or both. The baby can be seen as eating up all their parent's time, a nuisance, and possibly an embarrassment if they think their parent is over the hill. Other children are able to enjoy the new baby and see themselves as the big brother or sister.

Each of these special issues should be handled with careful thought. Creating an atmosphere where communication is facilitated so that feelings don't get bottled up is key. Making sure that your children have the physical space, privacy, and respect they need to feel comfortable and secure will prevent problems before they develop.

Silver Linings

Blended families can be an asset to your children if everyone has the right attitude. Additional family relationships will enrich your children. Children close in age can become fast friends and will provide mutual support throughout their lives. Stepparents can be positive role models who can give added perspective to your children's world view. As long as the children have adjusted to their new family structure, they can begin to accept and even enjoy the new additions to their world.

The Least You Need to Know

➤ Children handle life better when they are faced with predictable situations and environments, although occasional disruptions are tolerated.

➤ When you have met the person you think will be your next spouse, introduce him or her to your children and let them get to know each other over a period of time. Allow their relationship to grow naturally.

➤ If your children feel that their importance to you has been overshadowed by your new family, reassure them that their relationship with you is special and that nothing and no one can replace them.

➤ Children should be parented by their biological parent, unless there is an emergency. The stepparent should not take on the role of the children's parent.

➤ Don't expect your ex-spouse to maintain the same house rules as you do. Teach your children to respect the rules in the other parent's home.

➤ Blended families thrive when everyone—including the children—has his or her own space and privacy and is treated with respect.

Part 5
Getting On with Your Life

The lawyers are gone. The papers are signed. Your marriage is truly over. The task before you: rebuilding your life to integrate all the important elements, including work, friends, family life, and, eventually, love.

In the chapters that follow, we provide some guidance for the arduous steps ahead. Look here for help in dealing with grief, rejection, and guilt so that you can lead a fulfilling life alone. Learn how to divest yourself of your old life so you can go on to the exciting and new. Whether you must find and decorate a new apartment, seek a new job, find new friendships, or negotiate the pleasant dangers of a new love, the chapters ahead will light the way.

Good luck with your new life. You deserve it. We wish you well!

Facing Your Feelings

Your spouse has moved out, you've negotiated a settlement, and the documents have been signed. The divorce decree has arrived in the mail, and even your attorney has gone off to fight other battles for new generations of clients in the war zone called divorce.

You've been to another country—the land of divorce—but now your flight has landed, and you're coming home. Having divested yourself of the luggage of dysfunction and pain, you are about to deplane free and clear, ready to enter the world of regular people—those untethered by lawyer's phone calls, judicial decisions, visitation squabbles, or battles over the ownership of the crystal chandelier and the dog. After all, your spouse is now legally your ex; the war you have waged for so long, during your marriage, and again, in your effort to untie the knot, is at an end.

Or is it? The truth is, on an emotional plane, you might still have some vital issues to resolve. Much of the time, the newly divorced still carry residue from the experience. Only after you have truly severed not just the legal, but also the emotional ties of your marriage are you free to rebuild your sense of identity and begin anew.

The Heart of Darkness

In the aftermath of your divorce, along with a feeling of relief you might continue to harbor guilt, pain, and anger. You must resolve these feelings so that you can move on.

Remember, pain and anger following divorce are quite natural. The ability to feel pain—as long as it doesn't go on endlessly—may be the measure of your emotional depth. Rest assured that once the pain ends, you will have the ability to love again. But dwelling on these feelings is doing yourself a disservice by sustaining a relationship—at least in your mind—with a partner who has probably already let you go. It is time to move on.

Yes, of course, if you've been mistreated, anger is appropriate. You'll need a little fire in your belly as you move on in the world. May such mistreatment never befall you again!

Red Alert

Some people have so much trouble coping with the pain of divorce that they resort to alcohol or drugs. Often, these people are immersing themselves in emotional numbness to escape their feelings. A word to the wise: It's better to feel the pain and get through it to the other side, where life begins anew, than to linger in emotional limbo.

Into the Light

For some people, the feeling of rejection experienced in the aftermath of divorce is simply overpowering. It goes without saying, of course, that some people simply recover more quickly than others. But if you are still suffering mightily by the time the papers are signed, you are in need of professional help.

"As you look into your feelings with the help of a professional," states psychologist Mitchell Baris, "you may even find that the problem is deeper than the divorce itself." Perhaps you are unable to recover because of a particularly difficult experience during childhood. Perhaps there is a long-standing reason, unrelated to your marriage, for your sense of failure and low self-esteem. If so, take this opportunity to learn about yourself. You deserve it! And through such insight, you will succeed at marriage the second time around.

Silver Linings

It's common to pass through life without stopping to consider the consequences of our actions, or to be truly introspective. Given the stress of life today, exploring the inner self is often a luxury we feel we cannot afford. In the wake of divorce, it behooves you to go through such exploration. This is a gift—it may be painful, but it will enrich you for the rest of your days.

A Life of Your Own

Our friend Shanna had spent five years away from her family in her hometown of Binghamton, New York. Her mission: pleasing an irascible, critical husband—a professor of business at Harvard, no less—who found fault with her eating habits and reading habits, her clothes and her weight, her philosophy of life and her friends. Fortunately for Shanna, she had no children, and after a year of therapy, she felt ready to sever the bond.

For six months after her divorce was finalized, Shanna lived in a studio apartment near the Charles River. For furniture, she used cardboard chests from Woolworth's. Her bed was a cot, picked up on sale from Sears. Art on the wall included a single cartoon: the picture of an Earth man, surrounded by aliens, in a bar in some godforsaken section of the cosmos. The caption: "When I've made it, I'll go back to Earth."

You Can Do It!

Sometimes, you *can* go home again. In the wake of divorce, it may be helpful to return to your roots. There, you might find nurturing of old friends and family as well as inner strength you thought you had lost. You might also find some insight into your own role in your divorce.

To Shanna, that said it all. She couldn't help feelings of anger, even rage, at her ex. At the same time, she felt a twinge of guilt: Her husband couldn't help his nature, and he had been truly devastated when she walked out.

Shanna did, eventually, move back to Binghamton, New York, but not before she had bolstered her emotional resources. She had many issues to deal with in the aftermath of her divorce, and it took months before she was able, in the truest sense of the word, to return to the "singles" world to which she now belonged.

Silver Linings

Yes, you're divorced from your spouse. But your emotional self might still be in the process of letting go. Here are three helpful tips for regaining yourself:

1. See other people and events on their own terms and avoid the tendency to project your past relationship onto these new experiences.

2. If you feel exhausted or overwhelmed by your divorce, give yourself some time and space before jumping into another relationship.

3. After the divorce is final, sit back and reflect on what went wrong in your marriage. Perhaps if you can really understand what happened, you will be less likely to repeat the mistake.

Rediscovering Your Sense of Self

The issue for Shanna and most other survivors of the land called divorce was a true loss of identity. After years, or sometimes decades, of living with another person, it is easy to accept, without question, their sense of who you are. In Shanna's case, that meant seeing herself as somehow stupid and lazy.

For Matt, a commodities trader on Wall Street, it meant something else. Addicted to creature comforts, he left his house in his black BMW for the commuter train at 7 a.m. each morning, and after a day of tussling in the trenches, he returned each night at 8 p.m. Ursula, his wife, seemed to spend her day working out at the gym and cleaning the house. She met Matt at the door with a cocktail and chatter about the neighbors while classical music drifted out from the stereo in the den. Sure, they had two kids—Samantha and Jordan—but organized Ursula had them in bed and asleep before Matt walked in.

Ursula convinced him he could not navigate the complexities of what she called "real life"—buying the groceries, meeting with teachers, going to the dry cleaners, and even boiling eggs. "He's great with numbers but clueless about surviving," she often told their friends. With a taste for the most expensive furniture, clothing, cars, and vacations, Ursula prided herself in what she referred to as "class." Despite Matt's advanced degrees and high-powered income, Ursula insisted, he did not know the difference between true quality and "crap."

Ultimately, Matt came to agree with the classification. A working-class boy from Queens, he had, he often thought, ascended to a kind of royalty in his marriage to Ursula. When it came to the art of elegant living, he told himself, she would be his guide. He dressed the part with enthusiasm, and although he'd once loved his family and friends, he now felt justified in shunning them as "crude" and "low class."

One idyllic summer day, Matt sat on his deck, mimosa on the table and cigar in hand. It was the perfect backdrop for Ursula's announcement; he had to leave immediately because her affair with Samantha's piano teacher was, as she put it, "a symphony of passion I can no longer control." There could be no discussion and no resolution, Ursula said. "I never loved you anyway, from the moment I married you. You're overweight, you're boring, you're nervous, and you have no taste."

That was it. After 15 years of marriage, Matt was out and the piano teacher, in. To Matt, it was like being cast out of the castle. He would now descend, he thought, to the wretched, untouchable world from which he had sprung.

In short, it was difficult for Matt to see value in what were once his virtues—his honesty, his grittiness, his long-term friendships, his ability to work like a dog. Instead, despite his high-powered career, he saw himself through Ursula's lens—a clumsy, inept pauper who had aspired too high and now must take the fall.

Matt's image problem was typical. "After years of living with a spouse, you tend to internalize the labels and messages that you've heard repeated over time," says New York clinical psychologist Ellen Littman, a member of the faculty at Pace University and an expert on intimacy and self-image, among other issues. "Messages like 'You're no good' and 'You're incompetent' tend to reverberate in your mind. If you've let your spouse define who you are, you are faced with the tremendous task of redefining yourself in a divorce."

Your new task: shedding the labels and creating new ones that fit the image of the person you have become.

Often, Littman notes, "people choose spouses who have qualities in common with people in the family of origin. Your role in your new family may echo your role in the old. Even if the labels are unpleasant, they can, therefore, feel safe." In a strange way, this was even true of Matt—whose parents suffered a lack of self-confidence they managed to instill in their kids. When Ursula reiterated that sense of inadequacy, it was all too easy for Matt to agree.

The trick, of course, is to replace a negative image with one that is more positive instead of sliding back, once more, into patterns of old. After all, if you are changing your life, this should be the place to start.

Silver Linings

Once you consider how your marriage has perpetuated the worst in you, you may well view your divorce as the chance of a lifetime. When you finally get out of the environment in which negative images of yourself have been reinforced, you can start to view yourself in a new light, reflecting on your strengths and weaknesses, free of outside expectations.

Now That It's Over, It's Okay to Feel Mad

Where does the anger come in? "A tremendous amount of anger builds as a marriage dissolves," Littman says, "yet it's not wise to express that anger in front of your children or to your spouse. In fact, being in touch with all the anger might even be dangerous for you. Nonetheless, this high level of anger is inside you and often gets turned inward in the form of self-blame."

In Matt's case, for instance, his wife had clearly been unfaithful. Yet she blamed the situation on his deficits, and this, in turn, overwhelmed him with self-doubt. Didn't he deserve this treatment? Wasn't he disgusting? Hadn't he aspired for more than he deserved?

You Can Do It!

When you face your anger, you will be able to let go of it eventually. As you let go of your anger, you will also release all the negative definitions of yourself your spouse had convinced you were true.

Matt was lucky, at least in one sense. Already seeing a therapist, he explored his anger and his self-esteem issues before venturing out for romance again. He came to understand that he was shouldering more than his fair share of the blame, and, without fear of repercussion in the therapist's office, expressed his inner rage.

"Directing your anger at the perpetrator rather than yourself is the first step toward recovery," Littman states. "Many people are frightened by the intensity of their rage and feel that it is in some way unacceptable. They need to know that rage is an acceptable response when the very moorings of your life have been shaken, and you have had very little control over the destruction."

By purging his anger and examining the constraints Ursula had imposed on him, Matt was able to move on. A year after the day he'd been "kicked out," he was fathering his children as he never had when he lived at home. Able to return to a looser style far more natural to him, he often kept the kids up late—by Ursula's standards, anyway—on weekend sleepovers, watching movies and playing games. Now, when he was with his children, he was really with them—not blitzed out on classical music and a drink.

For the next couple of years, Matt, now 40, was on a mission: Part excavation and part exploration, he pieced together a self he never could have been with Ursula in tow. He joined the Sierra Club and took hikes into the mountains; he reconnected with his family and friends from the old 'hood. (Happily, he discovered that many of these so-called "classless characters" had become major success stories—in business as well as the arts.) And he joined a community theater group, becoming a member of the chorus in a series of musicals.

Says Littman: The goal is creation of a new identity based on wisdom gained from the journey. This new identity should embrace your unique set of gifts.

There is a postscript to this story: Matt remarried and, unfortunately, divorced yet again. But the second time around, he never relinquished his new sense of self, and through it all, he sustained an ever-stronger relationship with his children. As for Ursula, she moved the piano teacher into the house she once shared with Matt, still playing classical music in the den and serving cocktails each night at 7:00.

Dealing with Feelings of Guilt

Self-righteous to the end, Ursula never suffered a moment of guilt for cutting off Matt so quickly or for lying to him for a full five years. But that is unusual. Most people feel terribly guilty for rejecting their spouses and hurting them deeply, not to mention destroying the nuclear family for their children. If you're doing the leaving, you are likely to feel guilt. Although the feeling is normal, we hope you will deal with it appropriately. At first, there's a lot of guilt involved, even if you know it's the right thing to do. Is there anything that can be done to help the "left" spouse deal with his or her pain and anger?

Guilt is a form of anger turned inwards. Through the most honest and open communication possible with your spouse, you should explain why this step is important for the part of you that needs to grow. The other person will see in time that this will also allow the healthy part of him to grow when he is freed from the overwhelming dependency. As to your own guilt, you must ultimately do what will make you the healthiest person. That will result in the most rewarding life.

Red Alert

To sacrifice your needs for someone else is contrary to the concept of personal growth. Ultimately, a successful relationship must be built upon a foundation where both people are coming from the position of positive personal growth.

The Life You Left Behind

Even when you're well out of your marriage, it's natural to miss your life—afternoons in the yard, evenings with friends, and especially the kids. Brian, for instance, left his primary home to his wife and children. He found himself paying for their life in the house, however, even though he had no access to the premises and limited contact with his kids. "I just feel overwhelmed," he told us. "I'm 45 years old, and I'm experiencing a loss of alternatives. My money is committed, and I'm working to sustain a family I'm not even living with—and I don't get any of the positives."

The solution for Brian and others in his situation? Generate the options yourself. Take a new career direction, or for those who have been out of the job market, go back and get some new skills that will enable you to become self-reliant again.

Paying work isn't all that's important. If you feel you've failed to develop the skills to take care of your children on your own, this is the time to take child development classes and read up on child safety issues. Then, when the children are on your turf, you'll be far more adept as a parent and better able to sustain your role in their lives.

Remember, widening your options and your skills—in short, branching out—is the key to fending off feelings of frustration and the sense of being trapped.

You Can Do It!

Remember, if you are the noncustodial parent, feelings of loss can be repaired by throwing yourself into making a home for the children when they are with you. Think of things to do with your children that are ongoing and constant, something that they want to come to your home to do. How about taking a cooking class together?

Letting Go and Moving On

Margo and Blake had been sweethearts since high school. To all their friends, a more incongruous couple could not be found. Tall and beautiful, with flowing black hair, Margo was often sought by a variety of would-be Romeos. Short and almost shockingly unattractive, Blake was the typical nerd. But to Margo, whose troubled home situation caused constant angst, he was a sea of tranquility. Witty and constant and very smart, Blake promised (even in high school) to take Margo from the turbulence of her existence to a calm picket-fence world where she would never have to worry about betrayal or anger again.

True to his word, Blake attended medical school. Unlike most of his fellow students, whose goals included personal career advancement, Blake had gone this route simply to woo Margo. Over the intervening years, she had many other boyfriends, although she also always had time and space for Blake. Without high points in income and respectability, he felt, she would never commit.

The wedding, when it finally occurred, was simple but elegant. For Margo, whose emotional fragility had prevented her from working, the ceremony implied the safety Blake had always promised. For Blake, it was a dream come true.

But somewhere along the line, things went wrong.

The stress of meeting Margo's standards as he competed in the medical world caused

Blake to seek succor elsewhere—in drugs. His cocaine habit grew severe and obvious, and he was dismissed from his job.

Unable to deal with the turmoil, Margo sought and easily found a replacement partner. Her new and willing lover in place, Margo told Blake she wanted to bail.

Devastated but always understanding, Blake agreed to the divorce and, with the help of a drug therapy program, worked his way back to health. Unable to part with Margo, he took what he could—status as "best friend and buddy" for her and her new husband and, eventually, their infant son. Indeed, when Margo injured her hip in an accident, it was Blake who rushed to her bedside. And amazingly, when her husband found it difficult to empty her bedpan after she came back home, it was Blake who stopped by every afternoon to do the honors himself.

It's a touching, tragic story. We have one word of advice for Blake: Get a life!

This story, although true, is obviously extreme. Few would agree to become a servant for their ex and his or her significant other just to stay part of their lives. But we must warn you: The temptation to be drawn back into the circle of your past relationship and all that it represents is real. Once the divorce is final, make it your business to establish your own life and center of activity. Make it your business to move on.

You Can Do It!

Do whatever you can to erase the image of your ex-spouse as the love object in your life. No matter how tempting, do not hang out with your former spouse—even as "friends"—or you may find yourself as a peripheral figure in a life where you deserve to be the star.

When Doubt Lingers

It's not unusual, in the aftermath of divorce, to wonder whether you have done the right thing. In fact, unless your marriage has been complete hell, and that is not usually the case, you will still harbor residual feelings of love for your spouse and the happy moments you spent together.

"Unless it's a situation of utter relief from the most adverse possible circumstances," says Dr. Mitchell Baris, "ambivalent feelings are likely to linger."

There is, quite simply, a period of wondering whether you could have worked it out or whether you simply gave up too soon.

One friend of ours began harboring such feelings, especially after his ex started calling him and asking him to be open, at least, to trying again. Her requests were especially tempting to him because she had been the one to end the relationship and push for the divorce in the first place. Just a year ago, he had pleaded with her to give the marriage a shot, and now, miraculously, she was doing just that.

But for our friend, things had changed. The experience had revealed to him his wife's fickle, callous side, and he had started dating someone new. Not only was he basically content again, but also he had no desire to plunge himself into the pain he had experienced as recently as a year before.

Red Alert

In the wake of loneliness, it is tempting to succumb to the fantasy that you can once more find comfort and love with your ex. While this is certainly possible, beware of this notion as a common, unrealistic wish among the newly divorced.

What should he do? A therapist wisely advised him to get together with his ex-spouse. "Don't be afraid," the psychiatrist told him. "You're thinking very clearly now, and you'll see things for what they really are."

Indeed he did. His ex-wife claimed she wanted a re-union, but within minutes of their meeting at a local coffee shop, she was commenting on his tie (too loud) and his hair (too short).

Our friend was cordial throughout the meeting but was able to walk away from it understanding he was well out of a relationship that meant nothing but pain. He had looked into the eye of the monster, after all, and he had prevailed.

The moral of the story: After your divorce, face your ambivalence head on. If your spouse has really been a louse or is just not right for you, you'll have the ability to see that, even if in your weaker moments you're still not sure.

How to Be Friends with Your Ex

The divorce has been finalized and you're on your own. Your marriage, and all the pain it represents, is part of your past. Yet part of moving forward, for many, is learning to deal in a friendly, amicable way with the ex.

It seems like an oxymoron—two angry, divorced people ending up friends. Yet it is possible, according to Bill Ferguson, an attorney-turned-divorce consultant and author of *Heal the Hurt That Runs Your Life* (1996) and *Miracles Are Guaranteed* (1992). The key, says Ferguson, is to end the cycle of conflict and restore the feeling of love. "Not necessarily the husband and wife kind of love," he says, "but the kind of love that one human being extends to another."

This can seem like a daunting task if you are in the midst of conflict and angry feelings. How does one begin?

The first step, says Ferguson, is the realization that love is never enough to make a relationship work. In addition to love, a marriage also requires such elements as appreciation and acceptance—what Ferguson terms "the experience of love." That experience is destroyed by judgmental, critical behavior, he notes. Although it might be impossible to hold back such attitudes during the marriage, when the marriage is over, the cycle can end.

"To create and maintain this cycle of conflict," says Ferguson, "there must be two people participating, like a tennis match. When one person stops playing the game—when one person stops the non-acceptance—the cycle ends."

The key, he notes, is truthfully seeing your ex for what he or she is. "That person is the way he or she is, like it or not," says Ferguson. "When you can be at peace with the truth, you can see what you need to do. Maybe you need to move on."

Yet how do you break the cycle of conflict when you're hurt? "The first step," says Ferguson, "is realizing where the hurt is coming from." His notion is amazingly simple: "Your upset was caused not by what happened between you and your ex, but by your resistance to what happened. Now you must take your focus off what happened and, instead, work on healing the hurt that was triggered when they cycle of conflict began. Your anger and resentment are avoidance of the hurt. By facing the hurt, and coming to a place of forgiveness, it will be easier to be friends in the years to come."

"Trusting is one of the keys to letting go and being free inside," Ferguson adds. "However, this doesn't mean to trust that life will turn out like you want it to. Often life doesn't. The key is understanding that however life turns out, you will be fine."

Red Alert

The divorce courts are full of people who love each other. You may still love your ex, even after the divorce. This does not mean you should try to put your marriage together. Instead, remember that the goal is literally putting your divorce together, so that you can move on with your separate lives as friends.

The Least You Need to Know

➤ Allow yourself to experience the pain. It's something you've got to get through, but don't hold onto it indefinitely.

➤ After the divorce is final, sit back and reflect on what went wrong in your marriage. Perhaps if you can really understand what happened, you will be less likely to repeat the mistake again.

➤ After your divorce, face your ambivalence head on. If your spouse has really been a louse or is just not right for you, you'll have the ability to see that, even if in your weaker moments you're still not sure.

➤ Do not try to reintegrate your ex-spouse into your life after divorce. It is time to let go.

Chapter 24

Learning to Live Alone

In This Chapter

➤ Finding a new residence and making the move

➤ Discarding accouterments of the old life to make way for the new

➤ Setting up house

➤ Your new customs and routines

➤ Traveling solo

➤ Establishing your emotional independence

One of the most difficult parts of divorce for many is not, in fact, the loss of a spouse, but rather the arduous task, after so many years as part of a couple, of living alone.

Next to signing the divorce papers, the most symbolic act you can make on behalf of independence is moving out and starting anew.

A Room of One's Own: Finding a New Place to Live

If you and your spouse have not parted ways before signing the papers, you will certainly do so now. The task ahead for one, if not both of you, will be to pack your things and leave. On most levels, finding a new house or apartment is the same for a divorced individual as for anyone else. You answer an ad in the newspaper, contact a realtor, or respond to a For Rent shingle on the street.

You Can Do It!

If you have children who will be living with you some or all of the time, make sure that the space you select works for them. Is there a bedroom—or at least an alcove—for the kids? Will there be a patch of grass where they can run? If possible, parents should select a new home relatively close to the old, especially if children are school age. That way, children will not have to give up social, school, or community events even when on "visitation."

Red Alert

Although many newly divorced people go "slumming" when they find their new living space, others do the opposite. We have one word of caution for you: Don't! This is not the time to plunk down every last cent on a $15,000-per-month penthouse—unless you are so rich that such expenditures mean absolutely nothing to you. Remember, you are in the midst of transition, and you might need to move once or twice more before you truly settle down.

At this time of emotional upheaval, however, the newly divorced individual might be tempted to take any room or apartment—including one that would normally be unacceptable—just to move. Do be aware, as you choose the setting for your new life, that it must serve you well. Even if you don't have much money, you can find someplace with sunlight, a decent kitchen, and a modicum of safety. Maybe not today, but some day in the future, you will bring a new date home to this simple abode. It doesn't need to be fancy, but the basics are key.

Gordon was in such a rush to move out following his divorce that he grabbed the first apartment he could find. The two-bedroom was, in fact, ideal—except for the train that rattled the walls, the mice and the roaches, and the windows facing alleyways, letting just a glimmer of sunlight in. He was particularly embarrassed when, while making a telephone call, the train would come roaring by. "Are you calling from the subway?" was the invariable question. "Oh, no," he'd mutter to himself, "I just have this tacky apartment across the street from the train."

Of course you need to move out quickly, but when you're looking for that new place, choose well.

Pack Up, You're Outta There

Our friend, Michelle, was in so much emotional turmoil following her divorce that, after hurriedly finding a new apartment, she rented a U-haul truck and asked a friend to help her load her things in a couple of hours one afternoon when she knew her spouse would be gone.

She grabbed her clothes and jewelry and some of the dishes, but she left the furniture—and numerous other possessions—behind. When the shock finally wore off, the items left behind included her Beatles albums and a valuable antique dresser she had bought before her marriage when a local hotel went bust. She did muster the courage to call her ex to inquire about these belongings, but his reply was curt: "The Beatles albums are mine; always were," he said. "As for the chest, if you want it, have your lawyer contact mine." Indeed, she had never even thought to mention the albums in her settlement agreement. As for the chest, she knew it was legally hers, but she was loathe to carry the old battles of this disastrous marriage into the here and now.

Michelle relinquished these cherished belongings. But she needn't have; all she had to do was pack them up in the first place, before she left.

We hope the items belonging to you will be denoted, in black-and-white, in a settlement agreement. But if you're just too heartsick to pack everything before moving day, recruit a friend to help with the job. Even if you've hired a team of movers, make sure that you are not the only one directing the operation. Seek support from a caring friend who can say, "Isn't this beautiful painting yours?" or "Are you forgetting the breakfront? It belonged to *your* grandmother, right?"

Red Alert

We know that someone suffering the pain of a broken marriage may give little thought to packing a record collection or an antique dresser. All he or she wants to do is leave. But take it from us and the dozens of people we have spoken with: You will live to regret these losses. Do pack up all that is of personal value and bring it with you when you leave.

The Art of Divesting: Shedding the Baggage

When Nina married Whitney, she'd been swept away by his worldliness, his erudition, his impressive knowledge of everything from psychoanalytic literature to gold bullion to art. Older than Nina by two decades, in fact, Whitney had spent his 20s and 30s traveling through Europe, Asia, and Africa, learning Serbo-Croatian, studying with monks, and collecting original sculpture.

At first, Nina was thrilled to move into Whitney's stylish Greenwich Village apartment, a commodity he had had so long he was able to rent it for a song. She loved his bookshelves of signed originals and his walls of African masks. "The African artworks you find in the Manhattan shops are bogus," he liked to tell her. The masks and other pieces he had acquired in his travels through the subcontinent, on the other hand, were marvelously real.

Before long, however, Nina felt stifled. There was no room on these shelves, after all, for her paperback novels—and little tolerance for her music by Genesis and R.E.M. Even her Man Ray poster, a favorite from college, was relegated to the closet. "How can you think of removing the African art," Whitney sputtered, "to hang this cliché?"

Nina loved rock 'n' roll; Whitney preferred opera. She loved eating at Drake's Drum, a local Manhattan pub; he dined at the finest French restaurants—and never went anywhere without a comment about the chef.

In short, life for Nina had become insufferable.

When she moved out, after the longest 18 months of her life, she had no desire to take what she had collected during this short union—the precious antiques, the original paintings, even the $5,000 stereo system. Instead, she was thrilled to escape with her boxes of paperbacks, her cases of rock CDs, and her poster by Man Ray. Her new apartment, a small studio on the Upper West Side of Manhattan, contained no original art, but to Nina, it represented real life, at last.

For some people, of course, divesting the accumulation of a marriage might be a bit more difficult. As long as you are legally entitled, take what you want. But remember, you don't want everything. Symbolically and emotionally, acquiring new accessories, from shower curtains to tablecloths to artwork, can be cleansing, indeed.

Silver Linings

The loss of possessions from your marriage will give you the chance to accessorize anew. We suggest having fun without going into debt. Try one of the home accessory outlets like Ikea, Pier One Imports, or the Door Store. Take this chance to assert your style. If you have never been outrageous in style or decor, here's your chance.

Discover Your Own Style

Whether you embark upon the next leg of life's journey in your former marital home or a new apartment of your own, it is time to differentiate the present from what has come before. Now is the time to decorate your habitat in your own style. Now is the time to purchase art, music, and furniture that says something about *you*.

After her divorce, one woman we know hired an interior decorator to redo her Malibu condo in a Santa Fe motif. Another friend furnished his new apartment in contemporary style entirely from Ikea, the reasonably priced home furniture and accessory store.

Both confided that the new furnishings gave them a lift—and the feeling that they were moving toward personal growth instead of wallowing in an experience that had, frankly, failed.

Life Skills 101: Basic Training

After a number of years of marriage, it's easy to allocate some tasks to your partner, relinquishing your ability to negotiate some basic life skills. Jeffrey, for instance, let Laura take care of the clothing; not only did he not know how to work the washer and dryer in their basement, but also he did not even now how to deal with a dry cleaner. Laura, on the other hand, let Jeffrey deal with the cars; unbelievably, she did not even understand how to use the local car wash.

As simple as it seems, the first thing you must do when you are living on your own is ascertain that you have the basics down:

➤ **Shopping** If you don't know how or where to shop for food, clothing, hardware supplies, or medicines, we suggest you take the time to learn now. It is amazing how many people have told us they've never done a major supermarket shop, never used a coupon, never taken advantage of a sale. One man we spoke to did not know how to shop for underwear. Another, a high-powered attorney, went to the office in a ratty suit because he did not know where to go to buy the appropriate attire.

➤ **Cooking** Do you know how to boil water for coffee or an egg? (Sounds ridiculous, but we have discovered a number of men in their 40s and 50s who seem confused on these issues.) If you are among the secret society who cannot make a sandwich, broil a steak, or toss a salad, you must go through the learning curve now. Read a book, take a course, or just wing it with some instructions from a friend. It's not that hard, and it is part of the core curriculum if you are an adult.

➤ **Cleaning your house** Make sure you know how to vacuum the carpet, run the dishwasher, and clean the bathroom. Even if you hire a professional cleaning service, you will need these everyday skills.

➤ **Caring for your car** If you cannot check and change the oil, keep track of check-ups, or monitor fluids, including antifreeze and windshield wiper fluid, you have a problem. Now is the time to make sure you have the appropriate accessories in the trunk, and by this, we mean a flashlight, cables for recharging the battery, some sand for colder climates, and a spare tire. We have one friend who had been driving for the duration of her marriage—20 years—yet had not, in all that time, filled the tank with gas. If you drive, make sure you know how to care for your car.

➤ **Handling your money** We know we covered the basics in the financial section, but it bears repeating here. Make sure you know how to write a check and deduct the sum from the balance, as well as balance a checkbook. Make sure you know how to pay your bills, and do establish credit in your own name. Many divorced people we know, men and women alike, have confessed they don't understand how to handle the mutual funds in their IRAs and don't even know the number and code they need to exchange their funds in their personal account.

➤ **Taking care of your clothing** This includes washing, drying, and folding, as well as hiring professionals to assist in these tasks.

➤ **Taking care of the property outside your house** If you have a yard, you must be aware of basic issues such as mowing the lawn and watering the flowers. Even if you have a gardener, you must still know how to deal with these issues so you can be in control of what is going on. If you live in a colder climate, you must know how to deal with your property in instances of snow. Have you ever shoveled the driveway—or arranged for someone else to handle it? If not, consider this issue, and plan for it, before the first storm of the season. One friend of ours lost thousands of dollars when all of her pachysandra died in a heat wave. She had not realized that her husband had watered these delicate green plants whenever the temperature climbed above 90 degrees F.

➤ **Handling the infrastructure** Do you know how to operate the water heater, change a fuse, or replace the filter in your air conditioner or washing machine? Do you know who to call when the heat goes out, or when snow blocks the driveway? Make sure you can operate the basic equipment in your house—and that you know who to call when you need help.

➤ **Social skills** Many people tend to leave things in this arena to a spouse. Make sure you understand the social niceties. We hate to be sexist here, but one man we know invited a group of people over to watch the Super Bowl at his house yet forgot to supply beer, pretzels, and peanuts, not to mention sandwiches. A few of the guests ended up going for some take-out. (When they came back, they found the bathroom did not even have toilet paper!)

➤ **Basic care of the kids** If you are single parent and have never cared for a sick child or responded to an emergency call from the school, now is the time to learn.

Rites of Passage: When New Rituals Enrich Your New Life

In your new home, surrounded by your new possessions, you will slowly but surely let go of the past. One of the best techniques, experts have found, is to develop rituals and traditions of your own.

If you always celebrated Christmas with your spouse's family, this year visit your cousins from Omaha or your folks in Des Moines. If you habitually woke up to morning coffee and the paper, now may be your chance to start the day with a ritual—and healthy—jog.

One way of inventing new customs for your new, single life is through travel. If you and your spouse made a habit of skiing in Vail each winter, this year take a cruise. If your habit was Memorial Day at Martha's Vineyard, this year try Disney World. Establish your own rituals and customs through your travel so that these events are markedly different from vacations you've had before. We have one friend who always wanted to visit Hawaii, but his spouse, who loathed beach vacations, simply refused.

After the divorce, however, our friend was able to see the islands, and for him, that was at least one bright spot—and something he sustained as a mental image as his life went on.

Finally, remember that establishing new rituals for your new home may be especially meaningful to the children. Sunday breakfast at McDonald's or the old-fashioned neighborhood coffee shop, for instance, may become an important part of weekends with Dad. Making glass bead jewelry or sand art to sell at the local craft fair, on the other hand, may become something the children learn to do only with Mom. They will carry the memories of these family customs forward as they move into adulthood, and the knowledge that their parents have been able to move forward constructively will serve them well.

Flying Solo

Unless you have left your spouse for a new relationship, you will, after the papers have been signed, find yourself alone. Of course, whether married or single, we all drift in and out of loneliness. The newly divorced, however, are particularly prey to such feelings, and the sooner they learn to tolerate and transcend them, the better off they'll be.

You Can Do It!

Reinventing your life means coming up with new ways of vacationing, too. Even if you can no longer afford those cruises to Tahiti or weekends in Paris, you can still take time to recharge your engine and gain new perspective in life. Your best bet may be contacting a travel agent for the latest singles package. These are often quite reasonable and may provide a chance to meet new friends.

How does one learn such transcendence? According to psychologist Mitchell Baris, you reframe the context in which the emotion is viewed. Instead of telling yourself, "Now that I'm left alone, what should I do with myself?" for instance, you might say, "Now that I'm free, I'm no longer bound by all these constricting rules and traditions. I don't have to do it someone else's way. I can do it my way and express the person I really am."

Instead of drowning in despair, allow yourself to experience some definition as an individual. Spend your newfound time alone deciding what you value, what you think, and what you like to do. Then, take some positive steps to integrate those elements into your life as best you can. If you enjoy athletics, join a gym. If you value culture, season tickets to the local theater is your due. If you love music, join a choir and meet people who like to sing.

As you move out of your cocoon to pursue your true interests, you will meet other, like-minded people. Your new life alone in society can begin.

The Least You Need to Know

➤ Even if you don't have much money, find a new apartment with some basic qualities—such as a decent kitchen, cleanliness, and light.

➤ Don't stretch the budget too much when seeking a new apartment or home. Remember, you are in the midst of transition, and you might need to move once or twice more before you truly settle down.

➤ Experts have found that one of the best ways to let go of the past is to develop rituals and traditions of your own.

➤ After your divorce, spend your newfound time alone deciding what you value, what you think, and what you like to do. Then, take some positive steps to integrate those elements into your life as best you can.

Chapter 25

The Ties That Bind: Family and Friends

In This Chapter

➤ Sustaining valued relationships with your ex's family

➤ Who keeps the friends?

➤ Developing a support structure

➤ Making new friends: joining clubs and taking classes

➤ All in a day's work: change your job, change your life

When Jerry met Celia in high school, his family was in disarray. His parents were in the midst of divorce and, caught up in their own problems, had little time for him. Perhaps that was just as well. His dad, a martinet and a perfectionist, had constantly corrected his dress, speech patterns, and taste in everything from TV shows to friends. His mother, a perpetual adolescent, was most interested in Jerry when she could flirt with his friends. As far as Jerry was concerned, Celia's supportive family, with their penchant for political discussion and picnics, had saved his life. He was thrilled to take Celia's younger brother under his wing and teach him baseball. He was flattered when Celia's mother asked him for help with packages or when her Dad invited him to play tennis at the club.

When he married Celia, it's fair to say, he was at least as involved with her family as he was with her.

As often happens when people marry young, Celia and Jerry grew apart. Jerry was able to deal with that, but the thought of losing Celia's family—the only real family he had—left Jerry bereft.

When You Can't Let Go of the In-Laws

In Jerry's case, things worked out well. Celia's family continued to consider Jerry an insider, even after their daughter remarried and had children with her second husband. No, Jerry was not a fixture on Christmas Eve, but through phone calls, cards, and occasional lunches, he managed to sustain contact with this surrogate family through the next two decades of his life.

Of course, this is not always the case. Often, divorce is bitter, and family members may take sides. When push comes to shove, it's hard to find a father- or mother-in-law who will side with his or her child's spouse. When Ursula left Jonathan in the dust for his business partner, all Ursula's mother could say was, "Jonathan had it coming." Even though she and Jonathan had once been close, she now refused to take his phone calls. "Of course Ursula left him," she liked to say, "He was just dull."

Jonathan's mother, for her part, was livid at Ursula and her extended family. "She ate my son for breakfast," was one of her favorite phrases. Another: "She threw him out with the trash." She told anyone who would listen that Ursula had a personality deficit—a disorder, really—conferred by a poor upbringing. God only knew how her grandchildren, now in Ursula's custody, would survive.

Unfortunately, when two people divorce, they don't just divorce each other; they divorce their mutual families, too. Often, there's no love lost between an ex-spouse and his or her in-laws, but when relations have been intimate, complications abound.

In general, it's virtually impossible to sustain relations with your ex's family exactly as they were before. Even Jerry, a beloved "son and brother" figure, had to lower his expectations. Only by pulling back and giving his in-laws space to form bonds with Celia's new spouse, in fact, was he able to make those relationships last.

We've seen some pretty strange relationships develop in our journey though the outback of divorce. Sometimes, the ex-spouse can, for a time, end up closer to the ex's family than the blood relation himself or herself. But take it from us, 99 percent of the time, things self-correct. It's very difficult and very unusual to maintain the same kind of connection to in-laws that you had before. Eventually, the ties loosen; the relationship becomes more distant and casual and even more businesslike. You go on to celebrate your holidays somewhere else, and even if these people were closer to you than any other group on earth, they will soon take on a different, less ubiquitous, role in your life.

Helping Children Maintain Family Ties

While your relationship with the in-laws will inevitably change, these relatives will be more likely to remain a permanent part of your life if you have kids. This can be a positive for you and your children if you are able to maintain these relationships without invoking the negative energy you may still harbor for your spouse. Your children's grandparents are still their grandparents, and cousins still cousins, after all, despite their parents' divorce.

You Can Do It!

You should feel comfortable in helping your children maintain ties with blood relations, even if you yourself have little interaction with these people outside your role as liaison.

Remember, when your children are keeping up with your ex's relatives, those relationships do not obligate you to integrate these individuals as intimates in your own life as well. You do not need to introduce them to significant others, or invite them to family gatherings of your own. You do not even need to sign your name on a Christmas card—even as you ensure your children send cards and acknowledgements of their own. Instead, you may view yourself as facilitator or liaison. This role may become especially important if your ex has little interest in his or her own family—or is simply unavailable due to illness or work responsibilities.

Here are some tips for maintaining cordial relations with those who are related to your children, but not you:

1. Be sure your children send cards on holidays and other appropriate occasions.

2. Enable children to attend important family events like weddings or cousins' birthday parties.

3. Resist the temptation to disparage your ex's family in front of your children, just as you refrain from disparaging your ex.

4. Do not involve your children's relatives in continuing battles between you and your ex.

5. Try to avoid any situation in which you come to rely upon your ex's relatives for baby-sitting, loans, or any other "favor" that might make you beholden to them.

You Can Do It!

When you reach a point where your values and worldview change, you might decide you are no longer satisfied with your marriage. Likewise, you may feel it is time to move on and develop new friendships as well. If this is your feeling, be true to it. We issue just one word of caution: At this time, especially, you will need the love and affection of friends who are good to you. If you count among your friends such individuals, think long and hard before casting them aside.

6. If your children aren't free to participate in a particular family event, decline graciously.

His, Hers, Ours: Who Keeps the Friends?

When married couples talk about their friends, the phrase, "yours, mine, and ours" applies. There are, after all, the friends each of you had before you knew each other and then the friends you share.

Red Alert

Sometimes the friends you had as a couple choose sides—and not always yours. Some friends may find it difficult to continue their friendship with you based on information (true or not) that they have received from your ex. If the stories are upsetting enough, they may feel a friendship with you demonstrates disloyalty to your former spouse. In this situation, we recommend that you communicate your side of the story just once, and go your way. If these individuals refrain from contacting you thereafter, you will do well to let them drop from your social circle without further discussion. Fill your dancing card with new friends, instead.

In the event of divorce, it's virtually a given that your old college buds will flock to your side, while your wife's friends from the old neighborhood will rally behind her. But even friends you made mutually, after you were a couple, might find it difficult to befriend you both.

Kirk had always been something of a loner—serious, inhibited, intense. When he met Maura, however, it was as if he'd been transported by carriage to the ball. A former nightclub singer who was ebullient, effervescent, enthusiastic, Maura naturally attracted people and had a large circle of friends. With Maura, Kirk made the rounds of parties and barbecues and regularly attended dinners and theatrical events. When they had a child, Maura and Kirk were at the center of a close group of friends—all residents of a modest L.A. subdivision, all parents involved in the endeavor of raising their kids. Within this close group, Kirk lost some of his inhibitions and became known for the warm, generous man he was.

It's understandable, of course, that for Kirk, the divorce, when it came, hit particularly hard. Although his inner circle professed fondness for him, Maura had held the group together, and Maura maintained the friends.

Don't Hold On When Friendships Must Change

Ultimately, Maura herself grew apart from the parent group she had gravitated to when her marriage and her child were very young. Just as she had felt the need to embark on a new life with respect to her marriage, she felt a similar impulse toward her friends. Like Kirk, she found that without the construct of her marriage, friendships founded on the existence of that relationship were simply not the same.

If, like Maura, you find that your friendships no longer have emotional value, you must move on. If you feel that your friendships, like your marriage, have a pathological element—if they are somehow abusive, or overly dependent, or demeaning—it is time for you to leave your friends, too.

258

Your New Circle of Friends

In the best of all possible worlds, the newly divorced will maintain their most valuable friendships and forge new alliances, too. It is true, after all, that our friends are life's traveling companions and provide a mirror for who we are.

When Marla left her first husband in her early 30s, she counted among her friends a group of young, married, professional women like herself. Interested in spreading her wings and exploring her inner resources and talents as a single woman without a man for a while, she developed a second group of friends—women who lived more solitary lives, haunting the poetry workshops, fiction readings, and university lectures around town. Finally, when she felt ready to date again, she made friends with a couple of very social, single young women. Together they went to parties and clubs. Through it all, her very closest friends—those she had sustained throughout high school and college—remained ensconced in the background, supportive and loving, even if at a distance over the phone.

Married Friends: Friends Just the Same

Often, the newly divorced fear that their married friends will have no further interest in them now that they are divorced. Most of the time, nothing could be further from the truth. The world is far more diverse and varied than it was in the 1950s, and these days, groups of singles, marrieds, and other categories mix and match with ease.

In this day and age, with families taking so many forms and with divorce so prevalent, couples feel quite comfortable including single friends. Psychologist Mitchell Baris, an expert on divorce, says that in his experience, couples continue to invite their divorced friends along, just as they would if they were married. "It's usually the divorced individual who feels he or she does not fit in. The married couple is usually happy to have their friend along, with or without a date or spouse."

Remember, divorced people most often meet their next spouse through friends.

You Can Do It!

In the earliest days of the divorce process, especially in the aftermath of a separation, you may feel the need to talk. Sometimes this need can be so great that you don't realize how much you are imposing on your friends. If you suspect that you fall into this category, we suggest you spread the wealth around by calling a number of people, instead of just one. Even your best friend will feel resentful after two hours a day on the phone. But if you have three friends to call, you can reap that dose of comfort while taking the pressure off those you care for most.

> ### Silver Linings
>
> Sometimes, in the midst of life's pressures, we forget to value the friends and relatives most omnipresent in our lives. But the turbulence of a divorce may enable us to rediscover the value of these roots—especially when these people, above all others, are there to help us move on.

Joining In and Branching Out

In addition to friends, you might be able to find sustenance from support groups in your community or online. Check out Appendix B to locate groups for mothers, fathers, singles, and more.

One word of caution: Do avoid any group that thrives on anger and hatred instead of nurturing support. If you find a group with a political agenda on many of the issues swirling around the divorce world, you might find some like-minded souls. But you might not get help in coming to terms with your feelings of anger and rejection, a step you must take to heal. If your support group fosters externalization of such feelings around an issue instead of promoting understanding and inner growth, you may be in the wrong place. If your support group encourages you to continue to battle with your ex instead of letting things simmer down so that you can move on, you may be better off without the group at all.

Sometimes, the best way to drown your sorrows and move on with your life is to pursue a passion long ignored. Take a class in Chinese cooking; follow your dream of a career in journalism; take a trip around the world.

The point is to get out there—in ways that excite you—and meet new people who feel the same way you do.

When Your Career Can Jump-Start Your Life

For most people, work, whatever form it takes, is a source of identity. It defines us in society and the world. Especially for the newly divorced, a job that provides fulfillment is key.

If you are not currently working, or if you have put your career on hold, now is the time to avail yourself of the many training programs available to help you render yourself marketable or acquire new skills.

If you are not working at the time of your divorce and your obligations to your children permit, consider this an opportunity to get out in the work world. It's a great way to meet people. Of course, your divorce decree should allow you to earn some money without penalizing your support payments from your spouse.

Vocational counselors can help you find a direction. And myriad groups for displaced homemakers will aid you in finding starting positions that pay enough to support yourself and your family now.

What about just changing your job as a way of changing your life, even if you have a good job now? That idea might not be as good as it sounds. After all, you don't want to compound your losses, do you? For the divorced and the divorcing, the impulse to get up and flee is strong.

But if you've got a good job, and if that part of your life is functioning well, then you might look there for the stability and centering you most certainly need. Even if your job leaves something to be desired, do be wary about changing too many factors at once.

The Least You Need to Know

➤ No matter how attached you may have been to your in-laws during your marriage, clinging to this relationship now might make it difficult for you to move on with your life. The healthiest resolution is to distance yourself from your spouse's family.

➤ Some friends may find it difficult to stay in touch with both you and your spouse following divorce.

➤ Married friends will, in general, be happy to include you regardless of whether you have a date.

➤ Beware of support groups that work to sustain your anger instead of helping you move on.

➤ Don't quit your job too rashly in the aftermath of your divorce; familiar tasks and colleagues at the office may provide an important touchstone.

Chapter 26

Looking for Love in All the Right Places: Taking Another Chance on Romance

In This Chapter

➤ Coming out of your shell: deciding to date again

➤ Everything you wanted to know about dating

➤ Avoiding the rebound

➤ Don't make the same mistake twice

➤ In love again: making another commitment

➤ How to view your old relationship in the context of the new

For Marcy, the declining years of marriage had delivered nothing but pain. Her husband, always temperamental, even in the best of times, had begun to exhibit irrepressible rage when she deviated, even in the slightest, from his expectations. If she took a wrong turn while driving, he would scream and berate her until she thought she would crash the car. If she left a drawer ajar, causing him to injure his foot, he could be counted on to take her good vase and smash it on the wall across the room. His rage was so constant, finally, there was no place for her to hide. In any given discussion, she would do something so mortally offensive that her husband would turn red and purple, insult her relentlessly, and finally storm out the door. He regularly called her fat, robotic, boring, inhibited, dirty, cold, malodorous, and selfish—all in front of the children—and these are just the adjectives fit for print. Her inability to have sex in the wake of these constant outbursts enraged him still more.

Red Alert

Most people just coming out of divorce are struggling with personal redefinition. It is a vulnerable time. It is not the time to make another commitment. Before you reach out to commit to another relationship, live alone, inside your own skin. Gain a sense of comfort with the solitary player you are now.

Finally, Marcy had the courage to extricate herself from this abusive relationship. After she moved out, she was not only relieved, but also shell-shocked. After years of this psychological abuse, the last thing she could think of was finding a new romance. Instead, she cherished the evenings home alone and the silence of the inert walls. After she'd spilled some water or left a mess on the floor, she was continually shocked to hear nothing—no groaning or muttering or cursing at all. It was as if a poison fog had lifted. For the first time in a decade, she could talk freely, move freely, breathe freely.

Some two years after the divorce papers were signed (and some 208 psychotherapy sessions were complete), she happened to meet a man—the friend of friends—who found her delightful. She waited for the insults, the yelling, the anger, but they never came. Marcy never thought she would date again, let alone marry. But time and much reflection had in fact enabled her to let down her guard and open up to new emotion. With a man of greater calm and self-confidence and a larger capacity to accept her foibles and love, the second time around worked out fine.

Coming Out of Your Shell

How do you know when you're ready to find new romance? We think you just will. It's funny how people not on the market manage to project "stay away from me" vibes and keep love interests at bay. It's certainly not easy to find a new significant other, but you might find, once you're emotionally ready, that the candidates available for coffee, dinner, or a film are there.

Experimental Dating

Before you seek a truly serious relationship, it would be best to get back in the swing through what the experts call *experimental dating*. The chance to relive this exciting time of life, for many relegated to the teens and twenties, should not be missed.

Divorce Dictionary

Experimental dating: Dating many different kinds of people casually, without any deep involvement or commitment.

Toward this end, go out with friends, take courses in subjects that interest you, and join support groups. You will, in the course of this socialization process, meet others with similar interests. Whether these people are the same sex or the opposite sex, take some time to get to know them. Expand your circle of friends and acquaintances, and make sure to go out in groups. As you do, casual dates with members of the opposite sex should result.

As you begin to find and get together with partners for casual dates, your primary goal should be reevaluating your identity, your dreams, and your goals. Has your life been too materialistic in the past? If so, now is the time to get to know people without overwhelming monetary or acquisitive goals. Have you gravitated in the past to cold or insensitive individuals? Now is the time to surround yourself with people who are compassionate and warm.

Just because you are ready to go out for dinner and a movie doesn't mean you should now find a new life partner and tie the knot. Make sure to approach these dates with a light touch. This is neither the time nor place to detail the tragic failure of your marriage—or to dwell on your troubled childhood, your neurotic hang-ups, or your financial woes. If you have seen a movie, talk about the film. Talk about life on the job, your travel plans, the books you enjoy, your philosophy of life, your kids.

At dinner, take the time to listen. What does your date value in life? What are his or her goals and desires? This is the time to imagine what life might be like with these new acquaintances, were you to enter a more serious relationship. The point, at this juncture, is to envision the possible futures now open before you.

You are, after all, at a crossroads. Sure, responsibilities from child support to pressure on the job (not to mention the general need to stand up and be counted in the adult world and pay the bills) may have narrowed your options a bit. Still, the choices you make now could mean the difference between years of fulfillment or another round of marital discord and divorce. Your period of experimental dating does not need to last that long. After all, you are no longer a teenager; time might not stretch endlessly, lazily, as it did when you were 17 or 21. Still, in a certain sense, you have been given another chance to live through those young adult years, at least in spirit, and make better choices than you did before. Don't blow the opportunity to do a better job the next time around.

You Can Do It!

Consciously and explicitly decide upon the new course your life must take. If your spouse has been abusive, vow to yourself that any form of abuse will now be unacceptable; if you divorced because your spouse's refusal to work has placed you under too much financial stress, vow now to accept another partner only if he or she works to earn a living for themselves.

Red Alert

Beware that first kiss after divorce! If you're intimate too soon, you might be swept away and stumble down the wrong path, especially if you're rebounding from a failed marriage. Restrain yourself. It will be worth your while in the long run.

When the Idea of a Real Relationship Finally Feels Right

You've been in experimental mode for a few months now. But there will come a time when you feel ready to delve a bit deeper, exploring one-on-one intimacy with a special man or woman. There will come a time when you feel ready, once more, to entertain the notions of caring, closeness, commitment, and love.

If you've reached this point, no doubt you've also arrived at the following truism: Although hoping for a true love relationship can be relatively simple, finding a person to love can be pretty tough. You will not fall into such a relationship simply because you want to. Instead, you will probably engage in the arduous process of sifting through the candidates, having coffee with this one and seeing a movie with that one. You might spend months, even years, engaged in casual—though not experimental—dating, until you hit upon someone who just feels right.

If you keep meeting people, if you keep living your life, you'll meet your new life partner—as long as you are really ready to open yourself up to risk. The time and place of that meeting, of course, may be a matter of serendipity, written in the stars, not this book.

Be Prepared to Spend Some Time Looking for "the One"

Maggie was browsing in the bookstore near the relationships section when she happened to glimpse Jack. With his quick sense of humor and easy-going manner, Jack naturally joked about his need for a book on dating. Maggie was taken with his openness and continued the conversation. After a while, Jack asked Maggie whether she would like to have some cappuccino at the bookstore's cafe. The rest is history: They spent a couple of hours sharing their interests as well as their respective graduation from the school of hard knocks. They exchanged phone numbers and email addresses, and two years later, Jack and Maggie are now engaged.

We should all be so lucky, and many are. We have friends who met quite naturally on Sierra Club hikes, in writing workshops, in elevators, and even at the gym.

Yet we've found that the majority of people encounter more struggle. Many go to great lengths to engineer meetings, pursue their romantic interests, state their intentions, and find new love at last. If all you want is someone to love, then three years of "the dating thing" can feel like a stint in the Gulag. But it needn't be so. If you maintain a sense of optimism (and a sense of humor), you might find you enjoy your new quest for true love. After all, you are on a journey. Even if arduous and sometimes painful, it will still be exciting and interesting and—with the right attitude—a lot of fun.

Where to Go, What to Do

It might seem obvious, but if you want to find your soul mate, go to places where you'll meet the kind of people you want to know.

Religious organizations often help singles by offering special activities in a safe environment. Single parents groups in your community are a good way to network and meet others dealing with the same issues as you. Parents Without Partners is the most well-known group, but local organizations have sprung up everywhere.

Traveling with a group or to a destination catering to singles can lead to unexpected encounters in romantic, exotic locales. When traveling, it's easier to let go of the limiting thoughts you tend to carry with you in your work-a-day life. By transporting yourself to a new physical and mental realm, you can free yourself to possibilities you would not otherwise have considered, and thus unleashed, you might appear especially exciting and attractive to those meeting you for the first time.

Tom, one of our closest friends, met his wife this way. He had decided on a lark to join a tour going to Costa Rica. Even though he preferred to travel solo—he enjoyed absorbing the local atmosphere—pressures at his law firm made it impossible for him to organize a trip. The tour involved more air-conditioned bus rides than he liked, but the other members of the group were good-natured, the tour director had a sophisticated sense of humor, and he was able to relax while being chauffeured to the rain forest. After sharing meals with the group for a few days, he noticed that he was traveling with some genuinely interesting people. Eileen, in particular—also on her own—stood out from the crowd. An editor at a New York publishing house, she was tall, athletic, and just about Tom's age. They ate quite a few meals at the same table and ended up trekking through the jungle together comparing their lives while searching for wildlife.

The best way to meet a future spouse is often through introduction by family and friends. You might be most comfortable dating someone who has been recommended by your cousin; at least he probably won't be a serial criminal of some sort or marginally insane. Ask your friends to recommend

You Can Do It!

Taking adult education classes is a great way to meet people. Many adult learning centers confirm that students attend their classes to enhance their social life. Even if you don't find your future spouse, you'll meet new friends while learning a new skill or hobby or even finishing a degree.

Red Alert

Sometimes even the most well-intentioned friends can send you on disastrous blind dates. Perhaps they have not stopped to think about whether or not the match would even work. Let your friends off the hook in this case; they tried!

anyone who's available and appropriate. Although they're aware that you're single, your friends might not be thinking along these lines unless you ask the question directly. Or they might not know that you're ready to get back into action.

In case you need more ideas for meeting a future love interest, consider these:

➤ Volunteer work.

➤ A church or temple.

➤ A museum or art gallery.

➤ A concert.

➤ A retail establishment. (Yes, if you live in New York, we still recommend Bloomingdale's, but also bookstores, coffee shops, and even, dare we say it, the mall.)

➤ The office.

➤ A community theater group.

➤ Your children's activities. (You're not the only single parent, right?)

➤ Bars. (If you meet someone at a bar, apply the same standards of caution we apply to meeting in cyberspace, which we discuss a little later.)

A Word About Dating Services

Many new singles wonder whether using a dating service is worthwhile. Psychotherapist Frayda Kafka, a dating coach in the business for 17 years, answers this question with a resounding "Yes!" You can be assured that members of a dating service are interested in a serious relationship, she notes, because buying a membership to a service is a fairly serious commitment.

There are all kinds of dating services, many of them organized by interest—book lovers, classical music aficionados, sports enthusiasts, and so on. Dating services can also be organized by religion, age, or any other category. There are telephone services, letter-writing services, video services, and personal matchmaking services. Some or all may be right for you.

Frayda Kafka takes a hands-on approach to her dating service, "Lifeworks for Thinking Singles." She gives personal attention to each of her members and does her best to match compatible people. She urges her members to contact her with both positive and negative results.

As a first step, she sends each member a list of other members who might be good prospects, along with their stats—height, weight, marital status, location, occupation, and interests. Members can take their time considering each listing, so choices are based on what's important in choosing a potential mate, not a superficial physical attraction.

Not all dating services are this customized, and comparison shopping is a must when seeking an effective service for you. To find a good dating service, here are some helpful hints and a few questions you might want to ask:

➤ Is the service listed in the phone book? Sounds ridiculous, but most dating services don't stay around long enough to make it into the Yellow Pages. If you open the phone book, you will find that the better dating services are all there.

➤ Does the service have professional-looking brochures and applications? Call each one and compare the literature to make sure you are not getting involved with a fly-by-night operation.

➤ What do they offer and for how much?

➤ Will they be there for you should problems arise?

➤ Do they have suggestions about how to dress or behave on a first date?

➤ Will the service give you a list of happy customers as references?

Silver Linings

Dating services are generally safer than answering or placing ads in a newspaper. With a service, people are paying on a regular basis; that weeds out a lot of kooks and less serious people. Video services allow you to preview the person you might date, so you can decide ahead of time whether the effort makes sense. Despite the bad press dating services seem to get these days, we have several friends who met their significant others this way.

Dating for the Millennium

Our *Complete Idiot's Guide to Surviving Divorce* might not be much use for the gen-Yers—those 10–24-year-olds who shop online at dELiAs.com and rollerblade for kicks. The fact is that if you have gone through the vicissitudes of divorce, you have probably lived a little. Although many new divorcés have not been married that long, others have gone through decades with a single partner. We don't want to "date" our readers, but we know for a fact that some entered marriage when Elvis was in his prime, when a black and white TV was a luxury, or when the sexual revolution of the '60s was in vogue. Whatever your era, if you have been married for more than a decade, take it from us, times have changed. Today, you must deal with many more factors.

The Reality of AIDS

The threat of sexually transmitted diseases such as herpes and gonorrhea have been around for most of recorded history, but it is only in the last decade and a half that we have been faced with the killer AIDS. As a result, in a throwback to the "apple pie" age of the 1950s, dating couples do not expect to jump into bed after one or two dates. Instead, it is not uncommon for men and women to openly ask about other sexual partners, to insist upon safe sex, and even to request that a potential lover take an AIDS test. If someone asks about your sexual history, do not take offense. It's not personal, just prudent. It's a good sign that the person is responsible.

Cyberspace

The Internet has forever changed the way people communicate, and to some degree, the way they get to know each other or even meet. You must be extraordinarily cautious when meeting strangers in Internet chat rooms and on bulletin boards. That said, we know a number of people who have met close friends and future spouses online.

Without the usual physical factors that can cut short a potentially viable relationship or lead to a series of shallow, physical couplings, the Internet allows people to get to know the person inside the packaging—for better or worse.

Red Alert

If you meet a complete stranger online, you must be cautious in the extreme. Stories of psychopaths preying on the innocent are real. This should not discourage you from meeting potential partners in cyberspace, but if you do not know a new date through family, friends, or the office, always start by meeting in a public place. Never give out your address until you feel totally secure.

This is not a book about socializing on the Web, so we'll keep this brief. There are many guides to cyberspace, and we suggest you get one. Yet we do have a few specific recommendations: We do not necessarily recommend that you inhabit the many chat rooms intended specifically for singles. These can be worse than the proverbial snake pit, with predators galore. But you might find luck by visiting sites that reflect your interests—such as the environment, world politics, investing, or science fiction. The give and take in these venues work just like a course in the real world. As you pursue an interest, you just might find someone worth knowing well.

Finally, even if you meet your new love interest in the real—non-virtual world—he or she will want to send you jokes and tender thoughts through email. If you are hoping to nurture a romance in the new millennium and you lack an Internet account and email address, you might want to get one now. (After you set up an account, we also recommend going to Yahoo or HotMail for an extra, anonymous email address so that you can feel people out before you provide more personal information—such as your real email address or your phone number.)

The Women's Movement

These days, it's okay for a woman to call a man, ask him out, or even pick up the check. She can do all these things without being labeled aggressive.

Some men are delighted when a women approaches them, yet others—especially those from older generations—might feel their masculinity is threatened. Attention, women: Test the waters ever so gently, and keep your antennae up for any signs of discomfort coming your way. Hey, guys...enjoy!

Keep Your Cool

If you've been out there too long, you might start to feel a sense of desperation. Keep those feelings under control and never reveal them to potential dates. Only you know you're desperate to find a new companion. You do not need to alert the media.

You Can Do It!

When on a date, who pays? For those re-entering the dating scene after decades of marriage, the answer is confusing and unclear. Let us help: Nowadays, most people split expenses, at least in the beginning. After a certain comfort level has been achieved, a more relaxed give-and-take is appropriate. If there is a great disparity in income, bills can be weighted more towards the moneyed person.

Sometimes, a sense of desperation can cause you to compromise your standards or consider inappropriate prospects. You must resist the temptation to enter a bad or inappropriate relationship just because you do not want to be alone. Next week or next month, the right person might be standing in front of you at the local Starbucks, but you won't meet that soul mate because you have tied yourself up with someone you will never love.

Remember, another bad marriage and another divorce will be overload. Keep your cool and make sure you're on the right track before forging ahead. To help you stay focused, we present the following dating tips for "idiots":

➤ **Learn about your date's personal history** This might seem obvious, but besides asking what schools, jobs, and careers they've had or whether they have kids, be a sleuth and determine his or her relationship patterns: Are they serial and unsuccessful or enduring? One caveat—people do grow and mature; it is possible that a person who was not ready for commitment has now reached a new stage in life, so don't necessarily rule him or her out. Do make an effort to learn your date's values. Even casual conversation can tip you off about someone's attitudes on extramarital affairs, for instance.

➤ **Ask about friendships apart from romantic relationships** People who have lifelong friends are usually solid and can form lasting romantic relationships as well. Those who can't even keep a buddy are not promising companions.

➤ **Trust your instincts**   If something your date has said in a conversation over dinner bothers you, pay attention to your feelings of discomfort. Don't push them under the rug. Down the road, you'll be tripped up by the very characteristics that you buried in your enthusiasm to have someone in your life.

➤ **Compare attitudes toward children**   If you have children and your date doesn't, a well-intentioned beginning can turn sour once the reality of kids hits home. If you don't have children, but children are part of your life plan, make sure the goal is mutual.

➤ **Don't get physical too soon (unless that's all you want)**   We are not prudes, just cynics. Once the juices start flowing, it's easy to miss signs of incompatibility or personality flaws that would have emerged through spending time together.

➤ **If the relationship is not moving forward, cut your losses and move on**   Life is short, and there are other fish in the sea.

➤ **Do whatever you can to take your romantic focus off your ex**   Many people are able to experience deep romantic attachment—called libido in the days of Freud—for just one person at a time. If you're stuck on someone—your ex, for example, or your current date—but it's not reciprocal, you might have trouble mustering attraction for anyone else. If a dead-end relationship is preventing your libido from reaching an appropriate target, do all you can to eliminate the distraction.

➤ **Chemistry is not just for scientists**   You'll know whether the chemistry between the two of you is there. If there is no chemistry, chances are the relationship won't work. We're not talking about physical attraction here (although that is important, too), but rather, emotional attraction. Are you on the same wavelength? Are you simpatico and able to empathize and relate? Don't confuse neediness for a relationship with love.

➤ **Go with the flow**   If you find yourselves eager to telephone or email each other between rendezvous, you may be well on your way to a more serious relationship. If the signs are right, go for it! Your quest for true love may be at an end.

Focusing In: Loving Again

You've spent about six months reestablishing your sense of self and another three months "doing lunch" with a series of prospects. Now, about a year after your divorce, you have met a person who really interests you. You are ready to focus in.

Our friend, Kevin, a dermatologist, had been dating three women at once after his divorce. (We still can't figure out how he had the time.) About two years after the papers were signed, on a cruise to Alaska, he met "the woman of his dreams." Liz, an anthropologist, entertained him endlessly with discussions of ancient or isolated cultures, current film, and the Internet. Back home, in Boulder, she took him on walks through the wilderness and listened to his fervent hopes and dreams. In fact, although Kevin had gone to medical school, as his father desired, his true love was fiction. With Liz's encouragement, he cut his work schedule to four days a week and began writing.

Needless to say, Kevin didn't need any prodding to eliminate the three casual relationships he had sustained since the early days of his divorce. He moved in with Liz and after a couple of years married again.

Kevin was lucky. The time he spent engaged in casual dating was all the time he needed. As soon as he was ready for a more permanent commitment, one came his way.

Red Alert

Sometimes the period of experimental dating can last for years. It's not always that simple, after all, to meet someone with whom we connect. Especially after we have been hurt in a marriage, it's not always easy to trust or fall in love.

Multiple dating, like that done by our doctor friend, Kevin, is not the norm after the first year of divorce. Instead, people looking for new commitments tend to have serial relationships, each one a stab at something more permanent. If one relationship doesn't work, people just move on.

Don't Make the Same Mistake Twice

When Nat divorced his first wife, Reva, after coming home to discover her in bed with the doorman, the thought of dealing with things alone simply overwhelmed him. Without taking time to resolve his feelings of hurt and rejection, he involved himself with Sharon. She, too, was unfaithful. She had a series of affairs throughout their marriage and finally announced she wanted a divorce.

You Can Do It!

Accept responsibility for your divorce. Before you move into another relationship, make sure that you own up to the role you played in the demise of your marriage.

When Sharon left, Nat was devastated. He had been married to Reva for three years and Sharon for two, but in retrospect, it felt as if he'd been married to one woman—a Reva-Sharon hybrid—for five.

In the two years of relative solitude following the breakup of his second marriage, Nat went into therapy and was able to understand events in the context of his early life. His rejecting parents, he came to realize, had set him up for rejection in love. Using this realization, he had better defenses against making a devastating marital choice again.

Remember, it's easier to feel initial attraction than to stick it out through thick and thin. If a relationship is going to work, you must be able to solve some of life's problems together. You must also have respect and admiration for the other person. If the relationship is not headed in that direction, you might be making a poor choice.

Thought You Never Could: Trusting Again

"Once burned, twice shy," so the saying goes. After the one person with whom you have shared your most intimate moments, thoughts, and feelings now looks at you with cold, hard eyes as if those moments never existed, you are being asked by friends and family to trust again. "But how?" you think. "How can I even trust myself to choose someone who will not walk out on me again? How can I let down my defenses and take another risk when I am most vulnerable?"

We are not saying that trust will be easy, especially if you were the unfortunate victim of an extramarital affair. But no matter why you were divorced, here are some suggestions and thoughts that might help you trust again:

Red Alert

Stay attuned to the warning signs of trouble. If a person seems abusive, overly neurotic, or in any way unstable, believe us, they are. Don't give this individual another chance, vow to change them, or see how it goes. You've already had one failed marriage. This time, quit while you're ahead.

➤ Reflect for quite a while on any repeated patterns of negative relationships you have had.

➤ Take responsibility for your own part in the death of your marriage.

➤ When you meet someone you like, give that person a chance to show who they really are.

➤ It's okay to hold on to some defenses until you are entirely comfortable with the new person.

➤ Give yourself enough time to mourn the loss of your marriage and enough breathing space to heal. After you get to know yourself without your mate, you will feel rejuvenated and will be willing to take some small risks again.

➤ In time, if you are able to let go of the pain and put it into a larger perspective—a world where trusting relationships can exist—you will be able to trust again. Why shouldn't you be among the people holding hands walking down the street? It is not as impossible as it might seem to you today.

For 15 years after her marriage ended, Carey had brief, sporadic affairs. At first, her inability to trust caused these relationships to end. Later, it was sheer inertia. But she was happy and quite productive at work and never gave a lot of thought to her scattered love life. One day, she went on a business trip to California. She sat next to a good-looking man, Michael, on the plane and struck up a friendly conversation. It turned out they had a lot in common, especially astrology and new-age theories. They didn't stop talking for the entire trip. At the end of the flight, they exchanged phone numbers. When they returned to their respective homes, Michael phoned and they talked for hours. Carey experienced feelings she thought were long gone, never to emerge again. They married soon after and are still madly in love!

The Second Time Around

Roberta came from a family of doctors and lawyers, but she herself barely finished high school. She did have a special degree, though, from the school of hard knocks.

Her story provided the cautionary tale for others in her family who thought of marrying too soon, too rashly, or against the conventional family advice. Roberta had literally eloped with Frank, fleeing the judgment of her parents. For years, she worked as a dental assistant while Frank, always in search of his true calling, floated from job to job. When Roberta gave birth to Frank Jr. and then to Brian, however, the situation demanded that Frank Sr. go out and get a real, paying job. Bristling under the pressure, he drifted into an affair and then out of Roberta's life.

Although family members helped pay the bills, Roberta, determined to stay home with her children until the youngest reached age six, went on welfare. Lonely and depressed, she also put on weight, a great deal of it. Her children did, of course, grow up, but through the years, Roberta kept the weight on and looked to Prozac to get her through the day. Finally, at age 50, she took off the pounds and soon met a man, 10 years her junior, who had been divorced himself. Engaged by Roberta's wit and natural intelligence and comforted by her interest and empathy, he felt fortunate when she agreed to marry him. They are still married to this day.

You Can Do It!

If you cannot seem to recover your sense of your self, if you continue to feel uncertain about your identity or your direction, seek therapy. If you feel vulnerable to making the same mistake again, seek therapy.

Red Alert

Make sure to experience a bit of life with your prospective partner. How does this person deal with adversity? Is he or she supportive when life throws a curve—when you get fired from a job, for instance, or when you're ill?

Planning Your Prenup

If you're reading this chapter in a book on divorce, then you might be ready to tie the knot for at least the second time around. Especially if you have children from a previous marriage and want to make sure they receive most or all of your hard-earned assets, you might want to enter into a prenuptial agreement. Although many debate whether signing a prenuptial agreement gets a new marriage off on the wrong foot, most legal experts agree that for a second marriage with assets and children, a prenup is in your best interests overall. As you start the process, you might want to review the following checklist:

1. List all assets of both parties.
2. Provide direction for the disposal of assets should the marriage dissolve or in the event of death.
3. Define separate and joint property.
4. Review and sign the prenuptial well before the wedding date.
5. Make sure each party has his or her own attorney review the agreement.

Do you really need to go through all this? We think many people do. Having a new spouse waive inheritance rights provides more freedom to leave more of your estate to your children. Those who have been married before might also want to avoid the issue of alimony, especially if both spouses are working. Andrea and Barry, in their mid-50s, had both been married before, and each had children from their previous marriages. Although they loved and trusted each other, their main concern was that these children be financially secure. Because both worked and had money in their retirement accounts, they didn't feel it necessary to concern themselves with supporting each other. In the event of a divorce, they wanted to make sure their own children were entitled to their assets.

Andrea's and Barry's story is typical of couples going into a second marriage, but nowadays, first-time marrieds are asking their attorneys to draft prenups as well. With the divorce rate at about 50 percent, newlyweds do not necessarily assume their marriage will last a lifetime. With both the man and the woman working, each wants to protect what they bring to the marriage as well as what they earn during the marriage.

Remember, most states have equitable distribution laws on the books, and if you want to do something other than what the law stipulates, a prenup is a must. These agreements can alter not only the distribution of assets, but also inheritance rights and the amount and duration of support that one party can receive from another.

To Prenup or Not to Prenup?

What if you want to sign a prenuptial agreement, but your fiancée doesn't? It is not uncommon for one person to want a prenuptial agreement signed before getting married, whereas the other does not. Larry was a romantic, and more than that, he was convinced that his best friend's marriage failed because it got off on the wrong foot in the face of a detailed and offensive prenuptial agreement. His fiancée, Emily, had an executive position in a Fortune 500 company and wanted to make sure, in the event of a divorce down the road, that the fruits of her hard labor would remain with her and not be split 50-50. It wasn't that she didn't trust or love Larry, but she felt she was being realistic. What's a loving couple to do under these circumstances? There are no hard and fast rules, unfortunately. Each position has its own merits, and both people have to think over all the issues to make a decision. In such circumstances, it is best to reach a compromise. Larry and Emily finally drafted a limited agreement covering just Emily's stock options.

Making Your Second Marriage Work

Take heart in the number of divorced people who marry a second time. There are so many! Even if the tunnel seems endless now, there's likely to be a light at the end. If you make it your business to get out in the world and meet people, you have a fairly good chance of tying the knot the second time around.

The bigger issue, we believe, is making this second union work. Statistics show that second marriages are even more likely to end in divorce than first unions, but yours does not have to be among these. First, understand the special pressures inherent in many second marriages. Second marriages often bring the stress of auxiliary family members, including children and ex-spouses. Even without these stresses, those marrying for the second time carry excess emotional baggage and scars. You're not two kids starting out with nothing but your hopes and dreams; you now have possessions, careers, and the emotional debris of relationships past.

Red Alert

Don't rush into anything. Take the time to make sure that a prospective partner is truly right before committing.

Now, understand what you need to do to make your new marriage work. Those who succeed at second marriages have, for the most part, been able to come to terms with mistakes made during first marriages. Like Roberta, who realized she had thrived on the dependence of her first husband, Frank, they have been able to accumulate some self-awareness and insight and have come to understand their personal contribution to the marital failure that came before. These people have grown between the two marriages and have, in general, improved their problem resolution skills.

Out with the Old, in with the New

You have made the transition. You were divorced, and now you're remarried. Yet if you're like many people, the old relationship continues to lurk in the background, a ghost of the past. How can you reconcile your new life with the past? How can you put things in context? How can you continue to learn from your previous marriage yet leave it behind?

If you're a parent, of course, your ex will continue to be actively involved in your life through his or her relationship with the kids. If you have remarried, we hope you will have passed through the stages of separation; you will have worked through the anger to establish an ongoing, cooperative coparenting relationship. Now that you are remarried, you will not need to turn to your ex for intimacy, but you'll remain friends.

If you have no children, of course, you simply must let go. The important thing for you will be remembering that your new spouse is an individual in his or her own right. Do not project the foibles of your old spouse onto situations involving the new.

Silver Linings

There is, thankfully, life after divorce. But somehow, it's easier when you're the one to remarry. How do you deal with it when your ex remarries? According to psychologist Mitchell Baris, the most successful strategy is disengagement. If you don't have children, you can walk away and never see your ex again; if you do have children, you must sustain a working relationship with him or her. Your ex's remarriage might cause you to revisit the wound of the initial separation. It signals a finality even more final than the divorce. The healthiest reaction is to stay detached from your ex's love life and to put your energy into building new relationships for yourself as well.

You Can Do It!

Take the time to rebuild your self-esteem and your sense of self before considering a new commitment.

Remember, the best way to prevent history from repeating itself is to understand that history. Be as objective and as honest with yourself as you can. Know that life happens, but you also can make it happen and, to a great extent, direct its course. There is a lot of collective experience out there. You only have to listen, learn, and apply all our lessons to your own life. If you're familiar with the *Magic School Bus* series of books, just remember the overriding life philosophy: "Take chances! Make mistakes! Get messy!" Have fun!

The Least You Need to Know

➤ Before you reach out to commit to another relationship, live alone, inside your own skin. Gain a sense of comfort with the solitary player you now are.

➤ Before you seek a truly serious relationship, get back in the swing through what the experts call *experimental dating*. Don't miss the chance to relive this exciting time of life.

➤ Being ready for romance is a prerequisite to meeting good prospects. Detach from your ex, and focus on meeting one of the many fine people that are waiting in the wings.

➤ Dating in the new millennium brings some constraints (safe sex) but offers new opportunities, such as finding people on the Internet. Women and men can approach dating on more equal footing.

➤ Heed your instincts. Are you getting good signals or bad signals?

➤ Before you move into another relationship, make sure that you own up to the role you played in the demise of your marriage.

The Complete Divorce Lexicon

abandonment   The departure of one spouse from the marital home without the consent of the other spouse. In some states, this may constitute grounds for divorce.

action   A lawsuit. In matrimonial matters, it is usually a lawsuit for a divorce, an annulment, or a legal separation.

adultery   Engaging in sexual relations with someone other than one's spouse. In some states, this may constitute grounds for divorce.

affidavit   A sworn statement of facts. Affidavits usually accompany motions and are used to avoid having to personally appear in court to testify. However, sometimes you might have to appear in court even though you have prepared an affidavit.

alimony or **maintenance**   Payments made by one spouse to the other to assist with the support of the recipient spouse. Payments will usually terminate upon the earlier of the death of either spouse, the remarriage of the recipient spouse, or a date decided by a judge or agreed upon by the husband and wife. Payments received are usually taxable to the recipient spouse and tax-deductible by the paying spouse.

appeal   A presentation, usually in writing but sometimes supplemented by lawyers' oral argument in court, to a court a level above the court that has decided an issue. The purpose of the appeal is to have the higher court reverse or in some way modify what the lower court did.

appellant   The person who brings the appeal.

billing rate   The rate at which an attorney bills a client for work performed. Many attorneys bill on a hourly basis, charging a certain amount of money per hour. Some attorneys bill per project, regardless of how much or little time it takes to do the work.

brief   A written presentation of a party's position. Lawyers most often submit briefs to argue appeals. Lawyers also submit briefs to support points of law made at the trial court level.

child support   A sum of money to be paid by one parent to the other to assist with the support of the couple's children. Child support is sometimes paid directly to a third party, such as a private school or a healthcare provider, rather than to a parent. In some jurisdictions, child support is paid to a state support collection unit, which in turn pays it to the recipient spouse. Child support usually terminates upon a child's emancipation.

cohabitation   The act of living with someone. In some states, cohabitation may be grounds for the termination of support. In addition, some husbands and wives may agree when settling their case that cohabitation for a period of time (such as six months on a substantially continuous basis) will cause support to be terminated. However, cohabitation is usually difficult to prove.

community property state   A state where all property acquired during the marriage is presumed to belong equally to both parties.

constructive abandonment   The refusal of one spouse to engage in sexual relations with the other. In some states, this may constitute grounds for divorce.

contempt   The act of willfully violating a court order. Nonpayment of support when a spouse has the means to pay such support frequently gives rise to contempt adjudications in divorce cases.

cross-examination   The act of being questioned by the attorney representing the person on whose behalf the witness is not testifying.

decision   The judge's reasoning for why he or she directed something to be done or not done. Decisions usually accompany orders. Findings of fact and conclusions of law are the same as a decision.

defendant   The person who defends the lawsuit.

deposition   Answering questions under oath. In matrimonial matters, a deposition usually centers on a party's finances and is conducted in a lawyer's office or in the courthouse, but a judge will not be present. In some jurisdictions, the grounds for divorce may also be the subject of the deposition. A stenographer takes down everything that is said and later types it up for review by the parties and their attorneys.

direct examination   The act of being questioned under oath by the attorney representing the person on whose behalf the witness is testifying.

discovery   The act of revealing information so that both parties are fully informed of facts before trial. Discovery can pertain to finances or to one's physical or mental condition when those issues are relevant, such as when a spouse claims an inability to work due to an injury. Depending on the jurisdiction, other areas may be discoverable as well. Discovery methods include taking depositions, answering interrogatories, producing documents, and undergoing a physical.

dissolution   In many states, divorce is now called dissolution.

emancipation   The age at which a parent is no longer responsible for a child's support. The age varies by state. In some states, it may be 18; in others, 21. In addition, other events, such as a child getting married, joining the armed forces, or working full-time, if such events occur before the emancipation age, may also be deemed emancipation events.

equitable distribution   A system of dividing property between spouses based upon what the judge considers to be fair. The law and precedent provide the judge with the factors to consider in making that determination.

exclusive use and occupancy of the marital residence   The right one spouse has to reside in the home in which the parties had previously lived together. Such right may be agreed upon or may be directed by a judge while an action is pending.

forensics   The term sometimes used when a psychologist, psychiatrist, social worker, or other mental health professional is appointed to interview the parents and their children and make a recommendation to the court about who would be the better custodial parent. The mental health expert may also interview child caretakers, grandparents, teachers, and anyone else who has frequent contact with the children.

garnishment   A mechanism whereby support is sent by the paying spouse's employer directly to the recipient spouse and is deducted from the paying spouse's paycheck.

grounds   The legally sufficient reasons why a person is entitled to a divorce. Although many states are no-fault states, where no grounds need be asserted other than incompatibility or irreconcilable differences, other states require the plaintiff to prove grounds, such as adultery, abandonment, or mental cruelty.

interrogatories   A series of questions that must be answered under oath, usually designed to ascertain a person's financial holdings and means of earning income.

joint custody   Sharing of raising children despite a divorce. Joint custody can mean the children will live with one parent most of the time, but both parents will make major decisions. It can also mean the children will divide their time equally between the two parents' homes.

judgment of divorce   The written document that states that a husband and wife are divorced. In some states, this may be called a decree of dissolution. Typically, lawyers draft the judgment of divorce for the judge to review and sign.

law guardian   A person, usually a lawyer, selected by the judge and assigned to represent the children of the divorcing parents.

marital property   In general, property a husband and wife acquire during the marriage. Such property may also be called joint property. In some jurisdictions, inheritances, disability awards, and gifts received from a third party (that is, not the spouse) are not considered marital or joint property, even if a spouse received them during the marriage. Other exceptions may exist as well.

motion A request made of a judge at a time an action is pending or at trial. Motions can be made in writing for the court to consider, or orally, such as at trial. In matrimonial cases, motions are typically made for temporary support, temporary custody, or visitation rights or to enjoin someone from taking money or property. A motion may also be called an order to show cause.

noncustodial parent The parent with whom the children do not live. Such a parent might not make day-to-day decisions but, depending on the definition of legal custody, can have a great deal to say about decisions regarding the children.

order A ruling by a judge, made orally or in writing, directing someone to do or refrain from doing something.

order of protection An order directing one spouse to refrain from harassing the other. Violation of an order of protection can result in arrest and imprisonment.

perjury The act of lying under oath.

petitioner The person who first goes to court to file a request or petition for some kind of relief.

plaintiff The person who starts a lawsuit.

postnuptial agreement or **separation agreement** A written contract entered into by a husband and wife, which sets forth all their present and future rights in the event of a divorce or a spouse's death. The parties may or may not be involved in divorce litigation at the time they sign such an agreement.

precedent The use of previous decisions in cases factually similar to the case before a judge in order for the judge to decide how to adjudicate the present case.

prenuptial agreement A written contract entered into by a couple who intend to marry but want to establish, before marriage, their rights in the event of a death or divorce after marriage. The validity of such agreements depends on state law.

record All the testimony and exhibits upon which a judge based his or her decision. When a party appeals a decision, it is necessary to compile all the papers and transcripts of testimony that the lower court used to decide the case and to present that information to the higher court.

respondent The person who has to defend or object to the appeal. The respondent also responds to the petition in the trial court.

retainer A payment made to an attorney to secure his or her services. As the attorney works, charges are deducted from the retainer until the money is used up. At that time, the attorney will bill on a weekly or monthly basis or will ask for a new retainer.

retainer agreement A contract signed by an attorney and client setting forth the billing arrangement to be instituted between the lawyer and the client.

separate property   Property a spouse acquires before the marriage and after an action for divorce has begun. In some jurisdictions, inheritance, disability awards, and gifts received during the marriage by one party are considered separate property. Other exceptions may exist as well.

sole custody   One parent has the unilateral right to make decisions concerning the children without having to consult with the other parent. However, even in situations where sole custody exists, the other parent may have to be consulted before major expenses, such as college or healthcare, for which that parent may be responsible, are incurred.

transcript   The written presentation of testimony given at trial or in a deposition.

The Divorce Network: A Guide to Divorce Organizations

Given the number of divorces, it's no surprise that many thousands of divorce organizations exist around the United States. Some are for single parents, and some are just for singles. Some cater to the needs of parents without custody, others to the political agendas of divorced women and moms or divorced men and dads. We cannot list every organization in this appendix. However, we hope that the broad spectrum of national groups presented will enable you to link, either directly or through referral, to the information, support, and friendship that you need.

Children and Divorce

For issues regarding child rights, child custody, child support, and missing children, contact

National Association of Child Advocates
1522 K Street, NW, Suite 600 Washington, DC 20005
Eve Brooks, President
Phone: 202-289-0777
Fax: 202-289-0776
Email: naca@childadvocacy.org
Web site: http://www.childadvocacy.org/

NACA strives to change policy in areas of healthcare, education, childcare, child support, and juvenile justice. Although NACA and its 44 member organizations do not provide individual services, they can provide information on the most current legislation and policy. You can reach member organizations around the country by calling or faxing the Washington office. Link from there to local groups devoted to child support enforcement, single parents, noncustodial parents, stepfamilies, and father's rights.

Association quote: "Our mission is to provide a voice for children and their families on issues of critical concern—welfare reform; federal food assistance programs for children; healthcare; affordable, quality childcare; and enforcement of court-ordered child support—at the national and local levels."

Children's Rights Council
300 I Street, NE, Suite 401
Washington, DC 20002
David Levy, President
Phone: 202-547-6227
Fax: 202-546-4272

A national nonprofit organization dedicated to assisting children of separation and divorce through advocacy and parenting education.

Association for Children for Enforcement of Support (ACES)
2260 Upton Avenue
Toledo, OH 43606
Geraldine Jensen, President
Phone: 800-537-7072 or 419-472-0047
Fax: 419-472-6295
Web site: http://www.childsupport-ACES.org/

This self-help, nonprofit child-support organization teaches custodial parents what they need to do to collect child support. The association has 350 chapters located all across the United States. Call, write, or fax for information on how to contact a chapter in your area.

Committee for Mother and Child Rights
210 Ole Orchard Drive
Clear Brook, VA 22624-1647
Elizabeth Owen, Coordinator
Phone: 323-634-0543

This national organization offers emotional support and guidance for mothers with child custody problems. "We are concerned with the various abuses often associated with contested custody: mental, physical, and sexual," says Elizabeth Owen, coordinator. "Most times, if custody is contested, the man will get custody. We are strictly advocates for women and children." This group can provide names of attorneys and other experts in child custody issues, including sexual abuse issues.

National Center for Missing and Exploited Children
2101 Wilson Blvd., Suite 550
Arlington, VA 22201-3052
Ernie Allen, President and CEO
Phone: 800-843-5678 (24-hour hotline to report missing children) or 703-235-3900
Fax: 703-235-4067
Web site: http://www.ncmec.org/

According to Naheed Qureshi, NCMEC gives legal and technical assistance and can look into parental abduction cases if the parent reporting the abduction has custody and if the child has been entered into their computer system as a missing juvenile. If the child has not been so entered, that should be done first before a listing can be made. NCMEC also publishes a list of local, nonprofit organizations involved in recovering missing children throughout the United States. To get a list for a group in your area, call, write, or fax NCMEC.

Find the Children
11811 W. Olympic Blvd.
Los Angeles, CA 90064
Judy Sadowsky, Executive Director
Phone: 310-477-6721
Fax: 310-477-0731

A national nonprofit organization dedicated to the prevention, location, and recovery of missing and abducted children, this group provides educational materials and training, registers missing children, and manages specific cases, distributing photographs and descriptive information about missing children, working with other organizations in the field, maintaining a referral list of professionals all over the country who can help families of missing children, providing emotional support to families of missing children, and giving referrals for postrecovery counseling. All services to victim families and their children are provided free of charge.

Legal Resources

For matrimonial attorneys, mediation, conciliation, and dispute resolution, contact

American Academy of Matrimonial Lawyers
150 N. Michigan Avenue, Suite 2040
Chicago, IL 60601
Sandra Murphy, President
Phone: 312-263-6477
Fax: 312-263-7682
Web site: http://www.aaml.org

This organization provides referrals to board-certified attorneys specializing in matrimonial and family law. Chapters are located all over the United States and in other countries.

American Bar Association
750 N. Lake Shore Drive
Chicago, IL 60611
Robert A. Stein, Executive Director
Phone: 312-988-5000
Fax: 312-988-6281
Web site: http://www.abanet.org/family/home.html

This organization of 400,000 members can provide a list of state bar associations and can also provide numbers for referral services by state.

Association of Family and Conciliation Courts
329 W. Wilson Street
Madison, WI 53703
Christie Coates, President
Phone: 608-251-4001
Fax: 608-251-2231
Email: afcc@afccnet.org

This international association of judges, lawyers, counselors, custody evaluators, and mediators maintains a library of videos, pamphlets, and other publications on custody and visitation issues, child support, mediation, and more. Some titles include *Guide for Stepparents, Twenty Questions Divorcing Parents Ask About Their Children*, and *Preparing for Your Custody Evaluation*. Call, write, or fax for an order form. This group also sponsors parent education programs and conferences on a wide range of child welfare issues. AFCC's membership directory is available to nonmembers for $15.

Kayama
Web site: http://www.kayama.org

A non-profit organization that provides information and assistance for obtaining a Jewish divorce (get).

Single Parents

For issues relating to single parents, contact

Parents Without Partners
401 North Michigan Avenue
Chicago, IL 60611-4267
Kathleen Bell, Executive Director
Phone: 800-637-7974 or 312-644-6610
Web site: http://www.parentswithoutpartners.org/

Resources are provided through local chapters. (Call the toll-free number to get contact information for the chapter nearest you.) The organization provides information on child support and custody issues for both custodial and noncustodial parents.

National Organization of Single Mothers
PO Box 68
Midland, NC 28107-0068
Phone: 704-888-5437
Web site: http://www.singlemothers.org

"We offer support by providing our members a network dedicated to helping single parents face the challenges of daily life with wisdom, wit, dignity, confidence, and courage," group literature explains. The group also publishes a newsletter called *Single*

Mother, which can be ordered by sending $1 for postage and handling to the preceding address. A year's membership costs $12.97.

Single Parent Resource Center
31 E. 28th St., 2nd Fl.
New York, NY 10016
Phone: 212-951-7030
Suzanne Jones, Executive Director
Web site: http://singleparentresources.com/

This organization seeks to establish a network of local single parent groups so that such groups will have a collective political voice. It provides information and support on issues important to single parents.

Moms and Divorce

For legal and emotional support for divorced women with children, contact

National Women's Law Center
11 Dupont Circle NW, Suite 800
Washington, DC 20036
Nancy Duff Campbell, Co-President
Phone: 202-588-5180

This group works to guarantee equality for women under the law and to seek protection and advancement of their legal rights and issues at all levels. Areas of interest include child support enforcement, dependent care, and the family.

Women's Law Project
125 S. 9th St., Suite 401
Philadelphia, PA 19107
Carol Tracy, Executive Director
Phone: 215-928-9801
Fax: 215-928-9848

This nonprofit feminist law firm challenges sex discrimination in the law and in legal and social institutions. This group also maintains telephone counseling and referral services on women's legal rights concerns and community education.

Domestic Abuse

For support for adult and child victims of psychological abuse, violence, or rape, contact

AMEND (Abusive Men Exploring New Directions)
789 Sherman, Suite 580
Denver, CO 80203
Linda Pettit, Executive Director
Phone: 303-832-6363
Fax: 303-832-6364

This organization provides therapy for abusive men and advocacy for women as well as violence prevention programs in the schools. It can also provide specific information on help resources for women in violent relationships.

Child Abuse Listening and Mediation (CALM)
PO Box 90754
Santa Barbara, CA 93190
Elly Rumelt, Contact
Phone: 805-965-2376; 24-hour listening service (bilingual): 805-569-2255
Web site: http://www.calm4kids.org/

This group helps parents who are having difficulty coping with stress in their lives and are afraid they might hurt their children. It provides counseling for families in which abuse has occurred and for families at risk for abuse to occur; provides support groups for parents of children who have been abused and for children who have been abused by a family member; and also provides support groups for the purpose of educating parents and improving relationships between parents and children. Respite care is available. Referrals are provided to other organizations and services.

Child Welfare League of America
440 1st Street, NW, Suite 310
Washington, DC 20001
David S. Liederman, Executive Director
Phone: 202-638-2952
Fax: 202-638-4004
Web site: http://www.cwla.org/

This group consists of more than 800 member agencies in the United States and Canada. Call, write, or fax to obtain information on how to contact a group in your area.

National Clearinghouse on Marital and Date Rape
2325 Oak Street
Berkeley, CA 94708
Phone: 510-524-1582

This organization provides phone consultations for the fee of $7.50 for 15 minutes. Initial annual subscription fee is $15 for individuals.

National Hotline Number: 800-799-SAFE
(operated by the Texas Coalition Against Domestic Violence)
Web site: http://www.ncadv.org/links.htm

This organization operates the National Resource Center on Domestic Violence, one of the most active coalitions in the country in terms of number of battered women's shelters, treatment and education programs, and legislation initiatives.

Legal Aid for Abused Women
LAAW
3524 S. Utah St.
Arlington, VA 22206
Phone: 703-820-8393
Fax: 703-820-7968
Web site: http://ourworld.compuserve.com/homepages/LAAW/

LAAW provides legal aid for women and men trying to remove themselves from an abusive situation. Legal aid is often necessary to secure stay-away orders, obtain child support, settle child custody issues, initiate separation and divorce proceedings, and collect the court-required documentation of the emotional, sexual, and physical abuse. LAAW provides a revolving fund for legal aid. Recipients reimburse up to 100 percent of the monetary assistance provided and volunteer their time to assist others affected by domestic violence. Legal aid is provided regardless of race, nationality, gender, social status, orientation, or education level.

Dads and Divorce

For legal and emotional support for divorced men with children, contact

National Fatherhood Initiative
One Bank Street, Suite 160
Gaithersburg, MD 20878
Wade Horn, Ph.D., President
Phone: 301-948-0599

This organization is dedicated to improving the well-being of children through the promotion of responsible fatherhood in society. "Working with local media, community, church, and school," says David Blankenhorn, President, "we present to society the idea that fathers are a very important part of a child's life."

The Single and Custodial Father's Network
Web site: http://www.single-fathers.org/

Supports and provides information to single and custodial fathers.

The Fathers' Rights and Equality Exchange
701 Welch Road, #323
Palo Alto, CA 94304
Ann Mitchell, Founder
Phone: 500-FOR-DADS
Web site: http://www.dadsrights.org

Parenting is a 50/50 proposition. Fathers and mothers should share equally in the parenting and support of their children within and without the institution of marriage. This international group has members in the United States, Canada, United Kingdom, Germany, Australia, and Japan.

Blended Family Support

For issues related to stepparents and their spouses, contact

Stepfamily Association of America
650 J Street, Suite 205
Lincoln, NE 68508
Larry Kallemeyn, Executive Director
Phone: 402-477-7837
Fax: 402-477-8317
Web site: http://www.stepfam.org/

The organization has 60 chapters all over the United States and one in Canada. "Our mission is to provide education and support for people in the stepfamily situation," explains group spokesperson Jill Austin.

Stepfamily Foundation
333 West End Avenue
New York, NY 10023
Phone: 212-877-3244
Fax: 212-362-7030
Email: staff@stepfamily.org
Web site: http://www.stepfamily.org/index.html

Provides counseling, on the telephone and in person, and information to create a successful step relationship.

Financial Resources

For issues regarding finances and divorce, contact

Older Women's League
666 11th Street, Suite 700
Washington, DC 20001
Deborah Briceland-Betts, Executive Director
Phone: 202-783-6686
Web site: http://members.aol.com/owlil/index.htm

This group provides support and information on issues important to midlife and older women, including the effects of divorce on older women.

Pension Rights Center
1140 19th Street, NW, Suite 602
Washington, DC 20036
Karen W. Ferguson, Director
Phone: 202-296-3776

This group provides information concerning how divorce affects pensions and offers a lawyer referral service.

National Foundation for Consumer Credit
8611 2nd Avenue, Suite 100
Silver Spring, MD 20910
Durant Abernethy, President
Phone: 800-388-2227 or 800-682-9832 (Spanish assistance); 301-589-5600
Fax: 301-495-5623
Web site: http://www.nfcc.org/

A nonprofit membership organization whose purpose is to educate, counsel, and promote the wise use of credit, NFCC serves as an umbrella group for 200 member services with more than 1,100 counseling offices throughout the United States, Puerto Rico, and Canada. NFCC offers free or low-cost professional money-management counseling and educational services to consumers nationwide.

Psychological Support

For emotional help groups for divorce, contact

Ackerman Institute for Family Therapy
149 E. 78th St.
New York, NY 10021
Dr. Peter Steinglass, Director; Garda Spaulding, Director of Intake
Phone: 212-879-4900
Fax: 212-744-0206
Web site: http://www.spacelab.net/~ackerman/springwks99.htm

This organization provides family and couples treatment and helps divorcing partners resolve issues of childcare—such as how to tell children about a divorce and how to keep the child from the center of conflict. "Divorce is never a positive experience," says Garda Spaulding, director of intake, "but we try to show parents how to keep it as benign as possible."

International Association for Marriage and Family Counselors
c/o American Counseling Association
5999 Stevenson Avenue
Alexandria, VA 22304
John L. Jaco, Executive Director
Phone: 800-545-AACD or 703-823-9800
Fax: 703-823-0252

The association provides referrals to members working in the areas of marriage counseling, marital therapy, divorce counseling, mediation, and family counseling and therapy.

American Self-Help Clearinghouse
St. Clares-Riverside Medical Center
Denville, NJ 07834
Edward J. Madara, Director
Phone: 201-625-7101
Fax: 201-625-8848

This group serves as a resource center for self-help groups in the state of New Jersey and also lists out-of-state help lines and toll-free numbers for related organizations all over the United States.

Suggested Readings and Online Resources

Books and Magazine Articles

In the last 10 years, valuable books on divorce have been added to the shelves. We mention a few. Check your library or local bookstore for more. The more recent the publication date, the better—but some of the "classics" are well worth the read.

General

The Divorce Decisions Workbook: A Planning and Action Guide, Marjorie L. Engel and Diana D. Gould. New York: McGraw-Hill, Inc., 1992.

Discusses the practical, legal, and emotional aspects of divorce. Includes information on division of assets and liabilities, spousal support, responsibility to children, options other than divorce (such as legal separation decrees and annulment), no-fault divorce, adversarial divorce, uncontested divorce, and alternatives to adversarial divorce (such as mediation and arbitration). A great all-around guide.

When the Vows Break, Maria Costa with Rob Grogan. Fredericksburg, Virginia: MC&A, 1997.

Author's own story about her separation, divorce, and new life. How to survive divorce and move on to a new life.

The Divorce Handbook: Your Basic Guide to Divorce, James T. Friedman. New York: Random House, 1982.

Covers the basic issues of divorce in a clear question-and-answer format.

How to Heal a Painful Relationship: And if Necessary, How to Part as Friends, Bill Ferguson. Houston: Return to the Heart, 1999.

Learn how to end the cycle of conflict, heal the hurt, resolve issues, and restore the love—one human being to another.

Heal the Hurt That Runs Your Life, Bill Ferguson. Houston: Return to the Heart. Houston: Return to the Heart, 1996 .

Discover and heal the inner issues that destroy love and sabotage your life.

Second Chances: Men, Women, and Children a Decade After Divorce, Judith S. Wallerstein and Sandra Blakeslee. New York: Ticknor & Fields, 1989.

The preeminent researcher explains what happened to selected families during, after, and long after divorce, based on a 10-year study of 60 middle-class families. Some of the findings are controversial, but it's a classic and one of few long-term studies in existence.

The Divorce Book for Men and Women, Harriet Newman Cohen and Ralph Gardner, Jr. New York: Avon Books, 1994.

An experienced divorce lawyer explains how to gain your freedom at the lowest possible legal and emotional cost.

Practical Divorce Solutions, Ed Sherman. Berkeley: Nolo Press, 1988.

Pragmatic advice from a divorce lawyer, covering the gamut from emotional issues to legal costs.

Children and Divorce

Helping Your Kids Cope with Divorce the Sandcastles Way, M. Gary Neuman, Patricia Romanowski. New York: Random House, 1999.

This comprehensive book, based on Dr. Neuman's program "Sandcastles," discusses parenting after divorce, how children experience divorce, explaining divorce to children of different ages, recognizing depression, answering the tough questions, how to tell your children about your impending divorce, when a parent moves away, custody and visitation, dealing with two homes, parenting the child of divorce, dealing with divorce-related change, your new significant other, child abuse, the stepfamily, and more.

Voices of Children of Divorce, David Royko. New York: Golden Books, 1999.

Through the voices of children from kindergarteners through young adults, this book provides observations and insights to help understand what it is like for these victims of divorce. Dr. Royko offers advice for parents and other interested adults to help children better cope with the trauma.

Mom's House, Dad's House: A Complete Guide for Parents Who Are Separated, Divorced, or Remarried, Isolina Ricci. New York: Simon & Schuster, 1997.

Revised and updated with examples, self-tests, checklists, and guidelines. Looks at creative options and commonsense advice in the legal, emotional, and practical realities of creating two happy and stable homes for your children.

"Why Did You Have to Get a Divorce? and When Can I Get a Hamster?" A Guide to Parenting Through Divorce, Anthony E. Wolf. New York: Noonday Press, 1998.

Includes how to tell your children about the divorce, how to keep your children from being caught between you and your ex-partner, and how to help children cope with new partners or new siblings.

Rocking the Cradle of Sexual Politics, Louis Armstrong. Reading, Massachusetts: Addison-Wesley, 1994.

Explores the politics of incest and child sexual abuse. Discusses how we got from incest as a taboo to open discussion of sexual abuse and back again, to the backlash response in which society doubts the credibility of sexual abuse and incest reporters. Look here for a fascinating discussion of False Memory Syndrome.

Legal Rights of Children, 2nd Edition, Donald T. Kramer. New York: Shepard's/McGraw-Hill, 1994.

Explains various federal, state, and uniform laws, regulations, and procedures that now apply to children and their families. Specific issues covered include child support, child custody, visitation rights, child abuse, guardianship, public assistance for children, parental torts, and children as witnesses.

How to Collect Child Support, Geraldine Jensen. Stamford, Connecticut: Longmeadow Press, 1991.

Gives basic information on what steps parents need to take to collect child support: what child support enforcement should be doing, how to complain effectively, and so on.

Joint Custody and Shared Parenting, 2nd Edition, Jay Folberg. New York: Guilford Publications, 1991.

Examines the circumstances in which joint custody is appropriate. Second revised edition updates research and law in an accessible format. Aimed at professionals in the field, but parents can benefit from the information as well.

Caught in the Middle: Protecting the Children of High-Conflict Divorce, Carla B. Garrity and Mitchell A. Baris. New York: Lexington Books, 1994.

Provides parents embroiled in conflict—and the professionals who work with them—with tools to reduce tension and remove children from the center of fire.

For the Sake of the Children, Kris Kline and Stephen Pew, Ph.D. Rocklin, California: Prima Publishing, 1992.

How to share your children with your ex-spouse in spite of your anger.

Surviving the Breakup: How Children and Parents Cope with Divorce, Judith S. Wallerstein. New York: Basic Books, 1980.

Based on the Children of Divorce Project, a landmark study of 60 families during the first five years after divorce. Note: *Second Chances*, mentioned earlier, is the sequel to this book.

Children of Divorce: A Developmental Approach to Residence and Visitation, Mitchell A. Baris and Carla B. Garrity. DeKalb, Illinois: Psytec, 1988.

Drs. Baris and Garrity outline their recommendations for age-appropriate time-sharing for parents who are separating and divorcing. According to the authors, these recommendations are only for parents who have actively parented their children until the time of the parental separation; have competent parenting skills, where children are not in physical or psychological danger at either parent's home; are available and willing to parent the children; and when required, will put their children's needs ahead of their own.

Separate Houses: A Handbook for Divorced Parents, Robert B. Shapiro. Lakewood, Colorado: Bookmakers Guild, 1989.

A concise guide to handling difficult issues that arise at the time of divorce, especially as they relate to children. A child-focused guide to custody decisions and creation of a visitation plan.

The Divorced Parent: Success Strategies for Raising Your Children After Separation, Stephanie Marston. New York: Pocket Books, 1994.

A guide for raising well-adjusted children following divorce. Topics include preventing self-blame on the part of the child, helping children cope with the divorce, handling feelings of loneliness and frustration, using effective discipline, creating a life of your own, building a successful parenting partnership with your ex-spouse, dealing with difficult ex-spouses and stepparents, parenting long-distance, choosing an attorney, and becoming financially independent.

Parent vs. Parent: How You and Your Child Can Survive the Custody Battle, Stephen P. Herman. New York: Pantheon Books, 1990.

A child psychiatrist and court-appointed psychiatric evaluator, Dr. Herman focuses on what to expect during litigated cases. Moving from the beginning of the dispute to the judge's final decision and beyond to visitation and relitigation, Dr. Herman explains what to expect if you are in a litigated custody battle, including how to prepare for a court-ordered psychiatric evaluation and the emotional impact of custody proceedings on the family. The book shows readers what steps to take to safeguard their child's well-being.

"Home for the Holidays," Ellen Seidman. *Redbook Magazine*, November 1991, p. 168.

Two children are kidnapped by their mother. The father finally gets them back after 10 years, as the result of a television program.

Family Abduction: How to Prevent an Abduction and What to Do if Your Child Is Abducted, P. Hoff. Arlington, Virginia: National Center for Missing and Exploited Children, 1994.

Family abduction is another form of child abuse in which one parent uses the child as a pawn against the other parent. Frequently, that child bears the brunt of the anger felt by the abducting parent. This book tells parents what steps to take to reduce the risk of abduction when separation is imminent and discusses laws that exist to help parents recover children.

Single Parenting

Successful Single Parenting, Gary Richmond. Eugene, Oregon: Harvest House Publishers, 1990.

Divorce can be tough for children, but the effects don't have to be long-term. This book provides answers to tough questions single parents face about how to soften the blow of divorce for their children.

Coping with Marital Transitions: A Family Systems Perspective, Mavis Hetherington, W. Glenn Clingempeel, Edward R. Anderson, et al. Chicago: The University of Chicago Press, 1992.

A longitudinal study examining altered family relationships in the wake of divorce. Includes chapters on the adjustment of children in single-mother families and parent-child relationships in single-mother families. This book is targeted at professionals, but interested parents will also benefit.

Divorce and New Beginnings: An Authoritative Guide to Recovery and Growth, Solo Parenting, and Stepfamilies, Genevieve Clapp. New York: John Wiley and Sons, 1992.

Offers insight and help for those personally touched by a divorce, single-parent, or stepfamily situation. Takes parents and children step-by-step through each stage of divorce and discusses rebuilding a successful family by handling daily problems and long-term concerns.

"He Stole My Daughter," Jacqueline Trimarchi and Carla Cantor. *Redbook Magazine*, May 1992, p. 166.

Describes a mother's efforts to find and get back her two-year-old daughter after the child's father kidnaps her. This heart-wrenching story describes the mother's effort to rebuild the relationship after a separation of three years.

Dads and Divorce

Good Men: A Practical Handbook for Divorced Dads, Jack Feuer. New York: Avon Books, 1997.

Deals with single parenting from a man's point of view. Practical information on a wide variety of concerns—whether you are a divorced man seeking sole custody, joint custody, or visitation rights or you are still fighting with your ex for the right to see your kids.

Live-Away Dads: Staying a Part of Your Children's Lives When They Aren't a Part of Your Home, William C. Klatte. New York: Penguin Books, 1999.

Includes taking care of yourself, getting along with your children's mother and others, navigating the court system, fathering your children, building a network of support.

Fathers After Divorce, Terry Arendell. Thousand Oaks, California: Sage Publications, 1995.

A complete guide for dads.

Divorced Dads: Shattering the Myths, Sanford L. Braver, Dianne O'Connell. New York: Tarcher/Putnam, 1998.

A non-traditional view of the role of divorced fathers. Deals with concepts of deadbeat dads, no-show dads, standards of living, terms of divorce, emotional issues of divorce, who leaves the marriage and why it matters, the "parentally disenfranchised" dad, joint legal custody, keeping dads involved, custody policies that work, and more.

Stepfamilies

Stepfamilies: Love, Marriage, and Parenting in the First Decade, James H. Bray. New York: Broadway Books/Random House, 1998.

Based on a longitudinal study, a detailed guide to easing the conflicts of stepfamily life and healing the scars of divorce. Topics include types of stepfamilies and the three cycles of stepfamily life.

The Enlightened Stepmother: Revolutionizing the Role, Perdita Kirkness Norwood, Teri Wingencher, New York: Avon Books, 1999.

Taken from the stepmother's point of view, this book discusses what works and what doesn't.

The Courage to Be a Stepmom: Finding Your Place Without Losing Yourself, Sue Patton Thoele, Berkeley, California: Wildcat Canyon Press, 1999.

Hands on advice and practical skills for women who want to be good stepmothers while taking care of themselves.

Blending Families, Elaine Fantle Shimberg, New York: Berkeley Publishing Group/Penguin Putnam, 1999.

A guide to this complex family situation.

Just for Children

The Boys and Girls Book About Divorce, Richard A. Gardner. New York: Bantam Books, 1970.

Although published in 1970, Dr. Gardner's book still addresses universal issues faced by children of divorce. Written specifically for children, this book helps young ones deal with feelings and situations that affect them during and shortly after the divorce. Many of Dr. Gardner's positions are still advocated today, although some have become more controversial—such as his notion that you should be honest with children about negative feelings toward their other parent.

The Kids' Book of Divorce: By, For & About Kids, The Unit at the Fayerweather Street School with Eric Rofes, editor. New York: Vintage Books, 1981.

This book is the result of two years' work by 20 school children between the ages of 11 and 14 in an open school in Cambridge, Massachusetts. They offer advice on everything from how to avoid taking sides to how to deal with parents' new relationships, stepparents, and gay parents. They describe the legal process of divorce in language a child can understand and cover such subjects as handling a new living situation, holidays, and visiting arrangements and how to get support from friends, relatives, or counselors. Although published in 1981, this book is still interesting and relevant.

Steptrouble: A Survival Guide For Teenagers with Stepparents, William L. Coleman. Minneapolis, Minnesota: CompCare Publishers, 1993.

A product of divorce himself, Coleman explains to teenagers in a language to which they can relate how to cope with divorce and a new stepfamily situation. Important topics include how to relate to stepparents and stepsiblings, how to handle and understand your own feelings, how to communicate with your family and stepfamily, and how to deal with a parent's love life among others.

Dinosaurs Divorce: A Guide for Changing Families, Laurence Brown and Marc Brown. Boston: Little Brown & Co., 1988.

This children's classic will bring comfort to any child of divorce.

Women and Divorce

Fair Share Divorce For Women, Kathleen Miller. Bellevue, Washington: Miller, Bird Advisers, Inc. 1995.

Gives women the support and guidance they need to safeguard their marital assets. Too often, women find themselves at a disadvantage when their marriage ends and they have to fight for what is rightfully theirs. This book levels the playing field by arming women with the information and techniques they need to protect their valuable investment.

What Every Woman Should Know About Divorce and Custody, Gayle Rosenwald Smith, J.D., and Sally Abrahms. New York: Perigee, 1998.

What women need to know to come out ahead in divorce and custody battles. A complete insider's guide filled with crucial advice from judges, lawyers, therapists, and mothers who have gone through this challenging legal process. Designed for women at every stage of divorce, it covers a wide range of legal strategies, as well as financial and psychological issues.

The Illusion of Equality, Martha Fineman Albertson. Chicago: The University of Chicago Press, 1991.

Discusses the effects of no-fault divorce reform on women. Originally hailed as a victory for the ideal of gender-neutrality and equality, Albertson contends that, although reforms may have succeeded on a symbolic level, this success has been at the expense of the women and children such reforms were supposed to help.

Women, Work, and Divorce, Richard R. Peterson. Albany: State University of New York Press, 1989.

This book considers how women cope with the economic hardship that accompanies divorce, using national longitudinal data on a generation of women in the United States. Peterson employs sociological and economic approaches to the study of labor-market outcomes and to the study of life-cycle events, to analyze the experiences of women. He shows how most divorced women can make at least a partial recovery on a long-term basis but demonstrates that divorced women with children have a harder time making work adjustments and experience greater economic deprivation. Given the continuing high rates of divorce, Peterson's findings highlight the importance of work rather than marriage for women's economic security.

Grandparents and Divorce

Grandparenting Redefined, Irene M. Endicott. Lynnwood, Washington: Aglow Publications, 1992.

For grandparents now raising their grandchildren. Discusses children's lives, problems due to divorce and remarriage, and drug and child abuse. Provides hope despite painful challenges.

Domestic Abuse

Rape in Marriage, Diana Russell. Bloomington: Indiana University Press, 1990.

One out of seven American women who have ever been married has been raped by a husband or ex-husband. The author is the chief investigator for the study conducted by the National Institute of Mental Health that uncovered this statistic. The book dispels misinformation and illusions about a previously ignored aspect of family violence.

When I Call for Help: A Pastoral Response to Domestic Violence, The United States Catholic Bishops' Conference, 1992.

A pamphlet that gives practical suggestions for what abusive men, women who are abused, and the society as a whole can do to combat domestic violence. Contains specific suggestions for educators and for pastoral staff.

Legal Issues

Between Love and Hate, Lois Gold. New York: Plenum Publishing, 1996.

Advises on all aspects of conducting a divorce as painlessly as possible. Covers such issues as trial separation, parenting, reestablishing yourself as single, and coping with an ex-spouse. Considers such legal matters as mediation, division of property, child custody, and choosing an attorney.

The Complete Guide for Men and Women Divorcing, Melvin Belli and Mel Krantzler. New York: St. Martin's Press, 1990.

Covers choosing an attorney, effectively managing divorce expenses, talking to children about divorce, establishing custody and visitation, and dealing with anger and the grieving process.

A Guide to Divorce Mediation, Gary Friedman. New York: Workman Publishing, 1993.

Lists four criteria necessary for every couple about to enter into mediation: motivation to mediate, self-responsibility, willingness to disagree, and willingness to agree. Friedman is an attorney. He explains the ground rules, legal ramifications, and where to find a mediator.

The Five-Minute Lawyer's Guide to Divorce, Michael Allan Cane, Esq. New York: Dell Publishing, 1995.

The founder of Tele-Lawyer (a legal phone service) provides answers to the most frequently asked questions on the topic of divorce.

Financial Books and Articles

Divorce and Money, Violet Woodhouse and Victoria Felton-Collins. Berkeley: Nolo Press, 1995.

A practical guide to evaluating assets during divorce. Discusses how to determine the real value of marital property, including houses, businesses, retirement plans, and investments, and how to negotiate a settlement that is fair to both sides. Step-by-step information covers deciding whether to keep or sell a house, protecting yourself against misuse of joint accounts and credit cards, preventing tax problems, handling alimony and child support, dividing debts, avoiding hasty decisions that could be financially harmful, and gaining financial stability as a single person.

The Dollars and Sense of Divorce: A Financial Guide for Women, Judith Briles. New York: MasterMedia Ltd., 1988.

Includes information for women who are divorced or seeking a divorce on such issues as choosing a lawyer, getting child and spousal support, and learning about taxes and investment opportunities.

Money and the Mature Woman, Frances Leonard. Reading, Massachusetts: Addison-Wesley, 1993.

Discusses how to hold on to your income, keep your home, and plan your estate.

Women and Money: The Independent Woman's Guide to Financial Security, Frances Leonard. Reading, Massachusetts: Addison-Wesley, 1991.

Intended to help women in midlife and older take a first step toward financial security. Chapters and sections deal with such issues as how to make the best of midlife divorce, the facts of life, and law for married women and homemakers. Also discusses what women need to know about pensions, Social Security, and health coverage.

The Pension Answer Book, Stephen J. Krass, Esq. New York: Panel Publishers, 1995.

Includes chapters on pension and retirement plans, life insurance and death benefits, 40l(k) plans, IRAs, rollovers, annuities, and more.

Bankruptcy and Divorce: Support and Property Division, Judith K. Fitzgerald and Ramona M. Arena. New York: Wiley Law Publications, 1994.

Includes a supplement published in January 1996. Covers such issues as bankruptcy and divorce, child support, property settlement, estate problems, pensions and retirement funds, and premarital agreements.

Smart Ways to Save Money During and After Divorce, Victoria E. Collins and Ginita Wall. Berkeley: Nolo Press, 1994.

Offers 70 tips for saving money in divorce, from uncovering and eradicating hidden expenses to saving on attorney fees.

Psychological Support

101 Interventions in Family Therapy, Thorana Nelson and Terry S. Trepper. Binghamton, New York: The Haworth Press, 1992.

Discusses a variety of family therapy interventions for such issues as marriage counseling, stepfamilies, and divorce therapy.

The Complete Divorce Recovery Handbook, John P. Splinter. Grand Rapids, Michigan: Zondervan Publishing House, 1992.

This book was written by people who have been through divorce; it discusses grief, guilt, forgiveness, children of divorce, codependence, dating after divorce, Biblical perspectives on divorce and remarriage, and divorce in longer-term marriages.

Crazy Time, Abigail Trafford. New York: HarperPerennial, 1992.

Charts the emotional journey of divorce, identifying the common phases in the evolution from marriage to separation to divorce and eventually to a new life. In three sections, entitled "Crisis," "Crazy Time," and "Recovery," the author tries to give readers a better understanding of her own experiences and conveys the message that readers are not alone in their pain and confusion.

Divorce Online: Make the Connection

Divorce Central (http://www.divorcecentral.com):

The best all-around source for divorce information and support online. A community for those going through the divorce process. State-by-state resources, bulletin boards, chat rooms, professionals classifieds, bookstore, resources, and personals with links to other personals sites.

Divorce Online (http://www.divorce-online.com/):

Topical information of a general nature. Created by a group of lawyers and psychologists to boost their businesses, but the factoids are valuable.

Divorce Helpline (http://www.divorcehelp.com/index.html):
Pro forma worksheets, a short divorce course, and a reading room. Particularly strong on California law. Tools to keep you out of court and out of conflict.

Men's Movement (http://www.vix.com/pub/men/orgs/orgs.html):
The World Wide Web Virtual Library connects you to the men's movement online. More than 123 listings of national and local fathers organizations.

GriefNet (http://www.griefnet.org/):
Divorce is about loss. Get the scoop on grief and recovery here. GriefNet is an Internet community of more than 30 email support groups and two Web sites. Provides support to people working through loss and grief issues of all kinds. Companion site, KIDSAID, provides a safe environment for kids and their parents to find information and ask questions.

Divorce Info (http://www.divorceinfo.com/):
General information on divorce topics. Some crude language.

Divorce Source (http://www.divorcesource.com/):
State-by-state information on divorce. Includes chat rooms and bulletin boards.

Divorce Magazine (http://www.divorcemag.com/):
Web version of the national magazine. Articles on various aspects of divorce plus resources, including professionals serving the divorce community.

My Two Homes (http://mytwohomes.com/):
Products to help children of divorce.

DivorceNet.com (http://www.divorcenet.com):
Information and resources by state, bulletin boards, chat rooms, and bookstore.

Single Moms and Single Dads (http://www.dragon-net.net/~smasd/):
A supportive place for single parents to come for reflections, advice, and fun.

Single Parents (http://www.parentsplace.com/family/singleparent/):
Part of Parentsplace; everything from soup to nuts for single parents.

Sole Mothers International (http://home.navisoft.com/solemom/index.htm):
A compilation of resources for single mothers. Everything from professional advice to resources. They also help women with child support needs.

Kathleen Miller Online (http://www.kathleenmiller.com/):
This certified financial consultant provides financial information for women going through divorce.

Support Guidelines.com (http://www.supportguidelines.com/links.html):
Created by Laura Morgan, Esq, Chair of the Child Support Committee of the Family Law Section of the American Bar Association. Officially for lawyers, laypeople can also use this site to find out the support guidelines in their state.

How to Divorce as Friends (http://www.divorceasfriends.com/):
Attorney Bill Ferguson walks you through a way to divorce as friends, if it's right for you. Information, telephone consultations, books, and a bulletin board moderated by Bill Ferguson.

The Internet Personals (http://www.montagar.com/personals/index.html):
Every combination under the sun.

Match.Com (http://www.match.com/):
Mingle anonymously in this singles den or ask the webmaster to find your match.

A Guide to Divorce Laws on the World Wide Web

Divorce laws change so rapidly, it would be impossible to render them in a book like *The Complete Idiot's Guide to Surviving Divorce*; many of the laws we report would be inaccurate a month after publication. Instead, we have decided to create a roadmap for finding the most accurate codes, laws, and case decisions possible—on the World Wide Web. Because divorce laws vary by state for the most part, we have created two sections. The first section, with a focus on search engines, law libraries, and other resources, will guide you through divorce law nationally. The second section will cover divorce laws for each of the 50 US states. Remember that online material varies from state to state, so one jurisdiction might have much more information available for its citizens than another. We know some of these Internet addresses are complex; government filing systems remain arcane, even on the Web. Nonetheless, this is a small price to pay to have the most accurate, up-to-date divorce laws at your fingertips.

A General Guide to Divorce Law on the Internet

The Best Legal Search Engines

FindLaw
http://www.findlaw.com/

LawCrawler
http://web.lawcrawler.com/

Search Law Reviews
http://www.lawreview.org/

The Law Libraries

World Wide Web Virtual Law Library
http://www.law.indiana.edu/law/v-lib/lawindex.html

Cornell Legal Information Institute
http://www.law.cornell.edu/

US Divorce Law from Cornell
http://www.law.cornell.edu/topics/divorce.html

Divorce Law Web Site Portals

Divorce Central
http://www.divorcecentral.com/

Divorce Source
http://www.divorcesource.com

Divorce Net
http://www.divorcenet.com/

Important Federal Laws

Indian Child Welfare Act
http://www.law.cornell.edu/uscode/25/ch2

Parental Kidnapping Prevention Act
http://www.law.cornell.edu/uscode/28/173

Hague Convention on Child Abduction
http://adams.patriot.net/~crouch/haguetext.html

Internal Revenue Code
http://www.fourmilab.ch/ustax/www/contents.html

National and State Legal and Bar Associations

American Bar Association
http://www.abanet.org

Canadian Bar Association
http://www.algonquinc.on.ca:80/cba/

Association of Trial Lawyers of America
http://www.atlanet.org/

Federal Bar Association
http://www.fedbar.org/

American Civil Liberties Union
http://www.aclu.org

American Association of Law Libraries
http://www.aallnet.org/

Electronic Frontier Foundation
http://www.eff.org

Electronic Privacy Information Center
http://www.epic.org

National Association of Legal Assistants
http://www.nala.org

National Court Reporters Association
http://www.verbatimreporters.com/ncra/reporter/ncrahome.html

National Federation of Paralegal Associations
http://www.paralegals.org

National Lawyer's Guild
http://www.emf.net/~cheetham/gnawld-1.html

Practicing Law Institute
http://www.pli.edu

Washington Legal Foundation
http://www.wlf.org

Federal Office of Child Support
http://www.acf.dhhs.gov/ACFPrograms/CSE/index.html

A State-by-State Roadmap to Divorce Laws and Legal Resources on the Internet

Alabama

Marriage
http://www.legislature.state.al.us/CodeofAlabama/1975/50692.htm

Divorce and Alimony
http://www.legislature.state.al.us/CodeofAlabama/1975/50752.htm

Child Custody and Support
http://www.legislature.state.al.us/CodeofAlabama/1975/50821.htm

Husband and Wife
http://www.legislature.state.al.us/CodeofAlabama/1975/51069.htm

Protection from Abuse
http://www.legislature.state.al.us/CodeofAlabama/1975/51269.htm

Family Violence Protection Order Enforcement
http://www.legislature.state.al.us/CodeofAlabama/1975/51306.htm

Domestic Violence Facilities
http://www.legislature.state.al.us/CodeofAlabama/1975/51333.htm

Child Support Overview
http://www.acf.dhhs.gov/programs/cse/fct/sp96_al.htm

Alaska

Marital and Domestic Relations Statutes
http://www.touchngo.com/lglcntr/akstats/statutes/title25.htm

Supreme Court Index for Family Law
http://www.touchngo.com/sp/s_family.htm

Uniform Child Custody Jurisdiction Act
http://www.touchngo.com/lglcntr/akstats/Statutes/title25/chapter30.htm

Arizona

Uniform Marriage and Divorce Act
http://www.azleg.state.az.us/ars/25/title25.htm#025 0311 00S

Revised Uniform Reciprocal Enforcement of Support Act
http://www.azleg.state.az.us/ars/25/title25.htm#025 0551 00S

Arkansas

Arkansas Bar Association
http://www.arkbar.com/

Arkansas Child Support Overview
http://www.acf.dhhs.gov/ACFPrograms/CSE/fct/sp96_ar.htm

The Alaska Court System
http://www.alaska.net/~akctlib/homepage.htm

California

Family Codes
ftp://leginfo.public.ca.gov/pub/code/fam/00001-01000/

Uniform Child Custody Jurisdiction Act
http://www.leginfo.ca.gov/cgi-bin/displaycode?section=fam&group=03001-04000&file=3400-3425

Uniform Divorce Recognition Act
http://www.leginfo.ca.gov/cgi-bin/displaycode?section=fam&group=02001-03000&file=2090-2093

California Courts and Judicial System
http://www.courtinfo.ca.gov/

California Judicial Council Forms
http://www.lawca.com/

The State Bar of California
http://www.calbar.org/

Colorado

Colorado Bar Association
http://www.usa.net/cobar/index.htm

Colorado Divorce Law Searchable Index
http://www.intellinetusa.com/statmgr.htm

Colorado Child Support Overview
http://www.acf.dhhs.gov/programs/cse/fct/sp96_co.htm

Connecticut

Statutes
http://www.cslnet.ctstateu.edu/statutes/title46b/t46b-p2.htm

Connecticut Divorce Home Page
http://www.ct-divorce.com/

Family Court Forms
http://www.jud.state.ct.us/external/super/forms2.htm#FAMILY

District of Columbia

Domestic Relations Code
http://www.lexislawpublishing.com/sdCGI-BIN/om_isapi.dll?clientID=525&infobase=dccode.NFO&softpage=doc_frame_pg

District of Columbia Bar Association
http://www.dcbar.org/

Delaware

Family Court System
http://www.ncsc.dni.us/court/delaware/family.htm

State Bar Association
http://www.laws.com/org.html

Child Support Overview
http://www.acf.dhhs.gov/ACFPrograms/CSE/fct/sp96_de.htm

Division of Child Support Enforcement
http://www.state.de.us/govern/agencies/dhss/irm/dcse/dcsehome.htm

Domestic Relations Code
http://www.lexislawpublishing.com/sdCGI-BIN/
om_isapi.dll?clientID=523&infobase=decode.NFO&softpage=browse_frame_pg

Florida

Statutes
http://www.leg.state.fl.us/citizen/documents/statutes/1997/ch0061/titl0061.htm

Court System
http://www.flcourts.org/

Family Court Initiative
http://justice.courts.state.fl.us/courts/family

Divorce Court Rules
http://justice.courts.state.fl.us:80/releases/enacted.html#family

Florida Guardianship
http://ww3.pwr.com:80/LEGAL/FLABAR/Consumer/general/Consumer.Pam/42PAMPH.

Attorney General
http://legal.firn.edu

Child Support Overview
http://www.acf.dhhs.gov/ACFPrograms/CSE/fct/sp96_fl.htm

Georgia

State Bar of Georgia
http://www.gabar.org/

Atlanta Bar Association
http://www.atlantabar.org/

Grounds for Divorce
http://www.ganet.state.ga.us/cgi-bin/pub/ocode/ocgsearch?docname=OCode/G/19/5/
3&highlight=marriage

314

Alimony
http://www.ganet.state.ga.us/cgi-bin/pub/ocode/ocgsearch?docname=OCode/G/19/6/5&highlight=marriage

Custody
http://www.ganet.state.ga.us/cgi-bin/pub/ocode/ocgsearch?docname=OCode/G/19/9/3&highlight=marriage

Support
http://www.ganet.state.ga.us/cgi-bin/pub/ocode/ocgsearch?docname=OCode/G/19/11/43&highlight=marriage

Supreme Court of Georgia
http://www.state.ga.us/Courts/Supreme

Department of Human Resources
http://www.state.ga.us/Departments/DHR/dfcs.html

Georgia General Assembly
http://www.state.ga.us/Legis

Official Code of Georgia
http://www.ganet.state.ga.us/services/ocode/ocgsearch.htm

Atlanta Legal Aid
http://www.law.emory.edu/PI/ALAS/

Atlanta Volunteer Lawyers Foundation
http://www.law.emory.edu/PI/AVLF

Child Support Enforcement
http://www.state.ga.us/Departments/DHR/CSE

Hawaii

Hawaii Child Support
http://www.hawaii.gov/csea/csea.htm

Hawaii Child Support Overview
http://www.acf.dhhs.gov/ACFPrograms/CSE/fct/sp96_hi.htm

Idaho

Uniform Child Custody Jurisdiction
http://www.idwr.state.id.us/idstat/TOC/32011KTOC.html

Interstate Family Support Act
http://www.idwr.state.id.us/idstat/TOC/07010KTOC.html

Illinois

Statutes
http://www.legis.state.il.us/ilcs/ch750/ch750actstoc.htm

Supreme and Appellate Court Opinions
http://www.state.il.us/court/

State Bar Association
http://www.illinoisbar.org/

Chicago Bar Association (Family Law)
http://www.chicagobar.org/public/diallaw/diallaw.html

Chicago Bar Assoc. (Lawyer Referral)
http://www.illinoisbar.org/

Child Support Enforcement
http://www.state.il.us/dpa/csenews.htm

Department of Children and Family Services
http://www.state.il.us/dcfs

Illinois Pro Bono Center
http://www.soltec.net/ipbc

Indiana

State Bar Association
http://www.iquest.net/isba/

Statutes
http://www.law.indiana.edu/codes/in/31/art-31-1.html

Duties of Support
http://www.law.indiana.edu/codes/in/31/art-31-2.html

Marriage
http://www.law.indiana.edu/codes/in/31/art-31-7.html

Uniform Child Custody Jurisdiction Act
http://www.law.indiana.edu/codes/in//31/ch-31-1-11.6.html

Uniform Premarital Agreement Act
http://www.law.indiana.edu/codes/in/31/ch-31-7-2.5.html

Department of Child Support Enforcement
http://www.ai.org/fssa/cse

Attorney General
http://www.ai.org/atty_gen/index.html

Child Support Division
http://www.indy.net/~night/marion.htm

Iowa

Searchable Index of Iowa Statutes
http://www2.legis.state.ia.us/Indices/IACODE-1997.html

Kansas

Kansas Bar Association
http://www.ink.org/public/cybar

Searchable Index of Kansas Statutes
http://www.ink.org/public/statutes/statutes.html

Kansas Child Support Overview
http://www.acf.dhhs.gov/ACFPrograms/CSE/fct/sp96_ks.htm

Kansas Attorney General
http://lawlib.wuacc.edu/ag/homepage.html

Kentucky

Title XXXV Domestic Relations
http://www.lrc.state.ky.us/krs/titles.htm

Child Support Enforcement Division
http://www.law.state.ky.us/childsupport/default.htm

Kentucky Bar Association
http://www.kybar.org/

Louisiana

Child Support Overview
http://www.acf.dhhs.gov/programs/cse/fct/sp96_la.htm

State Bar Association
http://www.lsba.org/

Maine

Domestic Relations Statutes
http://janus.state.me.us/legis/statutes/19-A/title19-Ach00sec0.html

Child Support Overview
http://www.acf.dhhs.gov/programs/cse/fct/sp96_me.htm

Association
arm.net/msba/

ence
nform.umd.edu/UMS+State/MD_Resources/MDSP/domv.html

For family law statutes, select Family Law in the top menu box and start with section 1–101 in the lower menu box. Keep clicking Next to go to the next part of the text, and note sections of importance for future reference.

Child Support Overview
http://www.acf.dhhs.gov/ACFPrograms/CSE/fct/sp96_md.html

Massachusetts

Statutes
http://www.state.ma.us/legis/laws/mgl/index.htm

State Bar
http://www.laws.com/org.html

Child Support Overview
http://www.acf.dhhs.gov/ACFPrograms/CSE/fct/sp96_ma.htm

Michigan

Michigan Child Support Services
http://www.mfia.state.mi.us/CHLDSUPP/CS-INDEX.htm

Child Support Overview
http://www.acf.dhhs.gov/programs/cse/fct/sp96_mi.htm

State Bar
http://www.michbar.org/

Supreme Court
http://www.supremecourt.state.mi.us/

Supreme Court Opinions
http://www.icle.org/misupct/index.htm

Minnesota

Marriage
http://www.revisor.leg.state.mn.us/stats/517

Marriage Dissolution
http://www.revisor.leg.state.mn.us/stats/518

Uniform Child Custody Jurisdiction Act
http://www.revisor.leg.state.mn.us/stats/518A

Domestic Abuse
http://www.revisor.leg.state.mn.us/stats/518B

Uniform Interstate Family Support Act
http://www.revisor.leg.state.mn.us/stats/518C

Rights and Privileges of Married Persons
http://www.revisor.leg.state.mn.us/stats/519

Mississippi

Division of Child Support Enforcement
http://www.mdhs.state.ms.us/cse.html

Child Support Overview
http://www.acf.dhhs.gov/programs/cse/fct/sp96_ms.htm

Missouri

The Statutes
http://www.moga.state.mo.us/homestat.htm

Child Support Overview
http://www.acf.dhhs.gov/ACFPrograms/CSE/fct/sp96_mo.htm

Coalition for Fathers and Children
http://walden.mo.net/~usher/ncf-stl.htm

Missouri Bar
http://www.mobar.org/

Child Support Enforcement
http://services.state.mo.us/dss/cse/cse.htm

Montana

Separation
http://www.nfoweb.com/folio.pgi/mtcode/query=*/doc/{@41088}?

Uniform Premarital Agreement Act
http://www.nfoweb.com/folio.pgi/mtcode/query=*/doc/{@41108}?

Termination of Marriage, Child Custody, and Support
http://www.nfoweb.com/folio.pgi/mtcode/query=*/doc/{@41168}?

Child Support Enforcement Division
http://www.dphhs.mt.gov/whowhat/csed.htm

Nebraska

Wife's Separate Property
http://unicam1.lcs.state.ne.us/folio.pgi/statutes.nfo/query=*/doc/{@34087}?

Divorce
http://unicam1.lcs.state.ne.us/folio.pgi/statutes.nfo/query=*/doc/{@34207}?

Separation and Dissolution
http://unicam1.lcs.state.ne.us/folio.pgi/statutes.nfo/query=*/doc/{@34227}?

Husband and Wife
http://unicam1.lcs.state.ne.us/folio.pgi/statutes.nfo/query=
marriage/doc/{34696,0,0,0}?

Domestic Relations Matters
http://unicam1.lcs.state.ne.us/folio.pgi/statutes.nfo/query=child+custody/doc/
{@22901}?

Child Support Overview
http://www.acf.dhhs.gov/programs/cse/fct/sp96_nb.htm

New Hampshire

Statutes
http://199.92.250.14/rsa/T43/INDEX.HTM

Child Support Overview
http://www.acf.dhhs.gov/programs/cse/fct/sp96_nh.htm

New Jersey

Searchable Index
http://www.njleg.state.nj.us/cgi-bin/
om_isapi.dll?clientID=10290&infobase=Statutes.nfo&softpage=Doc_Frame_Pg

Child Custody
http://www.njleg.state.nj.us/cgi-bin/
om_isapi.dll?clientID=10290&advquery=child%20custody&infobase=Statutes.nfo&record=
{F6}&recordswithhits=on&softpage=Doc_Frame_Pg&x=42&y=23

Child Support Overview
http://www.acf.dhhs.gov/programs/cse/fct/sp96_nj.htm

State Bar Association
http://www.njsba.com/

Child Support Overview
http://www.acf.dhhs.gov/programs/cse/fct/sp96_nj.htm

Nevada

Marriage
http://www.leg.state.nv.us/NRS/CH_122.html

Rights of Husband and Wife
http://www.leg.state.nv.us/NRS/CH_123.html

Uniform Premarital Act
http://www.leg.state.nv.us/NRS/CH_123A.html

Dissolution of Marriage
http://www.leg.state.nv.us/NRS/CH_125.html

Custody and Visitation
http://www.leg.state.nv.us/NRS/CH_125A.html

Obligation and Support
http://www.leg.state.nv.us/NRS/CH_125b.html

Parentage
http://www.leg.state.nv.us/NRS/CH_126.html

Termination of Parental Rights
http://www.leg.state.nv.us/NRS/CH_128.html

Reciprocal Enforcement of Support
http://www.leg.state.nv.us/NRS/CH_130.html

Child Support Overview
http://www.acf.dhhs.gov/programs/cse/fct/sp96_nv.htm

New Mexico

Statutes
http://www.lexislawpublishing.com/sdCGI-BIN/
om_isapi.dll?clientID=125&infobase=nmsa1978.NFO&softpage=browse_frame_pg

Child Support Overview
http://www.acf.dhhs.gov/programs/cse/fct/sp96_nm.htm

New York

Searchable Index for New York Divorce Laws
http://www.findlaw.com/11stategov/ny/nycl.html

Child Support Overview
http://www.acf.dhhs.gov/programs/cse/fct/sp96_ny.htm

New York Bar Association
http://www.nysba.org/

North Carolina

Uniform Child Custody Jurisdiction Act
http://www.rosen.com/1.htm

Domestic Violence
http://www.rosen.com/2.htm

Equitable Jurisdiction Statutes
http://www.rosen.com/3.htm

Post-Separation Support and Alimony
http://www.rosen.com/4.htm

Child Custody
http://www.rosen.com/5.htm

Child Support
http://www.rosen.com/6.htm

Absolute Divorce Statutes
http://www.rosen.com/7.htm

North Carolina Bar Association
http://www.barlinc.org/

Child Support Overview
http://www.acf.dhhs.gov/ACFPrograms/CSE/fct/sp96_nc.htm

North Dakota

North Dakota's divorce laws are at Title 14. Chapter 14-05 includes the divorce laws; Chapter 14-09 relates to custody; Chapter 14-17.1 covers domestic violence.
http://www.state.nd.us/lr/centurycode.html

For North Dakota's Supreme Court decisions relating to divorce, check the ND Supreme Court home page under "opinions."
http://www.court.state.nd.us/

(To view this information, you must download the Adobe Acrobat Reader at http://www.adobe.com/prodindex/acrobat/readstep.html.)

Child Support Overview
http://www.acf.dhhs.gov/programs/cse/fct/sp96_nd.htm

Ohio

Searchable Index to Divorce Laws
http://orc.avv.com/title-31/home.htm

Child Support Overview
http://www.acf.dhhs.gov/programs/cse/fct/sp96_oh.htm

Oklahoma

Oklahoma Legal Research System
http://oklegal.onenet.net/

Child Support Overview
http://www.acf.dhhs.gov/programs/cse/fct/sp96_ok.htm

Oregon

Searchable Index
http://landru.leg.state.or.us/ors/

Child Support Overview
http://www.acf.dhhs.gov/programs/cse/fct/sp96_or.htm

Pennsylvania

Statutes
http://members.aol.com/StatutesPA/23.html

Child Support Overview
http://www.acf.dhhs.gov/programs/cse/fct/sp96_pa.htm

Rhode Island

Statutes
http://www.rilin.state.ri.us/Statutes/TITLE15/INDEX.HTM

Child Support Overview
http://www.acf.dhhs.gov/programs/cse/fct/sp96_ri.htm

South Carolina

Statutes
http://www.lpitr.state.sc.us/code/titl20.htm

Child Support Overview
http://www.acf.dhhs.gov/programs/cse/fct/sp96_sc.htm

State Bar Association
http://www.scbar.org/

South Dakota

South Dakota Domestic Code
http://www.lexislawpublishing.com/sdCGI-BIN/
om_isapi.dll?clientID=534&infobase=sdcode.NFO&softpage=browse_frame_pg

Child Support Overview
http://www.acf.dhhs.gov/programs/cse/fct/sp96_sd.htm

Tennessee

Domestic Relations
http://www.lexislawpublishing.com/sdCGI-BIN/
om_isapi.dll?clientID=112&infobase=tncode.NFO&softpage=browse_frame_pg

Tennessee Supreme Court
http://tscaoc.tsc.state.tn.us/

University of Tennessee Law Library
http://www.law.utk.edu/library/index.ht

Tennessee Bar Association
http://www.tba.org/

County Bar Associations
http://www.tba.org/Resources/net_tnbars.html

Child Support Overview
http://www.acf.dhhs.gov/programs/cse/fct/sp96_tn.htm

Texas

Statutes
http://www.capitol.state.tx.us/statutes/fatoc.html

Child Support Overview
http://www.acf.dhhs.gov/programs/cse/fct/sp96_tx.htm

Utah

Utah Statutes
http://www.lawutah.com/gb/docs/Statutes.htm

Utah Court Opinions
http://www.lawutah.com/gb/docs/Cases.htm

Frequently Asked Questions for Utah
http://www.lawutah.com/gb/docs/Topics.htm

Child Support Calculator
http://www.lawutah.com/gb/docs/Calc.htm

State Bar
http://www.utahbar.org/

Child Support Overview
http://www.acf.dhhs.gov/programs/cse/fct/sp96_ut.htm

Vermont

Statutes
http://www.leg.state.vt.us/statutes/title15/title15.htm

Child Support Overview
http://www.acf.dhhs.gov/programs/cse/fct/sp96_vt.htm

Virginia

Searchable Statutes
http://leg1.state.va.us/000/src.htm

Uniform Child Custody Jurisdiction Act
http://leg1.state.va.us/000/cod/code52.htm#1219085

Interstate Family Support Act
http://leg1.state.va.us/000/cod/code52.htm#1218713

Child Support Overview
http://www.acf.dhhs.gov/programs/cse/fct/sp96_va.htm

Washington

Statutes Summary
gopher://leginfo.leg.wa.gov:70/00/pub/rcw/title_26/26_title_digest

Dissolution of Marriage and Legal Separation
gopher://leginfo.leg.wa.gov:70/00/pub/rcw/title_26/chapter_009/rcw_26_09

Separation Contracts
gopher://leginfo.leg.wa.gov:70/00/pub/rcw/title_26/chapter_009/rcw_26_09_070

Temporary Parenting Plan
gopher://leginfo.leg.wa.gov:70/00/pub/rcw/title_26/chapter_009/rcw_26_09_004

Uniform Child Custody Jurisdiction Act
gopher://leginfo.leg.wa.gov:70/00/pub/rcw/title_26/chapter_027/rcw_26_27

Child Abduction or Concealment
gopher://leginfo.leg.wa.gov:70/00/pub/rcw/title_26/chapter_009/rcw_26_09_255

Maintenance Orders
gopher://leginfo.leg.wa.gov:70/00/pub/rcw/title_26/chapter_009/rcw_26_09_090

Child Support
gopher://leginfo.leg.wa.gov:70/00/pub/rcw/title_26/chapter_009/rcw_26_09_100

Modification of Child Support
gopher://leginfo.leg.wa.gov:70/00/pub/rcw/title_26/chapter_009/rcw_26_09_173

Retirement Benefits
gopher://leginfo.leg.wa.gov:70/00/pub/rcw/title_26/chapter_009/rcw_26_09_138

Failure to Comply with Decree
gopher://leginfo.leg.wa.gov:70/00/pub/rcw/title_26/chapter_009/rcw_26_09_160

Washington State Bar Association
http://www.wsba.org/

Child Support Overview
http://www.acf.dhhs.gov/programs/cse/fct/sp96_wa.htm

West Virginia

Child Support Overview
http://www.acf.dhhs.gov/programs/cse/fct/sp96_wv.htm

Wisconsin

Statutes
http://www.legis.state.wi.us/Statutes.html

State Bar
http://www.wisbar.org

Child Support Overview
http://www.acf.dhhs.gov/programs/cse/fct/sp96_wi.htm

Wyoming

Statutes
http://legisweb.state.wy.us/titles/97titles/title20.htm

Child Support Overview
http://www.acf.dhhs.gov/programs/cse/fct/sp96_wy.htm

Sample Settlement Agreement

The following is a sample divorce settlement agreement signed in the State of New York. Agreements do not have to follow this format, and anything the parties wish to include is permissible, within the confines of the law. Keep in mind that each state has its own laws, and, while the laws of New York State guided this agreement, the laws of California, for example, are quite different and an agreement based on those laws would differ accordingly.

It is always advisable for each party to consult with his or her own attorney before signing a settlement agreement. This is for the protection of the parties and their children. Don't be "pennywise and pound foolish" when your future is involved.

SUPREME COURT OF THE STATE OF NEW YORK COUNTY OF NEW YORK

-------------------------------X

Catherine,

                                            STIPULATION OF

                                            SETTLEMENT AND

Plaintiff,

                                            AGREEMENT

- against - Index No.

Robert Smith,

Defendant.

-------------------------------X

AGREEMENT AND STIPULATION OF SETTLEMENT made this 5th day of March, 1993, between CATHERINE Smith, residing at New York, New York 10010 (hereinafter referred to as the "Wife") and ROBERT Smith, residing at New York 10021 (hereinafter referred to as the "Husband"),

WITNESSETH:

WHEREAS, the parties were duly married to each other at New Orleans, Louisiana on 1980; and

WHEREAS, there are two infant issue of this marriage, to wit: CHRIS Smith, born and ANDREW Smith, born (hereinafter referred to as "the Child" or "the Children"), and no additional children are expected; and

WHEREAS, an action for absolute divorce entitled "CATHERINE Smith, Plaintiff, against ROBERT Smith, Defendant" was commenced by the Wife on or about and is presently pending in the Supreme Court of the State of New York, County of

which said action the parties seek to settle in all respects within the confines of this Stipulation of Settlement and Agreement; and

WHEREAS, the parties desire to confirm their separation and to fix their respective financial and property rights, including the resolution of all questions involving the support of the respective parties and of the Children hereto and all other rights, privileges and obligations and all matters with respect to each other arising out of the marital relationship of the parties and otherwise;

NOW, THEREFORE, in consideration of the premises and the mutual and reciprocal covenants hereinafter set forth, it is agreed as follows:

ARTICLE I

SEPARATE RESIDENCE

It is, and shall be, lawful for the parties hereto at all times to live separate and apart from each other and to reside from time to time at such place or places as each of such parties may see fit and to contract, carry on and engage in any employment, business or trade, which either may deem fit, free from control, restraint, or interference, direct or indirect, by the other in all respects as if such parties were sole and unmarried.

ARTICLE II

NO MOLESTATION

Neither party shall in any way molest, disturb or trouble the other or interfere with the peace and comfort of the other or compel or seek to compel the other to associate, cohabit or dwell with him or her by any action or proceeding for restoration of conjugal rights or by any means whatsoever.

ARTICLE III

MUTUAL RELEASE AND DISCHARGE

OF CLAIMS IN ESTATES

Except as otherwise provided in this Agreement, each party hereby releases, waives and relinquishes any and all rights which he or she may now have, or may hereafter acquire, as the other party's spouse under the present or future laws of any jurisdiction or under any Will or testamentary writing now in existence to share in the estate of the other party upon the latter's death; and to act as executor or administrator of the other party's estate. This provision is intended to, and shall constitute, a mutual waiver by the parties to take under any existing Will or testamentary writing of the other or to take against each other's Wills or testamentary writings, now or hereafter in force, under the present or future laws of any jurisdiction whatsoever. The parties intend, by the afore-described waiver and release, to relinquish any and all rights in and to each other's estate including the right of set-off now provided in §5-3.1 of the Estates, Powers and Trusts Law of the State of New York, any and all distributive shares presently provided in §4-1.1 of the Estates, Powers and Trusts Law and all rights of election presently provided for in §5-1.1 of said Law or any prior or subsequent similar provision of law of this or any other jurisdiction. However, the foregoing shall not bar a claim on the part of either party against the other for any cause or causes arising out of a breach of this agreement during the lifetime of the deceased party against whose estate such claim may be made. Moreover, the foregoing shall not be deemed a bar to either party naming the other as a beneficiary in any will he or she may hereafter execute.

ARTICLE IV

CUSTODY AND VISITATION

1. The Wife shall have custody of the infant issue of the marriage. The parties' mutual consent must be obtained with respect to the Children prior to a) undertaking major medical treatments, including but not limited to, surgical, major drug therapy, major dental, orthodontia, gynecological, dermatologist or ophthalmologist treatments and b) selecting or changing either Child's elementary, junior, high school or college. The parties shall mutually approve of physicians and educational institutions for the Children. In the case of an acute medical emergency and only after the person having the care of the Children at the time has made his or her best efforts, time permitting, to contact the other and has failed to reach that person, then the parent with the Child or Children may make any major decisions concerning the Children's health or welfare. In the event of the occurrence of an emergency, the parent who is with the Child or Children shall notify the other parent of the situation as soon as possible after the occurrence of the event.

2. The Husband shall have the following visitation rights with the Children as set out below:

(a)   Every other weekend from Friday night at approximately 7:00 P.M. until Sunday night until approximately 7:00 P.M., except that on one out of every four of his weekends he will keep the Children until Monday morning at 9:00 A.M., at which time the Husband shall bring the Children to school;

(b)   One mid-week evening each week from 6:00 P.M. to 9:00 P.M. provided that such period shall not interfere with the Children's scheduled school activities and provided that the Husband gives the Wife two weeks' advance notice that he will exercise such visitation;

(c)   Two one-week vacations per year. The Husband shall give the Wife at least four months notice of the specific vacations dates;

(d)   One-half of the Children's school holidays. The Husband shall give the Wife notice by August 30th of each year on which of the Children's school holidays he wishes to visit with the Children. For the purpose of this subparagraph, "school holidays" mean the winter recess beginning on December 26th and ending the day before school begins, the February recess and the spring recess including Easter Sunday.

(e)   In the even numbered years, Memorial Day, Labor Day, Veterans' Day, Christmas Eve (December 24th at 5:00 P.M. until 9:00 P.M.), New Year's Eve and Day;

(f)   In odd numbered years, Fourth of July, Columbus Day, Thanksgiving (from Wednesday after school until Monday morning at 9:00 A.M., at which time the Husband shall bring the Children to school), Christmas Day;

(g)   Holiday visitation shall commence at approximately 7:00 P.M. the evening prior to the holiday and end at approximately 7:00 P.M. on the holiday, except for New Year's Day, Christmas Day and Thanksgiving;

(h)   On the Children's birthday for not less than three hours, unless the Children are not at home, such time to be arranged so that the visitation will not interfere with the Children's educational or other activities; and the Husband's birthday, at such reasonable times when the Husband is not then working, such times to be arranged so that they will not interfere with the Children's education and for the day on Father's Day. There shall be no visitation on Mother's Day and on the Mother's birthday.

3. In the event the Husband is unable to be with the Children on a weekend visitation period, he shall pay the Wife Fifty Dollars ($50.00) unless at least three weeks prior to that weekend the Wife has notified the Husband of specific weekend plans away from her residence, the cancellation of which will cause financial loss. In such case, the Husband must make caretaker provisions for the Children for the entire weekend. The Husband's caretaker obligation shall be limited to one weekend per month and the Wife shall provide the Husband with proof of financial loss.

4. Visitation by the Husband shall take place away from the Wife's residence, except in the case of a Child's serious, prolonged illness. The Children shall be picked up at and returned to the lobby of the Wife's residence by the Husband except when he brings the Children to school.

5. Each of the parties hereto agrees to keep the other as reasonably well-informed as practical of the Children's whereabouts when with the Husband or Wife, respectively, and that in the event either party has knowledge of any illness, accident or other circumstances seriously affecting a Child's health or general welfare the Husband or the Wife, as the case may be, will promptly notify the other of such circumstances.

6. The parties shall exert every reasonable effort to maintain access and contact with the Children and to foster a feeling of affection between the Children and the other party. Neither party shall do anything which may estrange the Children from either of the parties, or which may inhibit the free and natural development of the affection and respect of the Children for each the parties.

7. The Husband shall be entitled to complete, detailed information and reports from any school, pediatrician, general physician, dentist, consultant or specialist attending the Children and shall be entitled to be furnished with copies of any such information and reports directly from such institutions or individuals.

8. In the event of the death of the Husband or Wife, the surviving parent shall exert every reasonable effort to maintain access and contact and to foster a feeling of affection between the Children and the Children's immediate family relatives.

9. Any non-exercise or partial exercise of any visitation right by the Husband, or the Children's immediate family relatives, in the event of the Wife's death or the Husband's death, shall not be deemed a waiver of future rights. Visitation not exercised shall be deemed waived.

10. During their minority, as defined herein, the Children shall be continued to be known by their names and surname as set forth in the recital of this Agreement and by no other name, and the Children's names and surname shall not be changed from those set forth in the recitals of this Agreement.

11. The Wife shall permit the Children to utilize the telephone in the Wife's residence to call the Husband for a reasonable period each day. If the Children are on vacation with a party, in or outside of the United States, that party shall cause the Children to telephone the other party (as well as permit the other to telephone the Children) no less than once per week for a time period of no less than ten (10) minutes in aggregate. The Husband shall pay the cost of such call or calls.

ARTICLE V

BASIC CHILD SUPPORT OF

THE CHILDREN

1. (a) Commencing with the first time the 15th or first day of month occurs following the execution of this Agreement, the Husband shall pay to the Wife the sum of $37,500 per annum, to be paid in equal semi-monthly installments of $1,562.50 each, on the first and 15th day of the month, except as otherwise provided in this Agreement.

(b)(i) In order to offset any changes in the cost of living, the Husband agrees that beginning with the first anniversary of the execution of this Agreement, and on each anniversary following, except as provided in paragraph "2" of this Article, he shall pay to the Wife, as Basic Child Support, to be paid in semi-monthly installments on the first and 15th day of the month, an amount equal to $1,562.50 times an escalation factor being a quotient which uses the Price Index on each anniversary date as the numerator and the Price Index for the first month following the signing of this Agreement as the denominator. The Price Index shall be defined as an average of the Special Index "All items less medical care" for (1) Consumer Price Index for All Urban consumers (CPI-U); Seasonally adjusted U.S. city average and (2) CPI-U, Selected areas (NY-NJ-CT), published by the U.S. Department of Labor, Bureau of Labor Statistics in its publication entitled, "CPI Detailed Report". Thus, if the Price Index on the anniversary date was 142.6 and the Price Index for the month following the signing of this Agreement was 135.8, the escalation factor would be 1.05 (142.6 ÷ 135.8), and the Basic Child Support would be increased to $1,640.63 semi-monthly ($1,562.50 × 1.05).

(ii) Notwithstanding the foregoing, in no event shall the adjustment result in an annual Base Child Support award, for the year for which the calculation is being made, exceeding 25% of the Husband's Gross Income. "Gross Income" shall be defined as annual earned income from all sources including annual cash and stock bonuses, but excluding involuntary pension plan contributions, involuntary savings plan contributions, non-cash incentive award plans, stock options awarded at the market price, annual interest on savings, dividends and capital gains unless capital gains are the Husband's principal source of business. Thus, to the extent the afore-described calculation results in an annual child support sum exceeding 25% of Gross Income, the Basic Child Support award shall be capped at 25% of such income. The amount of adjustment shall be calculated on the anniversary date of the execution of this Agreement and shall be paid to the Wife as described above in semi-monthly payments. If the Husband claims that the adjustment yields an annual figure which exceeds 25% of the income described in the first sentence of this subparagraph, then he shall provide the Wife with his W-2, 1099 and K-1 forms, and Schedule C forms, if any, for earned income for the year for which the calculation is being made.

(iii) In the event the Husband's Gross Income drops below $150,000 per annum, the Base Child Support shall be reduced to 25% of the Husband's reduced Gross Income but in no event shall the Base Child Support be less than $31,000 per annum for one year thereafter. After one year, if the Husband's Gross Income continues to be less than $150,000, the support shall be set at the percentage required under the Child Support Standards Act as applied to the Husband's Gross Income, as defined herein, of up to $125,000.

2. The Base Child Support shall be allocated 50% to each Child, and shall terminate on a pro rata basis upon each Child's emancipation as defined herein.

ARTICLE VI

ADDITIONAL CHILD SUPPORT

1. (a) Commencing with the first semi-monthly payment due twelve months from the date of execution of this Agreement, and continuing for 48 months from the date of the execution of this Agreement, the Husband shall pay to the Wife, on a semi-monthly basis, a sum of Additional Child Support in an amount equal to one twenty-fourth of 5% of a maximum of $500,000 of his Gross Income less $250,000. For example, if the Husband earns $300,000 in Gross Income as defined herein, the calculation of Additional Child Support pursuant to this Article shall be $300,000 – $250,000 = $50,000 × .05 = $2,500. $2,500 ÷ 24 = $104.

(b) In order to ascertain the amount of Additional Child Support for the second year following the execution of this Agreement, (i.e., the first year of such payments) Gross Income shall be calculated for the calendar year 1992. Thereafter, the Additional Child Support pursuant to paragraph 1 of this Article shall be calculated based upon the Husband's Gross Income for the prior calendar year. For example, Additional Child Support for the year 1995 shall be calculated based on the Husband's calendar year 1994 Gross Income.

2. (a) From the 49th through the 60th month following the execution of this Agreement, the Husband shall pay the Wife, in semi-monthly payments, a sum in an amount equal to one twenty-fourth of 5% of a maximum of $250,000 of his Gross Income less $150,000, plus one twenty-fourth of 15% of a maximum of $500,000 of his Gross Income less $250,000. For example, if the Husband earns $300,000 in Gross Income as defined herein, the calculation of Additional Child Support pursuant to this Article shall be: $250,000 – 150,000 = $100,000 × .05 = $5,000. $300,000 – 250,000 = $50,000 × .15 = $7,500 ($5,000 + 7,500) ÷ 24 = $521.

333

(b) Commencing with the payment due on the 60th month from the date of the execution of this Agreement, the amount of Additional Child Support shall be recalculated so that the Husband shall pay to the Wife, in semi-monthly payments, a sum in an amount equal to one twenty-fourth of 5% of a maximum of $250,000 of his Gross Income less $150,000, plus one twenty-fourth of 10% of a maximum of $500,000 of his Gross Income less $250,000. For example, if the Husband earns $300,000 in Gross Income as defined herein, the calculation of Additional Child Support pursuant to this Article shall be: $250,000 − 150,000 = $100,000 × .05 = $5,000. $300,000 − 250,000 = $50,000 × .1 = $5,000 ($5,000 + 5,000) ÷ 24 = $417.

3. Additional Child Support shall be allocated 50% to each Child, and shall terminate on a pro rata basis upon each Child's emancipation as defined herein.

4. Additional Child Support shall not be subject to the adjustment described in Article V, paragraph "1" of this Agreement.

5. Upon the first payment of Additional Child Support, and upon each recalculation in the payment amount thereafter, the Husband shall provide the Wife with a written description of how he derived the sums due, and a copy of his W-2 form(s), 1099 form(s), for the year which is being used to calculate the Additional Child Support, as well as his most recent pay stub.

ARTICLE VII

OTHER CHILD SUPPORT

1. Until a Child's emancipation, as defined in this Agreement, the Husband shall maintain health and life insurance for the benefit of such Child. The Husband's life insurance shall be maintained in the amounts described in Schedule "A" annexed hereto, which are sufficient to meet the Husband's obligations described in Articles V and VII of this Agreement and assigned to a trust. Under the terms of such trust, in the event of the Husband's death prior to the emancipation of either Child, the insurance proceeds, with the exception of $50,000, shall be administered by Citibank or another financial institution selected by the Husband and dispersed in accordance with Articles V and VII of this Agreement. Fifty Thousand ($50,000.00) Dollars shall be paid directly to the Wife if she shall then be living. To effectuate this arrangement, the Husband, within ninety (90) days of the date of the execution of this Agreement, shall establish a trust to which such insurance shall be assigned, and the trustee of which shall be the beneficiary of the insurance proceeds. The Wife shall cooperate to the extent necessary to effectuate this trust. The trust shall provide for equal shares for each of the Children until a Child's attaining the age of 30. At that time, the principal of that Child's share shall be paid to that Child.

2. Within sixty (60) days of the date of the execution of this Agreement, and as a condition precedent to the establishment of the trust, the Wife shall obtain and provide to the Husband written verification of each Child's social security number.

3. The Wife, at her option and expense, may purchase life insurance on the Husband's life. The Husband shall undergo such physical as is necessary to enable the Wife to obtain such insurance.

4. Until each Child is emancipated, the Husband shall maintain medical insurance for the Children and shall pay the cost of the Children's medical expenses. The Wife shall submit to the Children's health care givers any insurance forms provided by the Husband and shall cooperate in having such forms submitted to the insurance company.

5. (a) The Husband shall be obligated to pay, directly to the provider of services, the cost of the Children's tuition and mandatory school-related fees and costs, school books and school supplies (exclusive of school meals, extracurricular school or after school activities, and transportation, which shall be the responsibility of the Wife) during the duration of the Child's elementary, junior high and high school education. Such costs shall hereinafter be referred to as "Pre-College Tuition". Notwithstanding the foregoing, and except as provided in subsection "" of this paragraph "5", the Husband's obligation shall be limited to $10,000.00 per Child per year.

(b) In order to offset any changes in the cost of education, the Husband agrees that beginning with the first school year following the execution of this Agreement, and each school year thereafter, he shall increase his contribution to Pre-College Tuition in the same proportion that the increase in the Basic Child Support for that year bore to the amount of Basic Child Support for the previous year for a total annual contribution in aggregate of up to a maximum of 13.3% of his Base Salary. For the purpose of this subparagraph, "Base Salary" is defined as the Husband's gross annual, taxable salary, excluding annual bonus, involuntary pension contributions involuntary savings plan contributions, or other incentive awards for the year in which the calculation is made. However, in no event shall such increase exceed the actual increase in the Children's respective tuition increases. Similarly, in the event Basic Child Support is decreased in any given year, the sum of Pre-College Tuition shall be decreased by the same percent-age that the decrease in Basic Child Support bore to the prior year's Basic Child Sup-port sum. Despite such potential decreases, the Pre-College Tuition contribution shall in no event be less than $8,333.00 per Child per year, for so long as the Husband's income from all sources is at least $150,000.

6. (a) Commencing on the date of the first Additional Child Support payment required under Article VI, paragraph 2, if a Child's Pre-College Tuition exceeds the amount of the Pre-College Tuition as adjusted in accordance with paragraph "3" of this Article (such excess shall hereinafter be referred to as the "Pre-College Tuition Overage") Additional Child Support payments, as calculated in Article VI of this Agreement, exceeding $22,500.00 per year, if any, shall be applied to offset the Pre-College Tuition Overage, if any, provided the Wife is earning taxable income exceeding $45,000.00 or the Wife has remarried. Such $45,000.00 figure shall be adjusted, on a yearly basis, in accordance with the adjustment mechanism described in Article V, paragraph 1(i) of this Agreement.

(b) "Remarriage" of the Wife as used in this Agreement shall be defined as an actual ceremonial remarriage (civil or religious) of the Wife, regardless of whether such remarriage is terminated by divorce, annulment, or otherwise and as the Wife's cohabitation with an unrelated adult male for a substantially continuous period of nine (9) months, or for an intermittent period of 270 days during any consecutive 12 month period. If the Wife shall remarry, she shall, within ten (10) days after the marriage ceremony, notify the Husband in writing of the date and place of such marriage.

(c) The Wife shall provide documentation of her income by supplying the Husband with her most recent paystub and W-2 form if she is a W-2 employee, and by supplying him with her most recent Federal income tax return, or, at her option, with a statement from a certified public accountant which shows all the 1040 Federal tax information for her alone, and, in addition to the foregoing tax information, 1099 forms if she is an independent contractor or is self-employed. In the event the Wife refuses to provide the Husband with such documentation by August 30 of the school year, the Wife's income shall be deemed to exceed $45,000.00, or $45,000.00 as adjusted in accordance with the mechanism described in Article V, paragraph 1(i) of this Agreement.

7. Additional Child Support Payments used in accordance with this Article for Pre-College Tuition shall be equally proportioned between each Child.

8. Each of the parties shall contribute to the cost of the Children's college education in accordance with their then financial means and shall, to the extent possible, utilize loans, scholarships and the Children's contributions to assist in mitigating such expense.

9. For the purpose of this Agreement, a Child shall be deemed to have become emancipated upon the earliest happening of any of the following events

(a) Attaining the age of 21 years;

(b) Marriage of the Child, even though such marriage may be void or voidable and despite any annulment thereof;

(c) Permanent residence of the Child away from the residence of the Wife, including residence with the Husband, other than temporary absence due to attendance at an educational institution;

(d) Entry of the Child into the Armed Forces of the United States;

(e) Engagement of the Child in substantially full-time employment, other than during the Child's school recess or vacation periods;

(f) Death of the Child; and

(h) Death of the paying parent.

10. The parties have been advised of the provisions of the Child Support Standards Act ("Act") (Chapter 567 of the 1989 Laws of the State of New York, as presently codified

in DRL §240 (1-b)). Each of the parties acknowledge that his or her attorney(s) have fully explained the provisions of said Act and that he or she fully understands the possible applicability of its provisions to issues of custody and/or child support which are otherwise determined by the provisions of this Agreement. The parties have been advised that under the Child Support Standards Act, this Agreement, as drafted and presently applied to the parties, may deviate from the Act because a Court, if applying the Act to these parties, is presumed to require the Husband to pay to the Wife, on an annual basis, twenty-five (25%) percent of his total income less New York City and social security taxes, as basic Child support, and may cap that total income at $80,000.00, thereby requiring the Husband to pay a basic Child support sum of as low as $20,000.00 per year, or may not cap that total income, thereby requiring the Husband to pay a higher sum. The parties, nevertheless, agree that the Agreement as written is equitable, taking into consideration the financial resources of the custodial parent and non-custodial parent, and those of the Children, the Wife's capacity to earn income, the physical and emotional health of the Children, the standard of living the Children would have enjoyed had the marriage not been dissolved, the tax consequences to the parties, the non-monetary contributions that the parents will make toward the care and well-being of the Children and the fact that the Wife's income is currently less than the income of the Husband.

11. To the extent permitted by law, each of the parties waive any rights he or she may have pursuant to the said Act and instead agrees to be bound by the terms and conditions of this Agreement. As such, the parties intend that this Article be deemed to be a waiver as contemplated by DRL §240(1-b)(h).

ARTICLE VIII

SUPPORT AND MAINTENANCE OF

THE WIFE

1. The Husband shall pay the Wife a sum of $10,000 in taxable maintenance twelve months after the execution of this Agreement, unless the Wife has died, or the Husband has died.

2. The Husband shall pay the Wife the sum of $20,000 per year in taxable maintenance, payable in semi-monthly installments of $833.33 each, commencing with the first time the 15th or first day of the month occurs following the execution of this Agreement. The payment shall be made until the earlier of the thirteenth month following the execution of this Agreement, the Wife's death or the Husband's death.

3. The Husband shall pay the Wife the sum of $11,250 per year in taxable maintenance, payable in semi-monthly installments of $468.75, commencing in the thirteenth month following the execution of this Agreement through the twenty-fourth month following the execution of this Agreement, and the sum of $13,750 per year in taxable maintenance, payable in semi-monthly installments of $572.91, commencing in the twenty-fifth month following the execution of this Agreement

through the thirty-sixth month following the execution of this Agreement. The foregoing payments shall be made until the earlier of the thirty-sixth month following the execution of this Agreement, the Wife's death or the Husband's death.

ARTICLE IX

SEPARATE OWNERSHIP

1. Except as may be otherwise expressly set forth in this Agreement, each party shall own, free of any claim or right of the other, all of the items of property, real, personal and mixed, of any kind, nature or description and wheresoever situate, which are now in his or her name, control or possession, with full power to him or to her to dispose of the same as fully and effectually in all respects and for all purposes as if he or she were unmarried.

2. It is the intention of the parties by this Agreement to effectuate a full property settlement between them and to divide equitably their property pursuant to the Laws of the State of New York as effective as of the date hereof.

3. Except as otherwise expressly set forth in this Agreement, each party waives any and all rights which he or she may have to a distributive award or an award of equitable distribution in respect of any property acquired by the other or acquired jointly either before or during the marriage or by either, individually after the effective date of this Agreement, and each agrees never to seek through judicial proceedings or otherwise a distributive award or an award of equitable distribution with respect to any property acquired by the other or acquired jointly either before or during the marriage.

4. Except as otherwise expressly set forth in this Agreement, the parties agree that any property acquired after the effective date of this Agreement shall be his or her separate property. Each party acknowledges that the division of the parties' property is fair and reasonable.

5. The antique chest given to the Husband by his father and the Husband's video camera shall be made available for the Husband, along with other personal effects to be removed from the Wife's residence, within thirty (30) days after the signing of the Agreement.

ARTICLE X

MUTUAL RELEASE AND DISCHARGE

OF GENERAL CLAIMS

Subject to the provisions of this Agreement, each party hereby remises, releases and forever discharges the other of and from all cause or causes of action, claims, rights or demands whatsoever, in law or in equity, which either of the parties hereto ever had, or now has, against the other, except any or all cause or causes of action for divorce, annulment or separation, and any defenses either may have to any divorce, annulment or separation action now pending or hereafter brought by the other.

ARTICLE XI

RESPONSIBILITY FOR DEBTS

1. The Husband represents, warrants and covenants that, except as specifically set forth herein, he has not heretofore, nor will he hereafter, incur or contract any debt, charge, obligation or liability whatsoever for which the Wife, her legal representatives or her property or estate is or may become liable. The Husband agrees to indemnify and hold the Wife harmless of all losses, expenses (including reasonable attorneys' fees) and damages in connection with or arising out of a breach by the Husband of his foregoing representations, warranties and covenants, unless same shall occur by reason of the failure of the Wife to perform the terms, covenants and conditions of this Agreement to be performed by her.

2. The Wife represents, warrants and covenants that, except as specifically set forth herein, she has not heretofore, nor will she hereafter, incur or contract any debt, charge, obligation or liability whatsoever for which the Husband, his legal representatives or his property or estate is or may become liable. The Wife agrees to indemnify and hold the Husband harmless of all losses, expenses (including reasonable attorneys' fees) and damages in connection with or arising out of a breach by the Wife of her foregoing representations, warranties or covenants unless same shall occur by reason of the failure of the Husband to perform the terms, covenants and conditions of this Agreement to be performed by him.

ARTICLE XII

REAL PROPERTY

1. The Husband waives any interest which he may have in the apartment located in Madrid which is owned by the Wife.

2. The Wife waives any interest which she may have in the Husband's property located in Arizona.

ARTICLE XIII

PERSONAL PROPERTY

1. Except as provided herein, the parties have acknowledge that they have agreed upon the allocation of all of their personal property to their mutual satisfaction and shall divide such property at a mutually convenient time and place to be arranged. Each party hereby waives any right, claim or title to the property of the other now standing in his or her name.

2. Within thirty (30) days from the date of the execution of this Agreement, the Husband, at a mutually convenient time, shall remove from the Wife's residence any personal papers, books, photographs and photograph albums to be agreed upon by the parties, or other personal effects belonging to him.

ARTICLE XIV

LIQUID ASSETS

Each party shall retain his or her own bank accounts, security accounts, investments in stock or other financial instruments and hereby waives any interest he or she may have in such accounts of the other.

ARTICLE XV

PENSION PLANS

The Wife hereby waives any interest in the Husband's interest in any pension plans, profit sharing plans, savings incentive plan, stock option plans, and the like, and shall execute, within ten days of receipt of the same, any documents necessary to effectuate such waivers.

ARTICLE XVI

INCOME TAX RETURNS

1. If, in connection with any joint income tax returns heretofore filed by the Husband and Wife, there is a deficiency assessment, the amount ultimately determined to be due thereon, including penalties and interest, shall be paid by the party whose income or whose deduction caused such deficiency. Each party agrees to cooperate fully with the other in the event of any audit or examination of the said joint tax returns by a taxing authority and agrees to furnish to the party being examined or his (or her) designees, promptly and without charge, such papers, records, documents, authorizations and information as may be reasonably appropriate in connection with said audit or examination.

2. The Wife shall reimburse the Husband for any tax assessed against him which he pays, which is attributable to her failure to report income, or to her taking deductions to which she was not entitled. The Husband shall reimburse the Wife for any tax assessed against him which she pays, which is attributable to his failure to report income as to his taking any deductions to which he was not entitled.

3. If, for any year in which the parties filed joint United States tax returns there is a refund arising out of the Wife's having paid taxes or additional taxes in France, then the Wife shall be entitled to such refund provided she can substantiate that the refund is due to her payment of taxes or additional taxes in France and provided the Wife indemnifies and holds the Husband harmless for any tax payments the Husband makes as a result of the Wife's having received that refund and provided the Wife allows the Husband to offset such liability, to the extent he pays the same, with any future refund otherwise due the Wife under this Article XVI.

ARTICLE XVII

DEFAULT

1. In the event that either party defaults with respect to any obligation under this Agreement and said default is not remedied within fifteen (15) days after the sending of a written notice by certified mail to the defaulting party specifying said default, the defaulting party agrees to indemnify the non-defaulting party against or to reimburse him/her for any and all reasonable expenses, costs and attorneys' fees resulting from or made necessary by the bringing of any suit or other proceeding to enforce any of the terms, covenants or conditions of this Agreement to be performed or complied with by either party, or to enforce any of the rights to recover any amount to be paid pursuant to this Agreement, provided such suit or other proceeding results in a judgment, decree or order in favor of the non-defaulting party.

2. For the purposes of this Agreement, it is understood and agreed that in the event the non-defaulting party, no less than fifteen (15) days after written notification to the defaulting party, shall institute a suit or other proceeding against the defaulting party to enforce any of the terms, covenants or conditions of this Agreement and after the institution of such action or proceeding and before judgment is or can be entered the defaulting party shall comply with such term or condition of the Agreement; then and in that event, the suit, motion or proceeding instituted by the non-defaulting party shall be deemed to have resulted in a judgment, decree or order in favor of the non-defaulting party.

ARTICLE XVIII

LEGAL REPRESENTATION

1. The Wife acknowledges that she has had independent legal advice by counsel of her own selection in connection with the negotiation and execution of this Agreement, having been represented by Sullivan and Jones.

2. The Husband acknowledges that he has had independent legal advice by counsel of his own selection in connection with the negotiation and execution of this Agreement, having been represented by Swank and Moore.

3. The attorneys for the Husband shall prepare those documents necessary for the parties to secure an uncontested divorce in New York County. The Wife agrees to cooperate with the filing of such documents.

ARTICLE XIX

LEGAL CONSULTATION

The parties have had full opportunity to consult at length with their respective counsel concerning the content of this Agreement. The parties acknowledge that this Agreement has not been the result of any duress or undue influence exercised by either party upon the other or by any other person or persons upon either. Both parties acknowledge that this Agreement has been achieved after competent legal representation and honest negotiations, and that its terms are fair and reasonable.

341

ARTICLE XX

INDEPENDENT COVENANTS

Each of the respective rights and obligations of the parties hereunder shall be deemed independent and may be enforced independently irrespective of any of the other rights and obligations set forth herein.

ARTICLE XXI

DISCLOSURE

Each party has had the opportunity to be fully informed of the income, assets, property and financial prospects of the other and has waived full disclosure. Each has had full opportunity and has consulted at length with his or her counsel regarding all of the circumstances hereof and acknowledges that this Agreement has not been the result of any fraud, duress or undue influence exercised by either party upon the other or by any other person or persons upon either. Both parties acknowledge that this Agreement has been achieved after disclosure to the extent demanded, competent legal representation and honest negotiations, and that its terms are fair and reasonable.

ARTICLE XXII

RECONCILIATION AND MATRIMONIAL DECREES

1. This Agreement shall not be invalidated or otherwise affected by a reconciliation between the parties hereto, or a resumption of marital relations between them unless said reconciliation or said resumption be documented by a written statement executed and acknowledged by the parties with respect to said reconciliation and resumption and, in addition, setting forth that they are cancelling this Agreement, and this Agreement shall not be invalidated or otherwise affected by any decree or judgment of separation or divorce made in any court in any action which may presently exist or may hereafter be instituted by either party against the other for a separation or divorce.

2. Each party agrees that the provisions of this Agreement shall be submitted to any court in which either party may seek a judgment or decree of divorce or separation and that the provisions of this Agreement shall be incorporated in said judgment or decree with such specificity as the court shall deem permissible and by reference as may be appropriate under law and under the rules of the court. However, notwithstanding such incorporation, the obligations and covenants of this Agreement shall survive any decree or judgment of separation or divorce and shall not merge therein, and this Agreement may be enforced independently of said decree or judgment.

ARTICLE XXIII

MODIFICATION AND WAIVER

Neither this Agreement nor any provision hereof shall be amended or modified or deemed amended or modified, except by an agreement in writing duly subscribed and acknowledged with the same formality as this Agreement, except as expressly provided herein. Any waiver by either party of any provision of this Agreement or any right or option hereunder shall not be deemed a continuing waiver and shall not prevent or estop such party from thereafter enforcing such provision, right or option, and the failure of either party to insist in any one or more instances upon the strict performance of any of the terms or provisions of this Agreement by the other party shall not be construed as a waiver or relinquishment for the future of any such term or provision, but the same shall continue in full force and effect.

ARTICLE XXIV

LEGAL INTERPRETATION

This Agreement and all of the rights and obligations of the parties hereunder shall be construed according to the laws of the State of New York as an agreement made and to be performed within said State.

ARTICLE XXV

IMPLEMENTATION

The Husband and Wife shall, at any and all times, upon request by the other party or his or her legal representatives, promptly share any costs thereof, and make, execute and deliver any and all such other and further instruments as may be necessary or desirable for the purpose of giving full force and effect to the provisions of this Agreement.

ARTICLE XXVI

ENTIRE UNDERSTANDING

This Agreement contains the entire understanding of the parties who hereby acknowledge that there have been and are no representations, warranties, covenants or undertakings other than those expressly set forth herein.

ARTICLE XXVII

CHANGE OF NAME AND ADDRESS

1. As long as any act remains to be performed under this Agreement, the parties hereby agree that each will notify the other by registered or certified mail, return receipt requested, of any change of address within five (5) days of the date of such change.

2 No later than six (6) months from the date of the execution of this Agreement, the Wife shall not, unless necessary, use the surname "Smith".

3 Upon the entry of a Judgment of Divorce, the Wife shall permanently cease to refer to herself as the "Wife" of Robert D. Smith.

ARTICLE XXVIII

NOTICES

Any notice given in connection with this Agreement shall be deemed by the parties to be sufficient if given to the other by registered or certified mail, return receipt requested, addressed to the last known address of the other. Notice should be sufficient if

343

addressed to the addresses above set forth or to such other address as may be supplied by like notice.

ARTICLE XXIX

BINDING EFFECT

This Agreement and all the obligations and covenants hereunder shall bind the parties hereto, their heirs, executors, administrators, legal representatives and assigns and shall enure to the benefit of their respective heirs, executors, administrators, legal representatives and assigns.

IN WITNESS WHEREOF, the parties hereto have hereunto set their hands and seals the day and year first above written.

_____

CATHERINE Smith

_____

ROBERT Smith

STATE OF NEW YORK)

: ss.

COUNTY OF NEW YORK)

On this   day of March, 1993, before me personally came CATHERINE Smith, to me known to be the person described in and who executed the foregoing instrument and who duly acknowledged to me that she executed the same.

_____

Notary

STATE OF NEW YORK)

: ss.

COUNTY OF NEW YORK)

On this   day of March, 1993, before me personally came ROBERT Smith, to me known to be the person described in and who executed the foregoing instrument and who duly acknowledged to me that he executed the same.

_____

Notary

Index

N

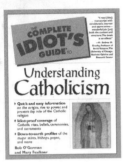

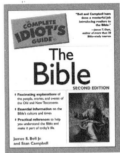

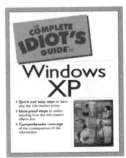